Dear Diana:

You remain an inspiration for me... from the day I met you have been in awe of your energy & perspective. I hope you find some entertaining energy & perspective in my book ... and some fun recipes!

With a bit of luck, Jori, Hudson & I will be cooking with you in the hills of Michoacan!

Eat with your hands & Cook with your heart

Love,
Ed

EAT WITH YOUR HANDS

ZAKARY PELACCIO

with JJ GOODE

ecco

An Imprint of HarperCollinsPublishers

HarperCollins books may be purchased for educational, business, or sales promotional use. For information please write: Special Markets Department, HarperCollins Publishers, 10 East 53rd Street, New York, NY 10022.

FIRST EDITION

Designed by Suet Chong

Library of Congress Cataloging-in-Publication Data has been applied for.

ISBN 978-0-06-155420-9

12 13 14 15 16 OV/QGT 10 9 8 7 6 5 4 3 2 1

TO JORI AND HUDSON

ACKNOWLEDGMENTS

Thanks to the Fatty Crew. Thanks to Rick Camac for his perseverance and strong partnership. Thanks to Corwin Kave for his wonderful creative drive, great taste, and dedication to the cause. Thanks to Jesse and Colin Camac for their energy and unwavering commitment. Thanks to Adam Schuman for his raw creativity. Thanks to my mom and dad for teaching me good taste. Thanks to my sister, Eva, for tolerating me all these years. Thanks to Michael Schrom for his talent and great generosity. Thanks to Daniel Halpern for his wisdom. And thanks to his team at Ecco for their patience and insight, particularly associate editor, Libby Edelson, interior designer, Suet Chong, and jacket designer, Allison Saltzman. Thanks to Kathryn Kellinger for getting this ball rolling. Thanks to JJ Goode for bringing this project to the finish line. Thanks to William Clark for shepherding in an unflappable and even-tempered manner.

Thanks to everyone who has worked with me through the years, to everyone who has offered me advice (good or bad), and to anyone who has humored me by listening to my long-winded rants.

Thanks to Huddy, my boy, for keeping me on my toes.

A very special thanks to the beautiful Jori Jayne Emde who not only worked with me, offered advice, and humored me (oh, the humor), but put her own time, labor, and passion into this book right alongside me. Thank you, baby.

CONTENTS

INTRODUCTION

"I never want to cook the same thing twice," I recently told a friend. He gleefully pointed out that I was working on a cookbook, a process that would force me to cook the same thing twice, three times, maybe more. For a minute I doubted myself. What the hell am I getting into? I thought—but barely a moment passed before I landed on the same reason I've made most of the questionable choices in my life: for the experience.

"Sure, let's do it" has long been my guiding principle. I've always rolled with the opportunities that come along, though they've produced varying degrees of satisfaction. I just can't shake the nagging desire to peer around the next corner, as if some newfound wisdom or enlightenment will reveal itself with the next move or project. Curiosity and stimulation—overstimulation if you can get it—that's the Kool-Aid I've been drinking for years now.

My first restaurant, the funky Chickenbone Café, was an early American version of a gastropub, with more focus on the "gastro" than the "pub." We served kielbasa bruschetta and braised goat on a deserted stretch of street in then relatively undeveloped South Williamsburg (this was back in late 2002–2003, before there was a cheese shop and a record store on every corner of Bedford Avenue). My next adventure? 5 Ninth. 5 Ninth was one of those projects that had a lot of promise, a lot of potential, but in the end it just wasn't the right restaurant in the right place at the right time. We were smack in the middle of the meatpacking district in the heyday of the heavy nightclub and partying scene there. Waifish models did not want to eat whole fish with chili and ginger, and geeked-out partiers weren't into sharing a roasted baby goat shoulder for two. My mission and the mission of the neighborhood were deviating, to say the least . . . so with one of my partners, I moved on.

In 2005, I opened Fatty Crab, a small, rollicking restaurant in the West Village. Fatty Crab was born when my business partner Rick Camac leased a tiny old laundromat on Hudson Street and asked me if I wanted to open a smaller, café-type restaurant in the space. I walked into the space one day and blurted out, "We should cook Malaysian-influenced food! It'll be cool, spicy, loud, rock 'n' roll, with great products and great flavors. I'll bring my crew from the Chickenbone . . . it'll be our party. Our party, and everyone will be invited!" (My Chickenbone crew were all creative rockers, writers, and illicit distillers who were totally out to lunch—like me.)

I was elated. I knew exactly what I wanted. A grubby storefront restaurant where, as soon as you walked in, you knew that you were going to drink more than you should and where new flavors, pungent profiles, and entertaining textures would bombard your mouth and completely fuck all your food-centric preconceptions. I sold Rick on the idea in a machine-gun-fire moment of inspiration. It was a combination of *Eureka!* and *Duh!* Why the hell wasn't I doing this before? Rick's verbatim answer was "That sounds great, but what's Malaysian food?" Still, he put some faith and some money into that little joint, and we went ahead, building it entirely on our own, fueled by the spirit of the project, cheap beer, and the reality that rent was coming due.

To this day, the Fatty world has managed not just to hold my scatterbrained attention but to stimulate it as well. Everything Fatty has kept me so engaged that I've finally been able to commit to just one restaurant (Okay, a few incarnations of one restaurant idea). For the first time in my life, I can slow down and enjoy cooking, eating, and simply living. These days, playing Frisbee with my son, Hudson, and planting chilies with my fiancée, Jori, tops my list of interests. And seeing those chilies used at Fatty Crab and Fatty 'Cue is incredibly satisfying.

In the Fatty world—two Crabs, one 'Cue, and more to come—I'm incredibly fortunate to be working with good friends I get to see every day. Building this new, nonblood family has become the most satisfying part of my career. While putting this book together I've discovered that writing down all the thoughts and recipes that have been simmering in my head has brought me even closer to the food and lifestyle I've been so passionate about, reminding me how lucky I am to have eaten so well over the years, to have grown up with fresh food prepared in an Italian style, to have had the good fortune to travel and live in many different places throughout Europe and Asia. So, yes, these days I'm cooking the same thing twice (or at least teaching someone to do it) and enjoying it.

Before I was a chef and restaurateur, I was a kid who ate a lot. I was raised on an Americanized approximation of the Roman diet. My folks lived in Rome for five years before I was born and returned to 1970s Westchester with a taste for prosciutto and Parmigiano-Reggiano. My mother made a great carbonara and always served salad after the main course. My father would stop at Arthur Avenue in the Bronx on his way home from work in the city, restocking our suburban cupboards with the makings of a good Italian pantry—thus saving my mother from full-scale cultural depression. So even though the produce sold at Mr. Green's on Post Road (an early iteration of the "gourmet" market) was sorry looking, and the absence of decent arugula was almost too much for my mom to bear, she raised me on food made almost entirely from scratch at a time when the microwave and ordering in were all the rage. My parents also encouraged me to ransack the fridge and concoct my own meals using whatever ingredients I could find, in whatever ways I wanted.

They instilled in me a tireless curiosity and a love for food that ultimately inspired me to head off to Southeast Asia, where I developed a firsthand understanding of the palate and techniques of Malaysian cuisine. In Malaysia I fell hard for lip-scalding chilies, unbelievably funky fermented condiments, and freshly made coconut milk. Over the years Malaysian cooks have integrated distinct Chinese, Portuguese, Indian, and Indonesian influences into the cuisine, especially in the urban centers and port cities. I felt a kinship with the motley cuisine, in part because it reminded me of the culinary mutt I was becoming, but also because Malaysians love to, as I've done since I was a kid, eat with their hands.

My mom's cooking, along with living and traveling in Asia and Europe, made me aware of the art, beauty, and flavor of great food. And once you know how great artfully made food can be—what an aesthetic and sensory experience it can offer—it's almost impossible to settle for mediocre grub. And since I didn't have the cash to finance a life of eating out day after day, I had no choice but to become a cook. To paraphrase the great architect Louis Kahn, "Art is not the fulfillment of a desire but the creation of a new one."

People still call me a chef, and I'm cool with that. But *I'm* reluctant to call myself a chef. I collect food experiences and ideas and reinterpret them. Sure, I do cook in my kitchens, and train my cooks to learn my taste, but mainly I convert experiences into dishes and into restaurants in collaboration with a team of skilled *real* chefs and cooks—true warriors.

Deciding what recipes to include in this book was a challenge, but it was even more difficult to actually write the recipes themselves. Thing is, I don't use recipes, unless I'm baking. And I never bake. They're funny things, recipes. They reduce cooking—movement honed through repetition that's responsive to subtle sensory cues—to words on a page. The blank spaces between words in a recipe shout to me the absence of all the subtlety I wish the recipe had been able to communicate and the heady memories I wish it could evoke. Recipes are form—not food, not cooking. Sixteen years ago, in the Aeolian Islands, for instance, I watched a long-haired Sicilian dude scarf down the sauce from *rigatoni alla norma* that I had just cooked. He was eating only the sauce, because the pasta was gone. I had oversauced the pasta. I never wrote this down. I never updated some "recipe" for the dish I had scribbled in some notebook. Instead, it remained a memory, and that particularly vivid memory is still how I judge the amount of sauce I mix with pasta. As far as I'm concerned, that *is* a recipe—a vague, proportionless, experiential recipe.

But until we harness the technology contemplated in the movie *Brainstorm* (come on, people: made in 1983, starring Christopher Walken and Natalie Wood), which lets us tap into one another's mind with some cables and a good pair of headphones, recipes are the best way I've got to share my taste memories and get my food on your dinner table.

I like to think that the recipes in this book are a glimpse into my mind, synapses firing wildly. I've included recipes from different phases of my life—from my restaurants, some still kicking, others late and lamented; some riffs on dishes I cook often at home; and others I wish I cooked more often. French- and Italian-inspired food shares the pages with grub from Malaysia and Thailand. There are dishes whose origins are impossible to pin down. Ingredients you may never have met before show up at the party. Don't give them the cold shoulder. But know you're going to have to flip to the glossary a lot. And if you must, feel free to substitute. Cooking is art, not science, after all. (Portioning is no science either—all serving sizes in this book are estimates. It all depends on your style of consumption.)

Some of these recipes you'll cook; others you'll simply read. Maybe one component or ingredient or technique will strike you, and you'll use it in your own way. Maybe you'll just enjoy reading them. What a concept.

I eat with my hands today, and not just because it would be a serious shame to let utensils slow me down. It has become a sort of philosophy of mine—a metaphor for life. When discussing life and its struggles, my father always told me to "just dig it" and I think I initially misheard his wise words as "just dig in." That's what I hope this book encourages and the way I hope you treat this book—unfamiliar ingredients, long cooking, and too much booze be damned!

Cooking is an intensely personal experience, though it's not a solo pursuit. Through cooking and eating we connect to the earth, to the seasons, to ourselves, our tastes, our family and friends. So if you're ready to have some fun, toast to it all and drink a big glass of something good.

BUYING: A WORK IN PROGRESS

Mangoes, pineapples, and coconuts don't grow in New York. No one here makes fish sauce or fermented shrimp paste either—well, not yet. These facts of Northeast living might present a problem for a fanatical locavore. Fortunately, that's not me. Conscientious, yes, but fanaticism isn't good for the blood pressure.

I first heard about the Slow Food movement, with its rejection of fast food and its emphasis on locally grown and raised meat and vegetables, from Patrick Martins, the peripatetic evangelist for the cause. This was the mid-nineties, when Slow Food was just getting started, and I was lucky enough to be in New York City, its American headquarters. As I worked alongside Patrick on the New York Convivium, articulating its early goals and missions, I was also developing my own philosophy about how to buy food responsibly. For most Slow Food converts, the answer was easy: a commitment to buying locally. But for me there was the whole tropical-cuisine-in-temperate-climate challenge.

But there's nothing like a good challenge to really push creativity, and the results of that dilemma have actually been quite extraordinary—a new cuisine that fuses equatorial gastronomy, local meats and vegetables, and New York City–driven eccentricity. When I started the Chickenbone Café back in 2003, I worked closely with local producers, asking upstate farmers to grow Asian herbs, butchering whole pigs from Violet Hill Farm, serving Brooklyn-distilled underground absinthe. As I explored the city, often led by my dear friend Robert Sietsema, a relentless street rat of the most elegant order, I developed a new take on "local." I began to haunt Weinberger Appetizers in South Williamsburg, a Hasidic family-run store with great matjes herring that I served with a chilled shot of Genever gin and a little square of black bread. I trekked to a tiny Bosnian butcher in Astoria to buy *suho meso*, smoked dried beef, that I sliced thin and served as a side to the Bone Shot, Dave Wondrich's fiery concoction of rye, simple syrup, Tabasco, and lime (page 201). I bought kielbasa from the oldest butcher shop in Greenpoint and made kielbasa bruschetta (page 272). For me, using my purchasing power to support not just farmers but also endangered family-run businesses was a natural part of the buy-local ethos: after all, you can't get more local than your neighbors. A certain selfishness motivates this too. If they close, *I* lose them for good. The ethnically diverse mom-and-pop stores are what makes NYC so unique.

My buying practices are constantly evolving, because I continue to be exposed to more bright ideas and bright people, who tirelessly study the impact and future of our food systems. I'm lucky to have been able to promote one of my cooks to the job of company "forager," which entails a constant search for what tastes best, what is local, and what is raised in a manner that dovetails with our philosophy. Our company invested in a huge, awesome commercial rooftop garden program called Brooklyn Grange. Truly local farming. I do buy mangoes and pineapples

from Florida and California and import obscure condiments shipped from far-off lands. But I worship local farmers who grow delicious produce and raise animals humanely. I buy tasty things from New York's unbelievably diverse array of artisans, from old Chinese women making hand-pulled noodles to unsung bakers kneading out loaves of fragrant bread to the young bucks experimenting with mustards and pickles. And I get down on all fours in the soft earth of my upstate garden, where each year we grow and harvest more and more of the produce for the Fatty Crew.

An American's Pantry

I'm 35 percent Italian, give or take, and the rest is Polish, Irish, Dutch, German, and whatever you'd call people from Indiana. In other words, I'm American, a true mutt. Therefore, there are no strictures or tenets of any particular culinary culture to which I have to adhere. Instead, my palate has been influenced primarily by simple, product-driven Italian-style cooking as well as the electric flavors, dynamic juxtapositions, and funky fermented fish products that characterize Southeast Asian cooking. My cooking is the result of a synergistic combo of these styles that might be summed up as "high-quality ingredients in highly flavored combinations." Executing this weirdly wonderful kind of cooking means shopping at farmers' markets to find the freshest, tastiest ingredients. Then there's the matter of delivering the promised big flavor, which is all about keeping a well-stocked pantry. Storing certain staples is the best way to ensure that, when the urge strikes, you'll have the resources to create something really tasty. So, what does an American of my hybridization and girth keep on hand? Over many years spent with the fridge door open, I've determined there are ingredients that I must always have around. I always have (or at least want) more. I just try not to have less than this:

Brown rice vinegar
Sherry vinegar
Good extra virgin olive oil
Lard and/or lardo

High-fat unsalted butter (it has less water and therefore more milk solids, which bring out flavor)
Anchovies (salt- or oil-packed)

Sea salt

Finishing sea salt (fleur de sel or Maldon)

Fish sauce, preferably the 3 Crabs brand

Palm sugar

Granulated sugar

Good local honey

High-quality capers (in salt or brine)

Raisins (dried on the vine or regular)

Lemons and limes

Whole dried Thai or cayenne chilies

Heads of garlic

Shallots

Yellow onions

Fresh chilies (Thai bird or red jalapeño)

Ginger (as fresh and delicate as you can find)

Herbs (always have something fresh: parsley, cilantro, basil, rosemary, thyme)

Black peppercorns

Rice (jasmine, short-grain Japanese, or basmati)

High-quality dried pasta (maybe Martelli, Latini, or Setaro)

Fresh local eggs

Cured meat of some kind

IT'S YOUR PARTY, BABY

Chefs are not gods—especially not the chef who wrote this book. And they can't divine absolute deliciousness, because it doesn't exist. I can't tell you how many times I've tasted something I made, then tweaked the seasoning until I thought it was perfect. And then watched a friend with a great palate squeeze on more lime or shake on more salt. All you can do is cook food that *you* think is delicious. And let that food convince other people.

To figure out what you think is delicious, you need to taste everything, everywhere you can. That's how I figured out that I love anchovies and cincalok and fish sauce. Throw your preconceived notions out the window or risk missing out on amazing food.

And when something you eat is awesome, don't just inhale whatever it is until you have to unbutton your pants and lie down and your eyes roll back into your head. Ask yourself *why* that particular combination of elements was so attractive to your mouth. How did your eyes influence what your taste and olfactory senses processed?

At thirty-seven, I've just begun to understand what I enjoy and how to get there. Getting to know your own palate is an ongoing adventure—and sharing food with other like-minded people can only help your quest.

Since I spend most of my time cooking, traveling, and eating, I'm constantly adjusting, refining, and trying to rearticulate what I like, what works, and what I want to cook. But once I settle down to cook something, I set my own goal, my own expectation for myself. I think you do a disservice to the food at hand when you try to cook without your own unique understanding of your goal. Even if you are working for someone else and have to re-create that chef's recipe the same way night after night, you should still set your own goal and expectation for that recipe, for the flavors and textures you seek to get out of it. Your own goal is unique . . . it is your interpretation of the chef's desire and palate . . . your own goal is the best YOU can get out of that dish.

The following is a list of sensations that bounce around in my brain when I eat, look at, cook, or contemplate food. In parentheses after each one, I list an example to provide a little clarification.

Crispy (nicely fried chicken skin)

Fresh and crisp (raw veggies and herbs)

Crunchy (corn nuts)

Chewy (tendon, jellyfish)

Tart (lemon, vinegar)

Roasty (the brown bits on the bottom of a roasting pan)

Charred (steak from a superhot charcoal grill)

Slick (sliced lardo)

Melting (jiggly cooked pork belly)

Bitter (coffee, bitter melon)

Viscous (oil)

Salty (anchovy)

Funky, stinky, or fermented (cincalok, budu)

Slimy (sea urchin)

Sweet (simple syrup)

Hot (chilies)

Earthy (black trumpet mushrooms)

Curry (mixed dry spices)

Garden (herbs, lavender to marjoram, borage to lemon balm)

Anise (basil, fennel)

Peppery (arugula, peppercorns)

Fuzzy (oregano, nepitella), in texture more than taste—how it rubs against the tongue

Mellow burn (raw ginger)

Fruity (fruits)

Vegetal (vegetables)

I always work to balance some of these sensations when I think about the food I cook. Rarely, if ever, are all sensations present, and more often than not a few sensations will act as the protagonists while a few others play supporting roles. Look at the pork with watermelon salad (on page 208). The hunks of belly are crispy on the outside and melting within. The fruit is crisp and sweet. Those are the two major players, but they share the stage with supporting—but necessary—players: tart pickle, sour and salty dressing, the mellow burn of ginger, and the heat of raw chili. The combination of flavors is layered and exciting and keeps you paying attention!

As I learn to manipulate these categories, I begin to refine what I am after and slowly make my way there.

Ultimately, it's your party: play the way you want to.

THE MORTAR AND PESTLE

Antique brass or copper mortars make really nice shelf ornaments. As for the smooth marble ones, you can use them to crush pharmaceuticals if that's your thing. But to make these recipes right, get yourself a rough, porous stone mortar and pestle. Ideally yours will be about 8 inches in diameter and will be able to hold about 1 cup of ingredients without ending up so full that the only place the food can go when you pound is up and over the sides. The coarse stone provides friction, which is essential when you're trying to break up fibrous ingredients such as galangal, lemongrass, and ginger. The pestle should be heavy, because the heavier it is, the more work it will do for you.

And yeah, I hear you: you *can* use a food processor, preferably a small one, though I can't stress enough the importance of smashing stuff into pastes in a mortar, at least until you get to know the texture you're after. Then, if you occasionally use a machine, you'll be able to approximate the look and feel of the pounded paste and avoid overprocessing.

The Higher Order of My Mortar

There are tasty pastes that you eat as dips. There are pastes that become marinades, and there are those you fry (in oil, lard, whatever) and then mix with stock or coconut cream to make curries, sauces, dressings, and soups. Most of these pastes will contain garlic, shallots, chilies, toasted dried spices, and fresh herbs. They'll be finished with lime juice, fish sauce, or some other liquid. Ingredients should be added in order of most fibrous to least. Think about it: if you added chopped tomato and some slices of lemongrass to your mortar at the same time and tried to pulverize the lemongrass, you would have quite a battle ahead of you. The pestle would ride a tomato skin slip, and you'd end up with barely bruised lemongrass and a shirt covered in bright red juice. Imagine if you were also trying to grind some coriander seed in that mess—forget it; game over. Now, if instead you add the lemongrass first, pulverizing it against the rough interior of the mortar with your heavy pestle, maybe even sprinkling in a little coarse salt for added friction, you'll be able to develop a nice coarse mash. Once you're satisfied with the mash, you toss in the tomato and achieve what you seek: a textured puree, a paste that's not quite a solid color but rather a variegated blend of ingredients, the flavors married by blunt force.

The Order for Your Mortar

1. Lemongrass
2. Cilantro root or herb stems
3. Galangal
4. Ginger
5. Chili
6. Turmeric root
7. Powdered or ground dried spices (see note) and belacan
8. Garlic
9. Shallot or onion
10. Tomato, tamarind paste
11. Liquids like juices and fish sauce

Note: I prefer using a spice grinder to reduce whole spices—coriander seed, cardamom, star anise, etc.—to a powder before adding them to the mortar. But if the mortar is your only option, make them the first ingredients you add to the mortar.

Pounding

1. First, cut, chop, and slice each ingredient into manageable pieces.
2. Second, put the mortar on a folded-up kitchen towel, which will absorb some of the impact and reduce the noise of pounding.
3. Third, put the most fibrous ingredient in the mortar first and pound, thoroughly pulverizing it (you might spend five minutes pounding each ingredient) before adding the second most fibrous. Pound to a beat, find your own rhythm, get into it. If you're like me, you'll probably end up coming at those ingredients with the pestle from the top at first. But when they've crept up the sides, you'll start scraping the walls with the pestle as you pound. And hold whichever hand you're not using to pound over the mortar to prevent jumpers.

Once you get into using a mortar, you'll become an addict. The fresh smells of the aromatic herbs, vegetables, and spices smashing open are invigorating. Food processor be damned! This is cooking. This feels right.

KITCHEN MUSIC

You don't have to be in no hurry
You don't really ever have to worry
You don't have to think about how you feel
Just keep repeating
That none of this is real
And if you're thinking something's wrong
Just remember it won't be too long
Before the director cuts the scene . . .
This ain't really your life
Ain't really your life
Ain't really nothin' but a movie . . .
—"B Movie," Gil Scott-Heron

You can be a serious cook without being too serious about cooking: You want the pork belly you're braising to be fucking tasty, but come on, you're *making dinner,* not performing a triple bypass. Cooking is a celebration—of ingredients, of friendship and family, of a Tuesday night, or of whatever the hell else you feel like commemorating. Instead of a silent kitchen, with all the vitality of a courtroom, you want a kitchen that's a party. So turn on some music.

Every professional kitchen I have ever run and every home kitchen I have ever spent time in has been filled with music. If you watch closely, you'll notice that everyone's cooking to the beat. Good cooks all have a natural groove to begin with—you can see it in their step, hear it in the way they chop or in the pound of their pestle. That groove is the subtle manifestation of a cook's connection with his ingredients. So turn the music up.

Not sure what beat will get the party started? Well, I've taken the liberty of suggesting the perfect music-recipe pairings. These suggestions are the result of rigorous experimenting and consultations with MIT sound scientists—actually, I just made them up. While I can't say with any certainty that listening to the suggested tunes enhances the flavor of the dish, I can tell you that you walk (and cook) taller when you have theme music.

ON DRINKING WHILE COOKING . . . AND EATING

Look, even the best food only gets better with a good drink. So after much actual experimenting, for which I have bravely sacrificed sobriety and probably the health of my liver, I have come up with beverage recommendations for each recipe. A good drink helps to alleviate stress and numbs you to the trivial concerns of a broken society—and to any possible burns or cuts that occur as a result of cooking drunk.

And the truth:

I can't seem to get used to myself. I don't even know if I am me. Then as soon as I take a drink, the lead slips away and I recognize myself, I become me again.
—Eugene Ionesco, *Rhinoceros*

A FROG

FROG LEG CLAY POT

Next to my house in upstate New York there is a pond. And in that pond there are some frogs. In the summer, when they're plump and ready for the pan, I go hunting. But damn, do those frogs move fast!

Whenever I have access to superfresh frogs' legs, I cook them the same way. I dredge the legs in flour, fry them, and then toss them in a simple sauce made with chilies, garlic, ginger, and chicken stock. I dump the saucy legs over rice cooked for a bit in a hot clay pot until the bottom is crispy. It's a simple preparation, so you need to use a fresh product—make it with frozen legs and it just won't be the same.

SERVES 2

2 cups Tamaki Gold or other short-grain white rice, well rinsed
8 small dried red chilies, such as cayenne
¼ pound guanciale, cut into lardons
1 cup peanut oil for frying, plus 3 tablespoons
½ cup all-purpose flour
½ cup rice flour
Sea salt and freshly ground black pepper

8 frogs' legs, not too big, not too small
½ cup Chicken Stock (page 324)
1 inch fresh ginger, peeled and minced
2 garlic cloves, minced
1 medium shallot, thinly sliced
2 tablespoons Shaoxing wine or dry sherry
2 cups pea shoots
Juice of 1 lemon

1. Prepare the rice according to your rice cooker's instructions or place the rinsed rice in a heavy saucepan and add 2 cups water. Bring the water to a boil, reduce the heat to produce the lowest simmer, cover with a tight lid, and cook for 15 minutes. If the rice isn't tender, add a few tablespoons of water and continue simmering, covered. When the rice is finished cooking, fluff it with a fork, stirring it around gently to allow the heat to escape and prevent the rice from overcooking and becoming a gloopy mess. Set aside.

2. Heat a dry sauté pan over medium-high heat. Add the dried chilies and toast, shaking the pan occasionally, until they begin to take on color, about 5 minutes. Take care not to inhale over the pan. Transfer the toasted chilies to a plate and set aside.

3. Put the guanciale in a cold sauté pan and turn the heat to medium-high. Render the guanciale until it's slipping in its own fat and it's golden brown and just beginning to crisp, 5 to 7 minutes. Use a slotted spoon to transfer the guanciale to a paper-towel-lined plate to drain. Pour off all but about 2 tablespoons of the rendered fat and take the pan off the heat.

4. Fill a small saucepan with the 1 cup peanut oil. Bring it to 375°F (measured on a deep-frying thermometer) over medium heat.

ON LIVE FROGS

If you don't have a pond to harvest, hit up your local Asian markets, some of which probably sell live frogs. If you're lucky, you can have them killed and skinned for your dining pleasure. Doing it yourself is a little messy but not really all that difficult. All you need is a couple of large bowls, a firm grip, and a good pair of scissors: Use the scissors to decapitate the frog and then use the tip of the scissors to lift the skin on the top of the frog's back (where the head once was) just enough so that you can slide one of the scissors' blades underneath. Snip the skin lengthwise down the back to the butt. Grab one of the cut corners, hold on to Kermit with your other hand, and pull the skin away from the body and legs; then do the same with the other corner. This skin will come right off. Use the scissors to snip off the hindlegs at the hip joint (that's what you'll eat). Discard the rest of the frog—that is, unless you want to make a tasty frog broth, and why wouldn't you? If so, discard the intestines, rinse the body, and proceed just as you would if you were making chicken stock. Or use the frog parts to reinforce a basic chicken stock, simmering as many of them as possible in a quart or two of chicken stock for a couple of hours along with a few cloves of fresh garlic.

5. Combine the flours in a shallow bowl, season generously with salt and pepper, and stir to combine well.

6. Pat the frogs' legs dry, dredge them in the seasoned flour, and set aside.

7. Heat two 8-inch flameproof clay pots or other heavy pans that hold heat well over medium heat. Add a slick of oil, about 1½ tablespoons, to each one, swirling them to coat. Divide the cooked rice between the clay pots and press down on the rice so it covers the bottom in an even layer approximately 1 inch thick. Reduce the heat to medium-low and cook until the rice forms a deep golden brown crust, 10 to 15 minutes.

8. Meanwhile, in another pot, heat the chicken stock over low heat.

9. Fry the dredged frogs' legs in the peanut oil, turning once, until golden, about 5 minutes total. Transfer them to a paper-towel-lined platter and season immediately with salt and pepper.

10. Put the pan with the guanciale fat back over medium heat. When it's hot, add the ginger, garlic, shallot, and wine and cook, stirring, for a minute.

11. Add the guanciale, toasted dried chilies, and 1½ tablespoons of the chicken stock and toss to combine. Throw in the pea shoots and stir until just wilted.

12. Pull the pan from the heat, add the frogs' legs, and stir to coat them with the goodness.

13. Pour the remaining warm chicken stock into each clay pot, top with the awesome, savory frog mixture, and finish with a squeeze of lemon. Serve immediately.

LISTEN
Ghostland Observatory, or any other cheesy, fun dance music, will keep you on your toes so you don't overcook that croaker. As you listen, hop around a bit in homage.

DRINK
Larmandier-Berrier Champagne. The soft bubbles work so well with these clean flavors and the little hit of chili.

FISH

Before I move toward piscine reality, let's talk about the *ideal* fish meal. You're in a market. The market is beside the water. All around you are piles of fish, many of which you've never seen before. All have firm, bright gills and clear eyes. They smell just slightly of the sea, the glistening skin suggesting the iridescent flesh below.

You sit down at a table. Just feet away, fish cook over a charcoal grill. A little bowl containing something bright and spicy—lime juice, fish sauce, chilies—is at the ready. Your eating implement—a fork, chopsticks—quickly yields to your hands, and you pick and suck and lick until only bones remain. In my version of heaven, those bones are whisked away to the deep fryer and return crunchy, completely edible, and entirely irresistible.

Unless you live in a hut in the Malaysian seaside town of Kota Kinabalu, your fish reality will probably be pretty damn different from my fantasy. But you'll be fine as long as you take the time to learn which fish are caught sustainably (visit www.montereybayaquarium.org for an up-to-date-list), and if you frequent a good fish market to learn what's in season and what's impeccably fresh. Then follow the commandment that Neptune spoketh unto Zakary: find that which is fresh, and around it build thy meal. Never force a fish into a recipe. If it's not calling out to you with its beauty, leave it be.

My first gastronomic reaction upon finding a perfect fish is lime juice, salt, and chili. Nothing beyond that is necessary. Anything else is just gravy. But I like gravy, so sometimes my mind wanders toward sambal belacan—a pungent mixture of fresh chilies and toasted dried shrimp—or an herbal broth packed with clams or a funky sauce made from crab roe. I love it when whatever sauciness that blesses the fish has notes of the sea itself—fermented shrimp paste, mussels, fish broths, anything that reinforces the flavor. Something porky is mighty fine too. Oh, and as usual, eat with your hands.

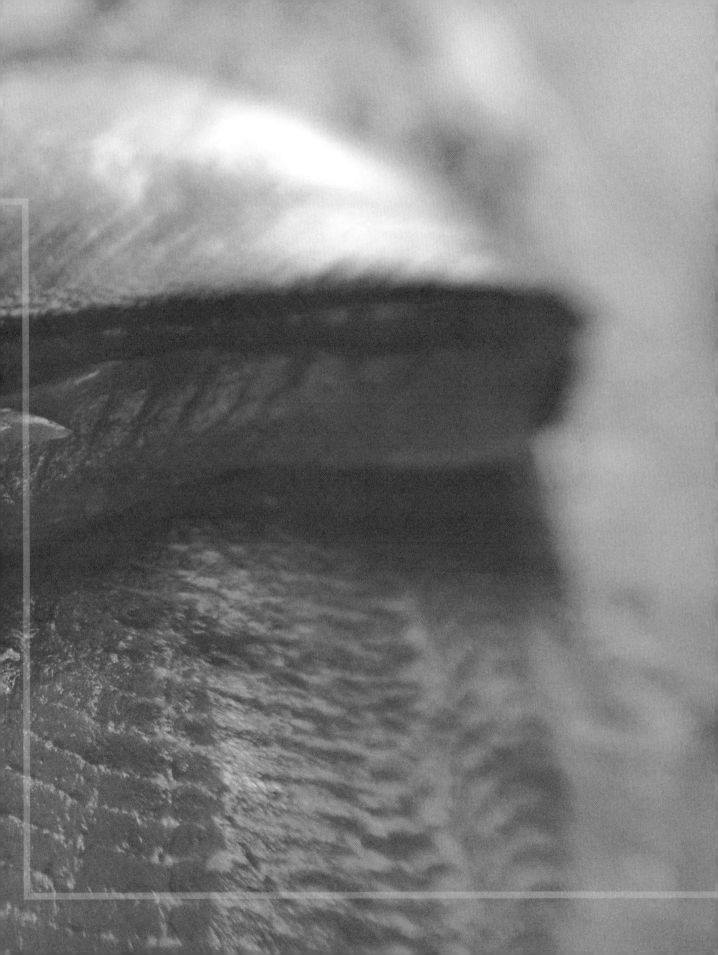

FISH HEAD CURRY

Like gnawing on a bone-in rib-eye, eating fish cooked on the bone is a little more work and a lot more delicious. There's no better example than the fish's head. The meat is so incredible—you have the lip-smacking gelatinous goodness and all those morsels that you discover when you really get in there among the bones. Why, then, are so many people reluctant to look a fish in the eye, demanding that waiters take away the whole fish and bring it back without the head?

The rejection of the head, bones, and other reminders of reality—this obstinate denial that what you're eating was once alive—is, as far as I know, unique to American culture. Eating the head, then, is not just obligatory for anyone concerned with deliciousness; it is also a profound affirmation that you don't take a creature's life for granted.

SERVES 4

FOR THE PEPPER PASTE
12 mild fresh chilies, such as
    Nardello, long red, or Anaheim
1 to 2 tablespoons olive oil (the best
    you can afford)
Salt

FOR THE CHILI-GARLIC PASTE
10 fresh Thai bird chilies, chopped   5 garlic cloves, chopped

FOR THE SPICE MIXTURE
1 tablespoon coriander seeds   1 teaspoon fenugreek seeds
1½ teaspoons fennel seeds   ¼ teaspoon whole cloves

FOR THE CURRY
½ cup ghee or clarified butter   2 sprigs fresh curry leaf
1 large white onion, thinly sliced   4 leaves daun salam (Indonesian
4 garlic cloves, thinly sliced   bay)
2 inches fresh ginger, peeled and   2 tablespoons unsweetened
    thinly sliced   tamarind paste, or more to taste
1½ inches fresh galangal, peeled   Juice of 1 lime, or more to taste
    and julienned   Sea salt
1 teaspoon belacan, toasted (see   2 large fish heads, well rinsed and
    page 333)   gills removed
Three 14-ounce cans coconut milk,
    preferably Aroy-D brand, shaken

MAKE THE PEPPER PASTE
Preheat the oven to 425°F. Spread the chilies on a baking sheet and toss with just enough olive oil to coat lightly (about 1 tablespoon) and some salt. Roast them

NOTE

Ask your fishmonger for two substantial heads, such as those from a salmon, striped bass, grouper, or large red snapper. If you must, you can use three or four smaller heads, but if they're not at least as large as a man's fist, they won't have enough meaty bits to be worth your effort. Make sure the gills are removed and rinse the heads well under plenty of running water.

in the oven, stirring once or twice, until the skins bubble and are slightly charred, about 10 minutes. Transfer the whole peppers to a blender and puree, adding just enough olive oil (about 1 tablespoon) to smooth things out. Press the paste through a medium-mesh sieve and set it aside. You should have about 2 cups.

MAKE THE CHILI-GARLIC PASTE

Use a mortar and pestle to pound (see page 12) the Thai bird chilies and the garlic cloves into a paste.

TOAST THE SPICES

Toast the coriander, fennel, and fenugreek seeds with the cloves in a dry pan over medium-high heat, swirling and shaking them until they crackle lightly, release their mysterious aroma, and color a little, about 3 minutes. Grind them to a powder in a spice grinder.

MAKE THE CURRY

1. Heat the ghee in a deep pot or large heavy skillet over medium-high heat. Add the onion, garlic, ginger, and galangal and cook just until translucent but not colored or fully soft, about 4 minutes.
2. Add the chili-garlic paste and cook, stirring a little, until very aromatic, about 3 minutes.
3. Add the ground spices and cook, stirring, until they're very fragrant. Add the toasted belacan and stir to incorporate, then do the same with the pepper paste and the coconut milk. Stir well and bring the liquid to a simmer.
4. Add the curry leaves and daun salam and season the liquid with the tamarind paste, half of the lime juice, and some salt. Return the liquid to a simmer and cook for about 30 minutes. Add more salt and lime juice to taste.
5. Add the fish heads to the curry and simmer, without moving them (you don't want them to fall apart) but basting often, until cooked through, 20 to 30 minutes, depending on size. When the cheeks feel loose when prodded gently, the fish heads are ready. Serve the curried fish heads in a large bowl with a bowl of rice on the side. Use your hands to get at the head's myriad goodies.

LISTEN
The Crusaders, "And Then There Was the Blues." An easy groove for a good time.

DRINK
Goutorbe Champagne. A few bottles for you and your friends.

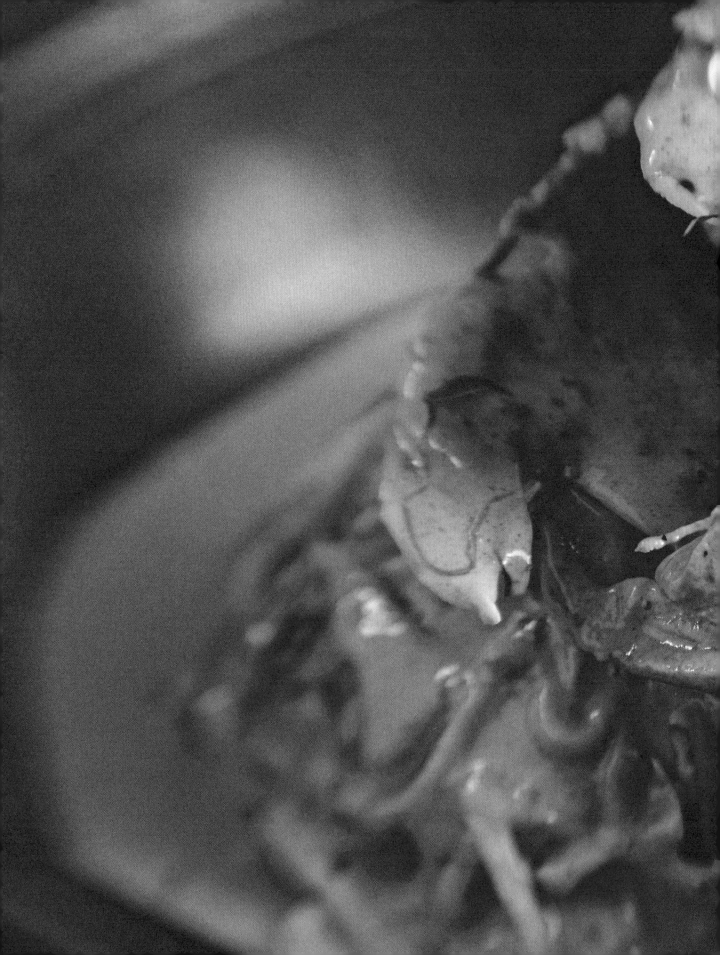

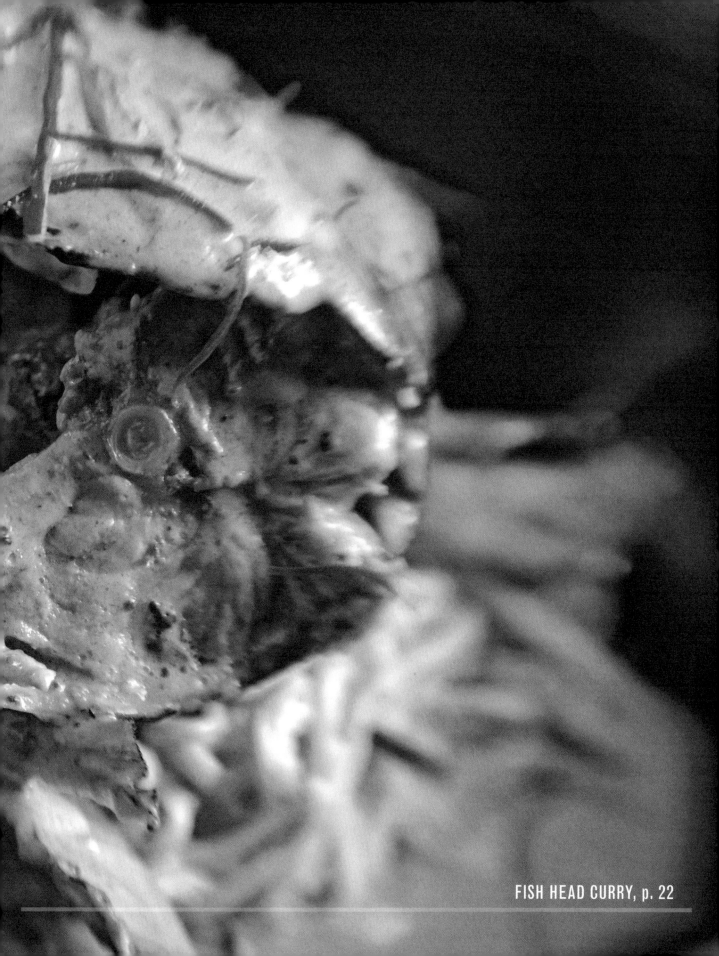

FISH HEAD CURRY, p. 22

GRILLED SARDINES WITH CELERY ROOT PUREE AND LEAF-LARD-POACHED RAISINS

The Good, the Bad, and the Oily. Starring Eli Wallach as the boozy, wrinkled raisins—not to be trusted but impossible to ignore. They team up with the celery root, played by Lee Van Cleef—white and insidious, its flavor threatening to envelop everything else. That is, until in rides our hero, Clint the sardine, a little roasted from the heat but with a glimmer remaining and enough flavor to tackle the whole plate and then some.

SERVES 4

½ cup rendered leaf lard (see page 196) or olive oil (the best you can afford)

½ cup raisins

2 medium celery roots, peeled and cut into 2-inch chunks

2 cups heavy cream

Sea salt

¼ cup nonvintage Armagnac

1 tablespoon granulated gula jawa (palm) or brown sugar

12 fresh head-on sardines, scaled and cleaned

Olive oil (the best you can afford)

Freshly ground black pepper

1 lemon

1½ cups loosely packed celery leaves

¼ cup sherry vinegar

1. If you're going to be a good boy and grill over hot charcoal, prepare the fire.
2. Render the lard in a saucepan over medium-low heat, add the raisins, and then keep them warm over very low heat.
3. In a medium saucepan, bring the celery roots, cream, and 1 tablespoon salt to a low simmer (be careful not to boil the cream). Cook until the celery root is tender enough to be pierced easily with a knife, 20 to 30 minutes. Strain the celery root, reserving the cream, and puree the celery root in a blender until smooth, adding a little bit of cream at a time to produce a smooth but not particularly runny puree. When you add the strained cream back to the puree, use just enough to form a tight, albeit lighter (due to the absense of gluten) puree, just like a fine pomme puree. Taste and season with salt if necessary. Set the puree aside and keep it warm.
4. Gently warm the Armagnac in a small saucepan over medium-low heat and add the sugar, mashing and stirring it with a metal spoon until it has dissolved. Remove the pan from the heat.
5. Just before you grill the sardines, strain the raisins from the lard, reserving the lard for another use (like pie dough!). Dump the raisins into a mixing bowl, pour in the Armagnac-sugar syrup, and toss to coat them.

LISTEN
Ennio Morricone, *The Good, the Bad and the Ugly* soundtrack.

DRINK
A fine vintage Armagnac. Perhaps with lemon zest and a splash of the Armagnac-sugar syrup (before you've added the raisins). A few cubes of ice, and I think we may have a new classic.

6. Heat a seasoned cast-iron grill pan, if you're not using a charcoal grill, over high heat. Brush the sardines with oil, then season the outsides and insides with a large pinch each of salt and pepper. Cook the sardines for about 1½ minutes on each side. Take care as you turn them, because the skin is very delicate and tears easily. Transfer the sardines to a plate as they're cooked and sprinkle them with a little more salt and a quick squeeze of lemon. Toss the celery leaves with the sherry vinegar and salt. Serve the sardines with a dollop of the celery root puree, a scattering of the raisins, and a sprinkling of the celery leaves.

SARDINE TEA SANDWICHES

The establishment of British hegemony in Malaysia began in the early 1800s and, to varying degrees, lasted until 1963 (although Malaysia remains part of the British Commonwealth, it seems to be a nominal relationship only), and one of the few colonial legacies I admire is the practice of high tea. So when I opened Fatty Crab, I decided I'd reinvent the whole British cucumber-finger-sandwiches thing, swapping sardines for the 'cukes. This is, in my opnion, a slightly elevated version of sardine tea sandwiches I have seen at some of the more refined Malay high tea affairs (I'd mention where and when I've sampled the dried-out offensive versions, but that would simply be scandalous!). The soft, sweet white bread, a funky sambal aïoli, and fresh sardines soaked in a tasty, acidic liquid (which you could call a Malaysian escabeche) are powerful little pillows that, with the right drink, will elevate any tea party from a stodgy affair to an affair of the senses. Sadly, we just couldn't move enough of them at Fatty Crab (people preferred tea sandwiches made with pork belly even though sardines are one of the universe's tastiest fish), so now they're on the menu only from time to time. The sardines are easy to make and keep well in the fridge, so you can eat them as they are or follow through all the way to sandwich completion.

MAKES 12 TEA SANDWICHES

16 fresh sardine fillets
¼ cup olive oil (the best you can afford)
1 small yellow onion, thinly sliced
3 garlic cloves, thinly sliced
½ cup tomato puree (see Note)
Juice of 1 lime
1 tablespoon salt

1 tablespoon Sambal Belacan (page 306)
1 tablespoon brown rice vinegar
8 slices Pepperidge Farm Original White Bread
¼ cup Sambal Aïoli (page 308)
16 fresh Vietnamese mint (rau ram) leaves

1. Place the sardines, skin side down, in a shallow, nonreactive dish just big enough to hold them in a single layer.

2. Heat the olive oil in a medium saucepan over medium heat until hot but not smoking. Add the onion and garlic and cook until translucent, about 3 minutes. Add the tomato puree, lime juice, salt, and sambal belacan, then raise the heat to medium-high and bring to a simmer.

3. Add the vinegar, raise the heat again to bring the liquid to a boil, and immediately pour the hot mixture over the sardines, spreading it to cover the fillets evenly. Let it sit for 10 minutes at room temperature, then cover and refrigerate overnight.

4. When you're ready to make the sandwiches, let the sardines come to room temperature. Then take the sardines out of their marinade, but don't wipe all of

NOTE

Tea sandwiches are all about the white bread: Moist, sweet, slightly dense, and very square like a *pain de mie*, or French sandwich bread—my favorite is Pepperidge Farm Original White. To keep this lovely bread from drying out, cover your finished sandwiches with damp paper towels and assemble the sandwiches no more than an hour before serving them.

NOTE

You can buy tomato puree or make it yourself by chopping up cored ripe tomatoes and cooking them in a pot over medium heat until they've broken down completely, about 30 minutes. Then mash them or give them a whirl in the food processor.

LISTEN
The deep sounds of early **R. L. Burnside** recordings.

DRINK
Moonshine (aka White Dog) stirred with ice, strained, and finished with a lemon twist, because sardines and sambal belacan can take it!

it off. Spread all 8 slices with 1 teaspoon of sambal aïoli. Lay four sardine fillets on each four of the bread slices, then tear the mint leaves and divide the pieces among them. Complete the sandwiches with the remaining bread slices and trim the crusts. Cut each sandwich into 3 equal rectangles and serve them on your grandmother's tray with shots of the moonshine in cordial glasses. Be classy while you get fucked up.

FISH COOKED IN COCONUT MILK WITH FIRE CHILI

This is such an elegant way to serve fish, known succinctly in Malay as *ikan masak lemak chili api,* fish cooked in coconut milk with fire chili. All you do is infuse coconut milk with Asian aromatics and enrich it with fish bones and heads, then strain it to get the luxurious broth you use to poach the fillets. My not-so-secret weapon? Dried *assam gelugor,* a Malaysian fruit that's almost always sun-dried, which adds an amazing acidity to the soupy sauce. The flavor is exciting and illustrates how refreshing a sour soup can be. You'll notice that I cook the stems of the herbs in the coconut milk, where they offer a more subdued version of themselves, and then use the tender, brightly flavored leaves as a garnish. That's something to consider, whatever you're cooking. I also use cilantro roots in the broth, an ingredient more closely associated with Thai than Malaysian cuisine, because I have no allegiances to tradition—just flavor.

SERVES 4

2 whole black bass (1½ to 2 pounds each), cleaned and filleted, heads and bones reserved

3 tablespoons olive oil (the best you can afford)

8 medium shallots, thinly sliced

10 fresh Thai bird chilies, 4 halved lengthwise and 6 thinly sliced crosswise

5 garlic cloves, thinly sliced

2 lemongrass stalks, outer layer removed and stalks crushed with a blunt object

1 cup ikan bilis

6 slices assam gelugor, well rinsed in cold water

6 fresh kaffir lime leaves, 2 leaves julienned (stems and center veins discarded) and 4 left whole

5 fresh Thai basil stems and about 12 leaves

5 fresh Vietnamese mint (rau ram) stems and about 12 leaves

4 fresh cilantro roots, rinsed, scraped, rinsed again, and trimmed

3 tablespoons coriander seeds

Six 14-ounce cans coconut milk, preferably Aroy-D brand, shaken

3 tablespoons fish sauce

2 teaspoons salt

Grated zest and juice of 1 lime

2 galangal flowers, julienned (optional)

1. Rinse the fillets, heads, and bones under cool running water. Pat the fillets and heads dry and refrigerate until you're ready to use them.
2. Heat the oil in a Dutch oven or large heavy saucepan over medium heat. Add the shallots, halved chilies, garlic, and lemongrass. Cook, stirring occasionally, until softened, about 5 minutes.
3. Add the fish heads and bones, ikan bilis, assam gelugor, 4 whole kaffir lime leaves, basil stems, mint stems, cilantro roots, and coriander seeds to the pot.

LISTEN
Billie Holiday (aka Lady Day) until you understand what it means to be seductive—or desperate.

DRINK
Lightly chilled Pommeau, because it's delicate but works with the richness of the coconut.

Cook, stirring well, for 3 minutes. Stir in the coconut milk, 1 tablespoon of the fish sauce, and the salt. Bring the liquid to a simmer and cook, covered, for 1 hour.

4. Strain the liquid into a bowl, discarding the solids, stir in the lime juice and zest, and season with more fish sauce until it tastes really good. Wipe the pot clean with a paper towel.

5. Place the fillets in the cleaned pot skin side down and gently pour in the coconut milk mixture. Bring to a gentle simmer over medium-low heat and cook until the fish flesh just begins to flake, about 10 minutes.

6. Use a spatula to transfer the fillets to shallow bowls and ladle some of the coconut milk mixture over each one. Tear the basil and mint leaves and garnish each dish with them, the sliced chilies, julienned lime leaves, and julienned galangal petals. Serve immediately with steamed white rice on the side.

STEAMED LOUP DE MER

The year is 1996. I'm sitting on the beach in Koh Phanggan, Thailand, drinking a Singha. The guy who runs the bungalow I'm renting for 50 baht a night comes over, offers me a drag from his spliff, and asks me if I'm hungry. Well, of course I'm hungry. He points to a small boat that just beached about a hundred yards away. "We have fish," he says. Fish is good; fresh fish is very good. About twenty minutes pass, and he brings over a plate on which sits a glistening hunk of fish bathed in lime juice and fish sauce and framed by crushed pieces of garlic and scattered bits of scud chilies. Life can be wonderful.

SERVES 2

FOR THE CHILI PASTE

4 fresh cilantro roots, rinsed, scraped, and rinsed again, or 16 cilantro stems

5 fresh Thai bird chilies, stemmed

6 garlic cloves, peeled

2 tablespoons fish sauce

Juice of 1 lime

FOR THE FISH AND BOK CHOY

Salt

1 pound baby bok choy

Two whole loups de mer aka branzino (1½ to 2 pounds each), cleaned and gills removed

One ¼-inch-thick slice lardo (see page 194 or store-bought), cut into twelve 2-inch-long matchsticks

3 tablespoons olive oil (the best you can afford)

Freshly ground black pepper

Ginger and Papaya Pickle (page 301; optional)

2 cups fresh cilantro leaves

1 cup thinly sliced scallion

MAKE THE CHILI PASTE

Use a mortar and pestle to pound (see page 12) the cilantro roots, chilies, and garlic, pounding each ingredient thoroughly before adding the next. Add the fish sauce and lime juice and pound to incorporate thoroughly. Set the mixture aside.

COOK THE FISH AND BOK CHOY

1. Bring a pot of water to a boil, salt it until it tastes like the ocean, and blanch the bok choy until crisp-tender, 3 to 4 minutes. Transfer the bok choy to an ice-water bath. Drain it well and set it on paper towels to dry.

2. Score each fish, making three ¼-inch-deep slashes from top to bottom on each side. Press the pieces of lardo into each slit.

3. Line a wide steamer basket with a large plate that fits snugly inside. Season each fish inside and outside with salt. Arrange the fish on the plate (it's okay if the head and tail hang off the plate a bit) and massage most of the chili paste all

LISTEN
The new Motown of **Mayer Hawthorne & The County,** who remind you that music is still fun!

DRINK
Neuberger from K. Alphart, a truly satisfying bottle of wine with just the right acidity for this dish.

over the fish. Set the steamer basket over simmering water and cover. Cook the fish until the flesh easily flakes away from the bones, 8 to 9 minutes.

4. While the fish steams, heat the olive oil in a sauté pan over medium-high heat. Add the blanched bok choy and sauté, tossing occasionally, to heat it through, about 3 minutes. Season with salt and pepper.

5. Carefully transfer the fish to a serving platter with the bok choy and pour all the chili paste liquid from the steamer plate over the fish. If there isn't much liquid, gently warm the leftover chili paste and spoon it over the plated fish.

6. Serve the fish topped with a tangle of the pickle. Garnish with the cilantro and scallions. Steamed rice on the side, fools!

SEA TROUT WITH MUSSELS, SAUSAGE, AND FERMENTED TOFU

This dish represents a watershed in my culinary life: the moment I finally figured out where fermented tofu fits in my cooking. When you whisk the little cubes of soft tofu with a liquid, they contribute a salty, hefty backbone to any dish—a quality that reminds me a bit of blue cheese. When I first made this dish, I thought I'd made a discovery on the level of Marie Curie's, the combo of fermented tofu and shellfish was just that delicious. But a few years later I learned that Chinese Malays cook small clams with fermented tofu. So though I might not win the Nobel Prize, I will keep promoting the frequent, though judicious, use of fermented tofu, which is not exactly common in restaurants in New York, or anywhere else for that matter. In this, my crew at Fatty and I walk alone.

SERVES 4

4 scallions

¼ cup olive oil (the best you can afford), plus extra for finishing

2 garlic cloves, minced

¾ cup dry white wine

3 stems each: fresh cilantro, basil, and Vietnamese mint (rau ram)

1 pound mussels, preferably bouchot, rinsed and scrubbed

½ pound sweet Italian sausage, removed from casings

4 skin-on sea trout, char, or wild salmon fillets (about 1¼ pounds total)

Salt and freshly ground black pepper

3 tablespoons unsalted butter

1 tablespoon fermented tofu (about two ½-inch cubes)

2 sprigs fresh Vietnamese mint (rau ram) leaves

2 fresh Thai bird chilies, thinly sliced

1. Preheat the oven to 400°F.
2. Cut the scallions into 2-inch pieces, halve them lengthwise, then julienne them lengthwise. Immerse them in ice water so they curl.
3. In a large heavy pot with a tight lid, heat 2 tablespoons of the olive oil over medium-high heat. Add the garlic and cook, stirring, for 30 seconds, then add the white wine and herb stems. Raise the heat to high and bring the wine to a boil. Add the mussels and cook over high heat, covered, until the mussel shells open, about 4 minutes. After 5 minutes, remove the pan from the heat and discard any mussels that did not open.
4. Place a colander in a saucepan or bowl big enough to fit the colander and strain the mussels allowing the saucepan or bowl to catch the cooking liquid. Remove half of the mussels from their shells, discarding the shells. Reserve these mussels in a small bowl and reserve the remaining mussels in their shells in another bowl.

5. Heat 1 tablespoon of the remaining olive oil in a medium sauté pan over medium-high heat and swirl it around in the pan. Add the sausage and cook without moving it around much but turning it occasionally until it has some nice color on it, 8 to 10 minutes, then break it up with a spoon. Turn off the heat and transfer the sausage to a paper-towel-lined plate with a slotted spoon. Discard the oil in the pan, then return the sausage to the pan and set it aside.

6. Pat the fish fillets dry and season each side with salt and pepper.

7. Heat the remaining tablespoon of olive oil in a large ovenproof sauté pan, preferably cast iron or black steel, over medium-high heat. Add the fillets to the hot pan skin side down. Sear the fillets, without moving the fish, until the skin is crispy and golden and the bottom $1/8$ inch of the fish is opaque, about 4 minutes. Add 2 tablespoons of the butter to the pan, let the butter foam, then spoon some of it over the fish. Place the pan in the preheated oven, just to warm the rest of the flesh, about $1\frac{1}{2}$ minutes. (This fish is best rare or medium-rare. If you like your fish hammered, then leave it in there longer.) Drain the scallions well.

8. While the fish cooks, add the shucked mussels to the pan with the sausage. Turn the heat to medium and toss the ingredients in the pan with a little bit of the olive oil. When they're warm, add the mussel-cooking liquid and the fermented tofu. Whisk to incorporate the cubes, mashing them up a bit at first, and bring to a simmer. Add the mussels still in their shells to the liquid, cook just until they're warmed through, and ladle this funky love fest into four bowls. Garnish each bowl with a sprinkling of the scallions, mint leaves, and chilies, and top with the trout fillets, skin side up. Serve with steamed rice. Grilled bread would also be nice.

LISTEN
Sonic Youth, *Goo*, because Chuck D is on it!

DRINK
A bottle of pastis, a bottle of water, and as many glasses as you need.

SEA TROUT WITH MUSSELS, SAUSAGE. AND FERMENTED TOFU, p. 34

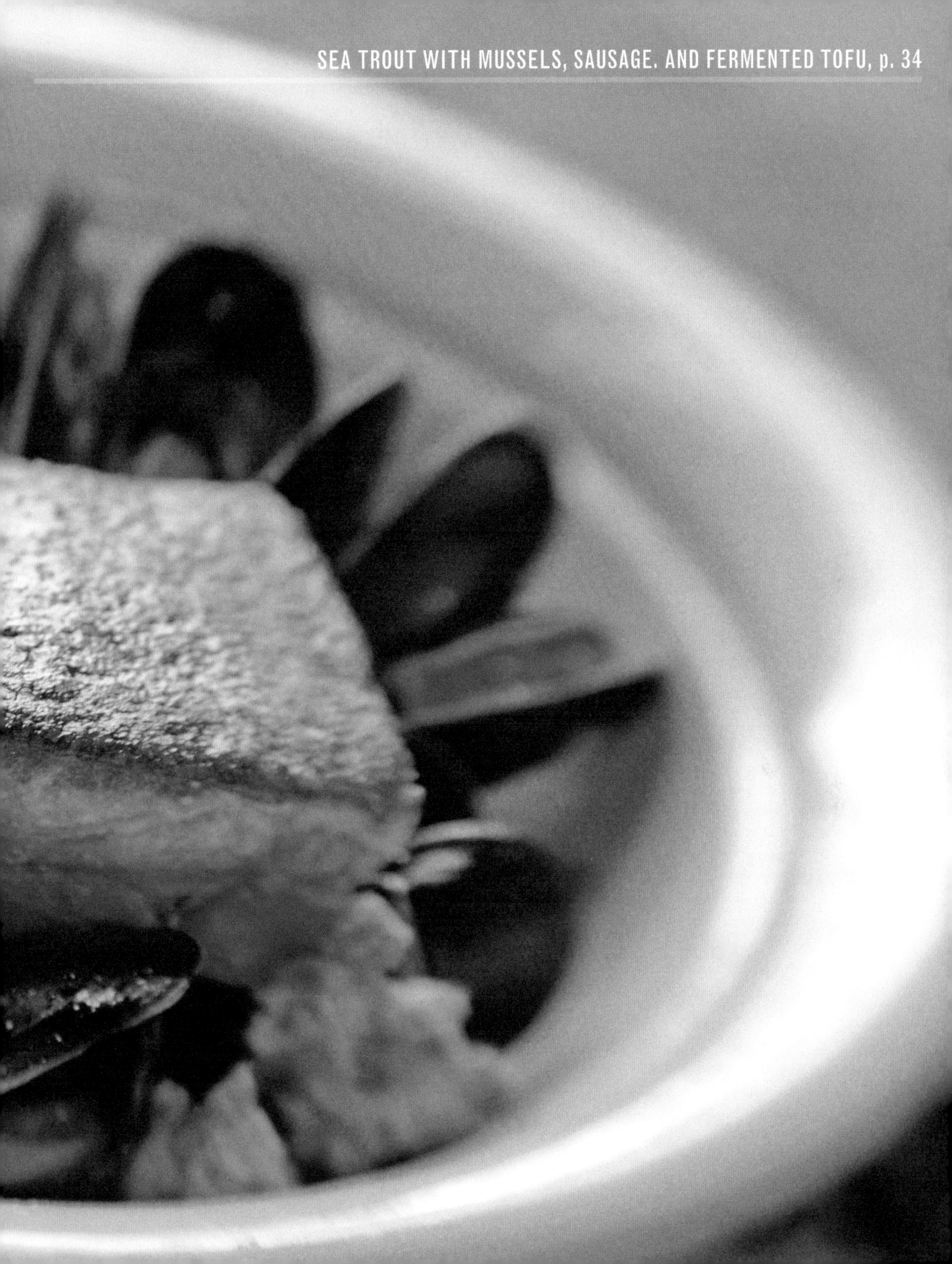

TUNA BELLY WITH AN APPROXIMATION OF A CLASSIC SAUCE DUGLÉRÉ

We usually encounter tuna belly at the sushi counter, so the idea of grilling it may seem odd to the uninitiated. But the belly, like a good steak, is streaked with beautiful, beautiful fat. When you grill tuna belly over a hot charcoal fire until charred and smoky outside and still cool and tender inside, the fat renders the flesh unbelievably silky. If you're going to skip the charcoal fire, a big cast-iron pan will do. Bluefin's best (try to get Kindai, the sustainable stuff), but you can use any kind of tuna as long as it's really, really fresh—or was just removed from one of those time-lock super deep-freezers that's the pride of superior sushi shops.

I came up with this dish after my friend Josh DeChellis came back from the Fulton Fish Market with an entire tuna belly. I looked to an old-school French sauce named for the chef Adolph Dugléré that I had once at an Alain Ducasse restaurant. But to call my version anything other than an approximation would be an insult to the original, because I turned the original flour-based sauce made with ripe tomatoes and fish stock into one made with green tomatoes, Master Stock, and a jalapeño. I also use a slightly oxidized white wine for the sauce, while the original employed Rancio, which is beyond oxidized and hard to find.

SERVES 4

2 tablespoons olive oil (the best you can afford)
4 garlic cloves, crushed and peeled
½ fennel bulb, outer layer removed and bulb roughly chopped, stalks chopped and saved for stock, fronds added as garnish if desired
2 shallots, roughly chopped
2 jalapeño chilies, 1 seeded and roughly chopped and 1 very thinly sliced for garnish
Sea salt
½ cup savagnin or sauvignon blanc
4 medium green (unripe) tomatoes, cored and chopped
12 medium clams, such as cherrystones or manila
3 cups Master Stock (page 322)
12 fresh parsley stems
1½ pounds tuna belly in one piece
Freshly ground black pepper
3 tablespoons unsalted butter
Splash of Banyuls vinegar (optional)
1 large red tomato, cored, peeled, seeded, and diced

1. Start a charcoal fire (or, fine, use a gas grill) and heat the clean grill grates over it. Let it get nice and hot.
2. Heat the oil in a large sauté pan with a lid over medium-high heat. Add the garlic, fennel, shallots, and chopped jalapeño along with a good pinch of salt and cook, stirring occasionally, until everything softens, about 4 minutes.
3. Add the wine to the pan and let it bubble up and cook down until it reduces to about 2 tablespoons, 1 to 2 minutes. Add the green tomatoes and then the clams. Cover the pan and cook the clams over high heat, shaking the pan occasionally,

LISTEN
Jackie Mittoo, "Merry Go Round." Mellow grooving for grilling.

DRINK
Savagnin (preferably made by Puffeney) from the Arbois. It's in the sauce!

until the clams open, about 6 minutes. After 7 minutes remove the pan from the heat and discard any clams that did not open.

4. Add the stock and parsley stems to the pan. Bring the mixture to a boil and reduce the liquid by about a third. Strain the liquid into a saucepan and keep warm, discarding the solids (including the clams).

5. By now your charcoal fire should be quite hot. Rub the grill with an oil-soaked towel.

6. Season the tuna belly with a light, even dusting of salt and pepper. Lay the fish on the hottest part of the grill and let it sit without moving until it develops a nice, dark char on the surface, at least 1 to 2 minutes. Gently flip onto the other side for 1 more minute. You want it really rare. If you have a great, beautiful big chunk, char the other two sides. If it's a thin piece, just char the two sides with the most surface area.

7. Warm the sauce over low heat and whisk in the butter. Season with salt and pepper and a touch of Banyuls vinegar if you like a little acidic kick.

8. Slice the tuna into nice ½-inch slices and coat with sauce. Garnish it with the diced red tomato, sprinkle with the jalapeño slices, and add the fennel fronds if you like.

ROASTED TURBOT WITH GARLIC PARSLEY PASTE, SWEET PEPPER PUREE, AND CLAMS

In the United States, fusion food typically operates in one mode—French technique, Asian ingredients. This recipe flips the script, applying an Asian technique to Western flavors. The method employed here is more or less the standard way of making a curry, only instead of coconut milk or stock the liquid is a mixture of wine, razor clam juice, and pureed roasted pepper. OK, fine, there are some Asian ingredients in there, too, like the Thai bird chili, which gives the dish a forward flavor, and a blend of fenugreek and coriander seeds, which add complexity and a touch of bitterness. And even though turbot, an amazing, justifiably pricey fish whose flesh exists in the magical land between meaty and delicate, can be served with just a touch of butter and lemon juice, it's also sturdy enough to withstand more aggressive flavors.

SERVES 4

FOR THE PEPPER PUREE

15 fresh Nardello, Anaheim, or Fresno chiles (about 1½ pounds total), stemmed

1 teaspoon olive oil (the best you can afford)
Salt

FOR THE CHILI-SPICE PASTE

1 tablespoon coriander seeds
1 teaspoon white peppercorns
1 teaspoon fenugreek seeds
10 fresh parsley stems

4 fresh Thai bird chilies, stemmed and seeded
8 garlic cloves, roughly chopped
5 shallots, roughly chopped

FOR THE RAZOR CLAMS

8 razor clams, cleaned well
2 tablespoons olive oil (the best you can afford)
4 garlic cloves, crushed

2 medium shallots, roughly chopped
½ cup dry white wine
3 tablespoons chopped flat-leaf parsley

FOR THE TURBOT

Four ½-pound bone-in turbot wings
Salt and freshly ground white pepper

3 tablespoons olive oil (the best you can afford)
½ pound (2 sticks) unsalted butter

TO FINISH THE DISH

¾ cup dry white wine
½ cup Simple Fish Stock (page 326)

Fleur de sel and freshly ground white pepper

MAKE THE PEPPER PUREE

1. Preheat the oven to 425°F and slide a large baking sheet in there to get hot. In a mixing bowl, toss the peppers with the olive oil and a pinch of salt. Put the

LISTEN
Death from Above, "Sexy Results." A driving, hard, funky, and fun song.

DRINK
Chartogne-Taillet Champagne. Turbot and Champagne—all night long!

peppers on the hot pan in a single layer and roast for 5 minutes. Turn them over and continue to cook until they're soft and their skins color and blister, about 10 minutes.

2. Scoop the peppers into the mixing bowl and cover tightly with plastic wrap for about 15 minutes. The peppers will finish cooking as they sit in their steamy bowl. Remove and discard the skins, stems, and seeds and puree the peppers in a blender until smooth. Transfer the puree to a bowl and set it aside.

MAKE THE CHILI-SPICE PASTE

1. Toast the coriander, peppercorns, and fenugreek in a dry pan over medium heat, swirling and shaking the spices until they start to crackle and release their mysterious aromas, about 3 minutes. Grind them together in a spice grinder.

2. Use a mortar and pestle to pound (see page 12) the parsley stems, chilies, garlic, and shallots, pounding each ingredient thoroughly before adding the next, until you have a fairly smooth paste. Scrape it into a bowl and stir in the ground toasted spices to combine well. Set aside.

COOK THE RAZOR CLAMS

1. Wash the razor clams very well under cold running water, lightly scrubbing the outside of the shells with a soft towel and letting the cold water run through the inside of the shells to remove any sand.

2. Heat the olive oil in a large sauté pan with a lid over medium heat. Add the garlic and shallots and sauté until fragrant and slightly softened, about 4 minutes. Raise the heat to high, add the white wine and parsley, and bring to a boil. Let the liquid boil for 30 seconds, then add the clams and cover the pan. Cook, shaking the pan once or twice, until the clams open, 3 to 4 minutes. Discard any that haven't opened after 5 minutes. Remove the pot from the heat. Strain the clams through a fine-mesh sieve, reserving the cooking liquid in a bowl. Remove the cooked clams from their shells, slice them on the bias so each piece is about ¼ inch thick, and set them aside.

COOK THE TURBOT

1. Preheat the oven to 425°F. Pat the turbot wings dry with paper towels and season well with salt and white pepper.

2. Heat a large ovenproof sauté pan, preferably cast iron or black steel, over high heat. When it's hot, coat the bottom of the pan with 1 tablespoon of the olive oil and add the turbot, skin side down. Reduce the heat to medium-high and add 4 tablespoons (½ stick) of the butter. When it starts to foam, add the remaining butter. When it starts to foam, slide the pan into the oven. Baste every 4 minutes or so, until the fish is just cooked through, 12 to 15 minutes. Each time you baste, tilt the pan with one hand (use a pot holder) and with the other quickly ladle the hot butter over the fish 7 to 10 times with a large metal spoon.

FINISH THE DISH

1. When the fish is about half done, heat the remaining 2 tablespoons of olive oil in another sauté pan over medium heat. Add the chili-spice paste and cook, stirring occasionally, until it's fragrant, about 2 minutes.

2. Add the wine, fish stock, and reserved razor-clam-cooking liquid. Cook, stirring, for a good minute, then add the pepper puree and cook for another minute.

3. Add the razor clams and cook just until they're warmed through, about 20 seconds, then remove the pan from the heat.

4. Spoon the clam mixture into 4 large bowls and top each with the turbot. Sprinkle the fish with a touch of fleur de sel and white pepper. Eat with some simple boiled potatoes.

SHELLFISH

One summer when I was young, my mom and dad rented a beach house in Maine. I liked to sit on the rocky shore and gawk at the lobstermen who baited their traps with whole crabs. One day I worked up the nerve to ask one if I could have a crab to play with. No, he said, but you can have this bucket of fresh crab claws. Great, I thought. What am I going to do with these? Little kids have great imaginations, but mine failed me. Dejectedly, I took them to my mom, who knew what glory was lurking inside. Later that night, we cracked the claws and dipped the sweet, delicate meat in drawn butter, tossing the shells over our shoulders into the ocean. And I was in love.

Soon my mom was taking lobsters from the traps herself (and paying for what she took, of course), revealing to me the splendor of another crustacean. Huge, rich chunks of flesh, with that irresistible tug to it, wound up in pasta along with chanterelle mushrooms from the woods nearby. Years later I had flashbacks to this dish while eating lobster with e-fu noodles in Taipei. In Asia, they eat the fuck out of everything with shells. Periwinkles, snails—any creature you can find—shells be damned, they'll find the meat in 'em. There's an infinite array of mollusks and crustaceans on offer in Italy too, tiny mussels and razor clams and bug-eyed little creatures that look like miniature legless lobsters and taste more succulent than shrimp.

And shellfish is inherently cool beyond its crazy flavor and succulence. When you eat shellfish, you get to experience firsthand one of man's greatest culinary discoveries: the surprise and delight that inside the spiny, hard, and generally unlovely shells of oysters, clams, lobsters, crabs, shrimp, and the rest lurks sweet deliciousness. And also? In this day and age, at least here in the States, we're rarely presented with the chance to kill our own dinner. When you send shrimp, crabs, lobsters, and mollusks to their grisly, delicious deaths, you get a deeper connection——whether you want it or not——to the food you eat.

Because the pristine flavor of shellfish is so distinctive, you have lots of options when you're cooking with them. You can tread lightly, making sure they're the main event, or you can go crazy and bomb them with chilies and sambal and ginger and garlic, knowing that though these brave creatures might have given their life for your dinner, when it comes to flavor, they don't back down.

PARCOOKING LOBSTER
(FOR EASY SHELL REMOVAL)

The Simplest Way: Bring a large pot of water to a boil, drop in the lobsters, let the water come back to a boil, and cook the lobsters for 1½ minutes. Remove the meat from the shell (see the method below for details).

My Way: I was first exposed to this brilliant lobster-meat-removal method while I was working for Thomas Keller at the French Laundry. The purpose of this method is to produce shell-less, flawless, barely cooked lobster meat—the tail and the claw meat are cooked for different amounts of time—that can be finished in a variety of ways before it hits the plate. Of course, some home cooks might just want to buy already-shelled lobster meat, so this is mainly for those who want to go the extra mile. Especially because before the cooking and the eating there is the killing. People don't usually slaughter their own dinner—unless they're making lobster. This method might seem a bit brutal at first, but it's no worse than dropping a lobster into a cauldron of boiling water.

This recipe is perfect for up to four 1¼- to 1½-pound lobsters. If you want to cook more than four, just scale up the water and vinegar amounts. If you want to parcook larger lobsters, just adjust your poaching time.

Use the lobster meat for Lobster Wontons (page 48), Lobster Wonton Mee (page 50), or Lobster Club Sandwich (page 54) and reserve the shells for Lobster Stock (page 328), which you'll need for the Lobster Wonton Mee.

2 cups distilled or white wine vinegar per lobster	Live lobsters, 1¼ to 1½ pounds each

1. In a pot large enough, bring 2 quarts water per lobster and vinegar to a boil.
2. Meanwhile, deal with the lobsters. Put three large bowls on a table. Using a towel to protect your hands from the sharp spines along the legs, remove the claws from the lobster by twisting them from the body, being careful to keep the legs and knuckles and claws intact. Remove the rubber bands from the claws, rinse the claws under cold water, and put them in one of the bowls.
3. Next, hold the body of one of your lively lobsters in your right hand and hold the tail in your left. Twist the body from the tail, rotating your wrists in opposite directions, with one sure, strong movement. Rinse the tail under cold water and put it in the second bowl. Rinse the body under cold water as well—after removing the grayish tomalley and, if you're lucky, the dark green coral.
4. Remove and discard the guts (everything you see inside the shell that's not tomalley, coral, or meat), and put the shell in the third bowl.
5. Set a timer, because the timing here is crucial to your success. Once the vinegar water has come to a boil, pour enough of it over the claws to fully submerge

The tomalley, which is the liver and pancreas of the lobster, can be rinsed, saved, and added to shellfish stocks or sauce just before they come off the heat and right before they get strained. The tomalley is best used in this way as it adds flavor, but some public health departments will recommend against eating it daily—or even often—as its role is to filter toxins. At the time of the writing of this book there is no red tide alert, but it's best to always double-check your research. As for me, I eat it all! The coral, or egg sacs, however, is even better and turns a brilliant red-orange color when heated. It makes a bangin' compound butter that can then be used to finish sauces, pastas, rice dishes—you name it.

them. After 2 minutes, pour enough of the remaining boiling liquid over the tails to submerge them. After 3 minutes, drain and discard the liquid. The claws should have been submerged for 5 minutes total, the tails for 3 minutes total.

6. Swiftly, to prevent the meat from overcooking from the residual heat, remove the meat from the tails: Put a tail bottom side up on a cutting board. You'll see a hard, translucent piece of exoskeleton. Use kitchen shears to clip it along the side of the shell all the way down to the tip of the tail. Repeat on the opposite side. Use your fingers to grab the tail flap at the top of the tail and peel it back to reveal the meat. It should pull off very easily. Remove the tail meat in one piece with your fingers (this too should just slip right out) and place it in a bowl. Repeat with the other tails, adding the shell scraps to the bowl with the other shells, setting the meat to the side.

7. Next, turn your attention to the claws. Twist the knuckle (the piece that connects the claw and the body) to separate it from the claw and set it aside. Use kitchen shears to snip off the very tips of the claw's pincers (about ¼ inch). Use the backside of a cleaver or knife (not the blade) to lightly crack the shell about ½ inch from the base of the claw. Turn the claw over and make a similar crack on the other side. Then you'll be able to peel the shell off the fat part of the claw, exposing some meat. Grab this meat with your fingers and gently wiggle and lightly twist it. Be careful not to tear the meat, particularly the tips, which are the most tender part. If the meat is resisting, resort to the blow method. Blow through the hole on the tip of each pincer and, while blowing, begin to gently pull the meat, tugging at the base end of the claw. Repeat with the other claws, adding the shell scraps to the shell bowl, and set the meat aside.

8. Finally, use kitchen shears to remove the knuckle meat by cutting along the length of each knuckle shell. Carefully pull the shell open and pry out the knuckle meat with your fingers. Add the shells to the shell bowl and set the meat aside.

The lobster meat can be stored in the fridge for up to 48 hours. The well-wrapped shells will last in the freezer for many months.

LISTEN
The *Jeopardy* theme song over and over and over again. Or, if you're not a masochist, "Jams I–V" from **Derek and the Dominos** off *The Layla Sessions*.

DRINK
El Tesoro tequila, neat. Sip it, don't shoot it, you philistine!

LOBSTER WONTONS

You'll discover that when you master this recipe, you've suddenly become very popular with your friends and family. I mean, who doesn't love a wonton? The wontons we serve at Fatty Crab are filled with a blend of shrimp and pork (a combo very popular with the secular crowd); these XO-sauce-spiked lobster-filled versions are equally awesome—and equally unkosher. One of the keys to awesome wontons is to remember that they are rather delicately filled—not overstuffed. The lobster wontons need at least 4 hours in the freezer before you use them—they'll stay there for up to a month—so make them ahead, whether you use them for Lobster Wonton Mee (recipe follows), eat them in a simple soup, or crisp them in a skillet.

MAKES 24 WONTONS

1½ teaspoons neutral oil, such as grapeseed or canola
2 garlic cloves, minced
1 large shallot, minced
1 inch fresh ginger, peeled and julienned
1 cup Parcooked Lobster Meat (preceding recipe)

1 egg white
3 fresh water chestnuts, drained and diced
1 scallion, thinly sliced
1 tablespoon XO sauce (recipe follows), drained of excess oil
2 tablespoons fish sauce
24 wonton wrappers

1. Heat the oil in a sauté pan over medium heat. Add the garlic, shallot, and ginger and cook, stirring occasionally, until translucent and aromatic, about 3 minutes. Remove from the heat and let cool completely.

2. Put the lobster meat, cooled vegetable mixture, and egg white into a food processor and pulse until pretty smooth. Transfer the mixture to a mixing bowl and add the water chestnuts, scallion, XO sauce (without the oil), and fish sauce. Use a rubber spatula to fold the ingredients together.

3. Put a wonton wrapper on a work surface with one corner pointed toward you. Put 1½ teaspoons of the lobster mixture in the center of the lower half of the wonton skin. Moisten the edges of the wonton with a wet brush or fingers, then fold the skin over the filling, corner to corner to form a triangle. Push out any air that surrounds the filling and then press the edges to seal. With the base of the triangle facing you, moisten the tips of each corner with water and fold the bottom two corners to the top corner, pressing firmly to seal.

4. Transfer the wonton to a parchment-paper-lined sheet tray and repeat this process with the remaining wrappers. Place the tray in the freezer. Freezing the wontons prevents them from getting soggy and tearing. Keep them in the freezer for at least 4 hours, until you're ready to use them or freeze on the tray for 4 hours and then transfer them to an airtight plastic bag and store for up to 1 month.

XO SAUCE

XO sauce is a fairly recent invention (it started showing up in Hong Kong in the eighties). It's named after a pricey cognac but tastes like the spicy sea. Dried shrimp and scallops are the base for this piquant condiment. Before you use it, drain the XO sauce in cheesecloth for 1 hour, occasionally gathering the corners to make a bundle and lightly twisting to force out the oil. The sauce left in the cheesecloth has a more concentrated flavor than it does straight out of the bottle. Plus, you can save the tasty oil to use in place of the chili oil in Lobster Wonton Mee, in case you don't have any premade in your pantry.

5. When you're ready to cook them, bring a pot of water to a tame boil. Drop the wontons into the water and cook until they float to the surface, about 5 minutes. Continue to cook for 30 seconds, then remove the wontons with a slotted spoon and divide them among bowls.

XO Sauce

MAKES 2 TO 3 CUPS

If you'd like to make your own, follow these loose guidelines.

¾ cup dried scallops (con poy)
¼ cup dried shrimp
¼ cup neutral oil, such as
    grapeseed or canola
4 medium shallots, minced
5 garlic cloves, minced

3-inch piece ginger, minced
7 dried red chilies, such as cayenne,
    ground
¼ pound thinly sliced and diced
    country ham
Sea salt

1. Soak the scallops and shrimp in hot water for 15 minutes. Drain, rinse, then mince by hand or in the food processor.
2. Heat the oil in a large sauté pan over medium heat. Add the shallots, garlic, and ginger, and cook, stirring occasionally, until they've softened, about 5 minutes. Sprinkle in the chilies and the scallop mixture. Cook for 5 minutes, toss in the ham, and cook for another 1 or 2 minutes. Season with salt to taste. Pour it into a bowl and let it cool. Store it in an airtight container in the refrigerator, where you can keep it for about 2 weeks.

LISTEN
The Menahan Street Band, mellow soulful shakin' just groovy enough to keep you going without fucking up the wontons.

DRINK
You can't drink and fold a good wonton—you're not Superman!

LOBSTER WONTON MEE

Wonton Mee is the bread and butter of the Chinese-Malaysian hawker stalls that line the streets of cities like Kuala Lumpur and other towns like Penang and Malacca. It's a heartstring-tugging soup of silky noodles and tender little dumplings. This recipe is a high-end twist on the basic version: a lobster stock, charged with a hit of chili oil, swimming with lobster-filled wontons.

SERVES 4

Sea salt
½ pound wonton egg noodles, vermicelli, or Hong Kong noodles
6½ tablespoons neutral oil, such as grapeseed or canola
Two 1- to 1½-pound lobsters, parcooked and meat removed from shells (page 46)
8 tablespoons (1 stick) unsalted butter

3 cups Lobster Stock (page 328)
24 uncooked Lobster Wontons (preceding recipe)
2 garlic cloves, minced
4 cups loosely packed fresh pea leaves, watercress, Chinese water spinach, or baby bok choy leaves

FOR GARNISH
2 teaspoons Chili Oil (page 318) or reserved XO Sauce oil (page 49)

½ cup thinly sliced scallions
4 fresh Thai bird chilies, thinly sliced

1. Bring a large pot of water to a boil and salt it until it tastes like the ocean. Have an ice bath ready. Blanch the noodles in the boiling water until al dente, about 4 minutes. Drain the noodles, reserving the water, and transfer them to the ice bath. Return the cooking water to the pot (you'll use it to cook the wontons), adding more water if necessary.

2. Drain the noodles, lay them out on a paper-towel-lined tray and pat them dry. Transfer them to a bowl and toss them with 1½ teaspoons of the oil to keep them from sticking together, then set them aside.

3. Split the lobster tails lengthwise. Heat the butter and 1 cup water together in a large heavy sauté pan over very low heat, whisking constantly as the butter melts to emulsify. When the butter has fully melted, add the halved lobster tails and gently poach until just cooked through, about 5 minutes. Transfer the tails to a cutting board and slice them lengthwise and then across so you have six pieces.

4. Add the claws to the pan and gently poach in the liquid until just cooked through, about 4 minutes. Return the sliced tail pieces to the pan and remove it from the heat. Set it aside.

5. Bring the stock to a strong simmer. Meanwhile, bring the pot of noodle-cooking water back to a tame boil. Drop the wontons into the boiling water and cook

TAKE NOTE

A lot happens at the stove toward the end of the prep. If you've got a friend in the kitchen, divide the cooking duties and cook in concert. If you alone are responsible for dinner, read the recipe well and have all your ingredients and pots ready. And work on finding some friends who like to help in the kitchen.

until they float to the surface, about 5 minutes, then continue to cook for 30 seconds. Remove the wontons with a slotted spoon and divide them among four bowls.

6. While the wontons are cooking, heat 3 tablespoons of the oil in a large sauté pan over medium-high heat. Add the garlic and cook until aromatic, about 1 minute. Scatter the pea leaves into the pan and toss just until they wilt. Season with salt to taste. Transfer the wilted leaves to a bowl and set it aside in a warm place.

7. Wipe the pan clean with a paper towel and return it to the stovetop. Add the remaining 3 tablespoons oil and turn the heat to medium-high. Add the noodles, shake the pan, and cook, undisturbed, until they start to crackle and the undersides have become crisp and golden (but not brown), 2 to 3 minutes. Lightly season the noodles with salt and transfer them to a paper-towel-lined plate to drain. Use kitchen scissors to cut the noodles into four even portions and arrange on the edge of large serving plates. Top each portion of noodles with the wilted pea leaves.

8. Pour the simmering stock into the bowls with the wontons in them. The broth should fully submerge the wontons. Drizzle each bowl with chili oil and top with sliced scallions. Sit that bowl next to the noodles on each plate.

9. Put half a lobster tail's worth of slices and a claw on each noodle mound. Sprinkle the lobster with salt and top with the chilies. Eat the noodles by themselves or moisten them with the stock—after all, it's your party.

LISTEN
Mandrill, *Solid*—yes, yes, it is.

DRINK
Fabio Lini's Metodo Classico Bianco, a white, sparkling pinot nero from Italy.

LOBSTER WONTON MEE, p. 50

LOBSTER CLUB SANDWICH

Everybody loves a club sandwich—if it's a lobster one, even better. But to make sure we brought something new to the pressed-and-creased world of club sandwiches, my crack (addicted) team of cultural anthropologists, market-research analysts, and focus groups got together and determined that the best way to inject a little ethnic fire into the beloved sandwich was to fuse it with that bastardized Chinese suburban specialty: shrimp toast! But since this is a *lobster* sandwich, we swapped one crustacean for the other, and thus a new American classic was born.

MAKES 4 SANDWICHES

FOR THE LOBSTER TOAST

About 4 cups peanut oil
1 cup parcooked lobster meat (page 46)
1½ teaspoons fish sauce
½ teaspoon MSG
½ cup all-purpose flour

Sea salt and freshly ground black pepper
½ cup rice flour
1 to 1½ cups sparkling water
4 slices Pepperidge Farm white bread, crusts removed

TO FINISH THE SANDWICHES

8 tablespoons (1 stick) unsalted butter
Two (1½-pound) lobsters, parcooked and meat removed from shells (page 46)
12 slices bacon
8 slices Pepperidge Farm white bread, lightly toasted

8 teaspoons Sambal Aïoli (page 307)
2 heads of Boston or Bibb lettuce, the best inner leaves only
4 slices medium gorgeous heirloom tomato, about ¼ inch thick

MAKE THE LOBSTER TOAST

1. Heat at least 2 inches of oil in a deep heavy pan over medium-high heat to 375°F (measured on a deep-frying thermometer).

2. In a food processor, pulse the parcooked lobster meat, fish sauce, MSG, 2 tablespoons of the all-purpose flour, 1 tablespoon salt, and 1 teaspoon pepper until a paste forms. In a bowl, whisk together the rice flour and the remaining all-purpose flour. Season it with salt and pepper. Then add the sparkling water, starting with 1 cup, whisking to incorporate evenly and ensure there are no lumps. Whisk in up to ½ cup more sparkling water if necessary to obtain the consistency of a slightly watery pancake batter.

3. Spread the lobster paste evenly over each piece of bread, all the way to the edges. The coating should be ¼ inch thick. Working with one piece at a time, dip the lobster-smeared bread into the batter and coat fully, shaking off the excess. Carefully add each piece to the hot oil and fry, flipping once, until golden and crisp on both sides, about 3 minutes total. Transfer to a paper-towel-lined plate to drain and season with salt.

What, you don't have servants?! Okay, then, your best plan of attack is this:

1. Make the sambal aïoli.
2. Parcook the lobster meat. You'll need a total of three lobsters to make the lobster toast and the sandwiches.
3. Fry the lobster toasts.
4. Assemble the sandwiches.

LISTEN
The **Beach Boys**, *Pet Sounds*, a classic—and well suited to gin and tonics and club sandwiches.

DRINK
G&Ts—club service, nudge, nudge.

FINISH THE SANDWICHES

1. In a medium saucepan, heat the butter and ½ cup water over low heat, whisking until the butter has completely emulsified. Cut the lobster tails in half lengthwise. Add the tails to the butter mixture and poach gently until just cooked through, about 5 minutes. Transfer them to a plate and gently poach the claws until just cooked through, about 4 minutes. Remove the pan from the heat, return the tails to the liquid, and set the pan to the side.

2. In a medium sauté pan over medium-high heat, cook the bacon until brown and crisp, then transfer to a paper-towel-lined plate to drain. Cut the cooked bacon slices to fit perfectly on the bread and eat the trimmings.

3. Trim the crusts from the toasted white bread. Spread each slice with 2 teaspoons of the sambal aïoli. Top each of four of the slices with a few lettuce leaves, a slice of tomato, a slice of lobster toast, and 3 slices of bacon. Put half a lobster tail and a whole claw on each stack. Top with the remaining toasted white bread, slice each sandwich diagonally, and serve immediately.

GRILLED LANGOUSTINES WITH BACON VINAIGRETTE

If I could eat langoustines every day, I'd never eat any other shellfish. Sweeter than lobster, as delicate and delicious as crab (but with a much more attractive meat-to-effort ratio), and easy to work with, langoustines have everything going for them—except you can't get them that easily. The best langoustines you can cook with are still alive when you buy them. Ask for them at the best fish market you know, and see if they'll place a special order. You'll pay dearly, but it'll be worth it. Or fine, substitute shrimp. There's easy-to-make tomato water in the vinaigrette, so note that you'll have to get it going at least twenty-four hours before you cook this dish.

SERVES 4

4 ripe tomatoes, cored
2 tablespoons rendered bacon fat
   (see Note)
1 garlic clove, crushed and peeled
½ inch fresh turmeric, peeled and
   crushed
2 tablespoons sherry vinegar

Sea salt and freshly ground white
   pepper
8 langoustines, fresh and alive, or 8
   large prawns (or large crayfish,
   marrons, or small spiny lobsters)
Oil for the grill

MAKE THE BACON VINAIGRETTE

1. At least 24 hours before you want to eat, pulse the tomatoes in a blender to make a chunky puree. Line a fine-mesh sieve with slightly damp cheesecloth. Put the sieve over a bowl large enough to fit the sieve and deep enough to accommodate the water that will drain from the tomatoes. Pour the tomato puree into the cheesecloth and let it sit undisturbed in the fridge for 24 hours. Discard the solids, reserving the liquid. Tomato water keeps for about 1 week in the fridge.

2. Preheat a charcoal grill or cast-iron grill pan until it's nice and hot.

3. Heat the bacon fat in a small pan over very low heat. Add the garlic and turmeric and cook for 12 minutes without letting the garlic brown. Remove the pan from the heat and let the mixture steep at room temperature for another 20 minutes.

4. Puree the infused fat in a blender while still slightly warm, then strain it through a fine-mesh sieve and discard the solids. Add the sherry vinegar and 5 tablespoons of the tomato water. Whisk until emulsified, season with salt and pepper to taste, and set the mixture aside.

WHAT?! YOU DON'T SAVE YOUR BACON FAT?

Fine, cook bacon slices (3 or 4 should do it) in a skillet over medium heat until most of the fat has rendered and the bacon is crisp. Transfer the cooked bacon to a paper-towel-lined plate to drain, snack on some, and crumble the rest over the langoustines right after you dress them.

PREPARE THE LANGOUSTINES

1. With a sharp knife, cut the langoustines in half lengthwise. Remove the gunk from the heads. If there's any roe, leave it in there—it's delicious! Sprinkle the langoustines with salt and a small amount of pepper. Rub the grill grates with an oil-saturated towel.

2. Put the langoustines, shell side down, on the hot grill and sear until the meat facing up is cooked through, about 5 minutes. Do not turn them or cover the grill. When the meat is cooked, it will start to pull away from the sides of the shell. Transfer the langoustines to a serving plate. Whisk the vinaigrette well, drizzle it over the langoustines, and serve immediately.

LISTEN
Lee Fields & The Expressions. Feel it, drench yourself in it, lick it up.

DRINK
Cornelissen MunJebel Bianco, a biodynamic white from Sicily as playful and enjoyable as langoustines and bacon.

CHILI CRAB

We came up with this sweet, sour, and spicy version of the crab in chili sauce you see all over Asia just before opening Fatty Crab. And I'm happy to report our customers dug it, boldly grappling with the crab to get at the meat and sagely sopping up the sauce with toasted white bread. To reward this courage and wisdom, we switched from blue crabs to Dungeness crabs, which yield a better meat-to-effort ratio. Still, this dish is seriously messy, so when you eat it, don't wear your good T-shirt.

SERVES 4

FOR THE GARLIC-GINGER PASTE
2 inches fresh ginger, peeled and
    thinly sliced
3 garlic cloves, crushed and peeled
3 shallots, thinly sliced

One 4-ounce jar crab paste,
    preferably Por Kwan brand
1 teaspoon Sambal Belacan
    (page 306)

FOR THE SRIRACHA LIQUID
¼ cup sriracha sauce
1 tablespoon rice vinegar
1 tablespoon oyster sauce
2 tablespoons sugar
2 tablespoons dark soy sauce

3 tablespoons tomato puree
3 tablespoons ketchup
2 teaspoons dark sesame oil
1 teaspoon tomato paste

FOR THE CRABS
Salt

4 live Dungeness crabs, about
    1 pound each

TO FINISH THE DISH
2 tablespoons peanut oil
8 tablespoons (1 stick) cold unsalted
    butter, cut into 8 pieces
1 egg, well beaten
1 cup fresh cilantro leaves

4 slices thick-cut white bread,
    preferably from a Pullman
    loaf, toasted and halved
    diagonally

MAKE THE GARLIC-GINGER PASTE
Use a mortar and pestle to pound (see page 12) the ginger, garlic, shallots, and crab paste to a paste, pounding each ingredient thoroughly before adding the next. Then add the sambal belacan, pound again, and set the mixture aside.

MAKE THE SRIRACHA LIQUID
In a mixing bowl, whisk together all the ingredients, from the sriracha through the tomato paste.

COOK THE CRABS
1. Bring a large stockpot of salty water to a boil. Rinse the crabs well (they should be lively) under cold running water. Drop the crabs into the pot and cook for

LISTEN
Deftones, *Adrenaline*—because it's what Corwin, Fatty Crew executive chef, plays in the kitchen.

DRINK
Marcel Deiss Engelgarten—a gorgeous Alsatian Riesling from one of the world's greatest winemakers.

exactly 5 minutes, starting the timer the moment the water returns to a boil. Use a slotted spoon to transfer the crabs to a rack to cool.

2. When they're cool enough to handle, put them on a cutting board. Using your thumb and forefinger, pull off the flap on the underside of each crab (pluck off any little gill bits too) and discard them. Then use a large chef's knife to cut each body in half. Rinse the bodies under running water as you remove and discard the entrails. Use the back of of your knife blade (the dull side) to gently crack the claws. Transfer them to a paper-towel-lined plate to drain.

FINISH THE DISH

1. Heat the peanut oil in a large sauté pan over medium heat. Add the garlic-ginger paste and cook, stirring, until aromatic, about 3 minutes. Add the sriracha liquid and bring to a boil. Remove the pan from the heat and stir to let some of the heat dissipate. Wait another 30 seconds or so and add the butter, piece by piece, stirring constantly. When all the butter has been added, slowly drizzle the well-beaten egg into the pan, whisking constantly to incorporate smoothly. The chili sauce should be thick but pourable, like gravy.

2. Add the crabs to the chili sauce and toss them so that they're well coated.

3. Put two crab halves in each of four serving bowls. Pour some of the steaming hot chili sauce (enough to coat the crabs generously) into each bowl. Sprinkle each with a good handful of the cilantro leaves. Serve with toast triangles to soak up the sauce you leave behind after scarfing up the crabs.

CHILI CRAB, p. 58

WHOLE SHRIMP WITH GUANCIALE AND PRESERVED LEMON

For me this dish is a casual affair, a no-recipe-necessary dish that you throw together with a few ingredients you have (or, ahem, should have) in the fridge. If you're not cut from that cloth, here's a simple recipe (still casual, not too precise) that you can commit to memory to fake culinary nonchalance in front of your friends. No plates, please. Eat from the pan—enamel cast iron looks particularly nice on the table.

Chinese celery leaves provide flavor and color and are easy to find. But you can also substitute regular celery leaves or lovage.

SERVES 4

Start with **two dozen nice, fresh (live if possible) head-on shrimp**—spot prawns if you can get them. Figure 6 or so large shrimp per person.

Pick up some **guanciale** (cured pig jowl) at the Italian gourmet store. A ½-pound chunk will do just fine. Slice it into thin, approximately ½-inch squares.

Round up **1 cup of celery leaves** from a bunch of Chinese or regular celery, tearing them up a bit as you pick them.

Pull out a bottle of **extra virgin olive oil, 3 garlic cloves, some fleur de sel, a peppermill filled with black peppercorns, a fresh lemon**, and **one of the preserved lemons** (page 302) I hope you're storing in your fridge. Cut the peel from the preserved lemon and discard the rest. Julienne the peel.

1. Heat a cast-iron or stainless-steel pan over high heat. Have a swig of that chenin blanc.

2. Pour just enough olive oil into your hot pan to thinly cover the bottom. Toss in the guanciale and cook until the pieces become translucent, maybe 3 minutes.

3. Add a few crushed cloves of garlic, swirl the pan, and cook for a minute or two.

4. Then toss in the shrimp. When they start to curl and the shells turn pink, flip them and pour in a splash of your white wine. Let the wine cook off while the shrimp cooks for another minute or two.

5. Then pull the pan off the heat and squeeze half of the fresh lemon over the pan, throw in the celery leaves, toss, and then sprinkle on the preserved lemon, freshly ground black pepper, and fleur de sel. Eat the shrimp from the pan: twist the heads off and suck out the goodness within, then drag the rest of the shrimp through the pan juices, grab a piece of guanciale with your thumb, and consume in one bite.

LISTEN
Neil Young, *Tonight's the Night*—chilly, raw, and some of the most honest music around.

DRINK
Christian Venier's chenin blanc, a bottle to sip—or gulp—from while you're cooking.

STEAMED LIVE SHRIMP WITH GREEN CHILI VINEGAR

Too often we are subjected to dead, flash-frozen shrimp with sad, mealy texture. Well, if you could find another way, wouldn't you want to? So, no excuses: If there's a Chinatown near you, you can find live shrimp, and their clean taste and firm texture are well worth the effort.

SERVES 4 AS A SNACK

½ cup chopped fresh green chilies, such as jalapeños
½ cup brown rice vinegar
Salt

¼ cup Shaoxing wine or dry sherry
2 tablespoons fish sauce
1 pound live shrimp
2 tablespoons dark sesame oil

1. Puree the chilies with the rice vinegar and 1 teaspoon salt in a blender and refrigerate overnight.
2. Set a large steamer basket over a few inches of water in a large pot, cover it with a lid, and get the water steaming.
3. Pour the Shaoxing, fish sauce, and 2 tablespoons of the chili vinegar into a large bowl. Add the wriggling shrimp and toss them around in this liquid. Let them imbibe for a moment as you do the same with your Miller High Life. Return them to the bowl when they flip out of it, as they will do.
4. Put the bowl in the steamer basket. Cook the shrimp until their flesh is opaque and firm but still yielding, 4 to 6 minutes. You'll be very pleasantly surprised by the texture.
5. When they're done, dump them onto a serving platter and sprinkle them with salt and the sesame oil. Serve the remaining chili vinegar on the side for dipping. No forks.

LISTEN
Roy Ayers, "We Live in Brooklyn, Baby." Even if you don't, Roy can make you feel like you do.

DRINK
Miller High Life with this delightful snack and with that delightful song.

WHOLE SHRIMP WITH GUANCIALE AND PRESERVED LEMON, p. 62

RAZOR CLAMS WITH PICKLED CHILIES, p. 68

RAZOR CLAMS WITH PICKLED CHILIES

Eaten alone, this quick-to-make dish is quite light and appeals to me on days that I pretend to diet. With a little rice or a hunk of bread on the side you've got a perfect meal. And in case you haven't caught on by now, I should mention that some quiveringly fatty porktastic love sitting next to these bright clams and chilies will turn heads and inspire poems—yes, poems!

SERVES 4

3 garlic cloves, crushed and peeled
1 medium shallot, peeled
4 fresh cilantro roots, rinsed, scraped, and rinsed again, or 16 cilantro stems
1 teaspoon fish sauce
2 tablespoons olive oil (the best you can afford)
2 tablespoons Shaoxing wine or dry sherry

2 tablespoons white wine
2 pounds razor clams, scrubbed, rinsed, and soaked in several changes of icy cold water for at least 1 hour
Leaves and tender stems from 8 sprigs fresh cilantro and/or basil
12 Pickled Thai Chilies (page 294)

1. Use a mortar and pestle to pound (see page 12) the garlic, shallot, and cilantro roots to a paste, pounding each ingredient thoroughly before adding the next. Add the fish sauce to loosen and season the paste.

2. Heat the olive oil in a large sauté pan with a tight lid over medium-high heat. When the oil shimmers, add the garlic paste and cook, stirring, until aromatic, about 3 minutes.

3. Add the Shaoxing and white wine. When the liquid begins to bubble, add the clams in more or less a single layer. Cover the pan and steam the clams until they open, about 5 minutes, giving the pan a shake after about 3 minutes.

4. After another 5 minutes remove the pan from the heat and discard any clams that haven't opened. Add the pickled chilies and toss them with the clams and liquid. Divide among 4 bowls and garnish with cilantro. Enjoy immediately.

LISTEN
Peter Tosh, *Stepping Razor.* In keeping with our mollusk of the moment.

DRINK:
Alesh Movia's Veliko Bianco. Buy a case; you can thank me later.

SINGAPORE BLACK PEPPER MUSSELS

Named for the city-state where I once enjoyed a similar preparation made with crab, this is for dedicated lovers of black pepper, which figures almost more prominently in this dish than the mussels. The grind of the pepper is key: it should be as coarse as you can get it and not at all powdery. My mussels of choice for this dish are plump bouchot mussels, originally from Poitou-Charentes in central-western France but now also farmed in Maine. Even though smaller mussels tend to be sweeter, the tensile surface of the attractively distended bouchot is textural perfection. Serve them in a large bowl with a few small bowls alongside—for the shells, not for serving. This is communal eating.

SERVES 4

3 tablespoons peanut oil
⅓ cup very coarsely ground black pepper
4 shallots, thinly sliced
6 garlic cloves, thinly sliced
½ cup Shaoxing wine or dry sherry
½ cup Chicken Stock (page 324)

8 tablespoons (1 stick) butter
¼ cup yuzu juice or lemon juice
2½ pounds mussels, preferably bouchot
Salt
2 cups fresh cilantro leaves

1. Heat the oil in a straight-sided sauté pan with a tight lid over medium-high heat. Add the black pepper, letting it toast in the hot oil for 1 minute. Add the shallots and garlic and cook, stirring often, until they're translucent but not browned, about 3 minutes.

2. Add the Shaoxing wine and, when it bubbles, add the chicken stock. Bring them to a boil and let the liquid reduce somewhat, about 2 minutes. Lower the heat to medium to maintain a simmer and add the butter to the pan along with the yuzu juice, swirling the butter in the pan until it melts.

3. Add the mussels to the pan and cover. Cook until the mussels open, about 3 minutes. After 5 minutes remove the pan from the heat and discard any mussels that don't open.

4. Taste the broth and season with salt to taste. Transfer the mussels and all the broth to a large serving bowl. Garnish the bowl with cilantro leaves. Devour.

LISTEN
The Supreme Genius of King Khan and the Shrines. Fill a giant bowl full of mussels and dance to the retro groove of this bad daddy.

DRINK
An albariño from Zarate.

COCKLE SALAD

You see this style of salad in endless variations throughout Thailand, and this version made with briny cockles (though the formula can be applied to flaked fish, raw fish, bacon, pickled vegetables, and more) makes a great side dish for anything from braised pork to a simple bowl of rice. The common thread in these salads is the glorious dressing, a mixture of garlic, chili, lime, palm sugar, and fish sauce, which is salty, sour, and a little bit sweet. In this case it's also really fucking spicy, the kind of heat that hits you like Mike Tyson's right hook. But just moments after the initial jolt, you'll crave more, shoveling it into your mouth until you're scraping the last traces of it onto some rice. You'll stop at nothing to get some more; you won't be able to control it. You've become a masochist.

SERVES 4

7 fresh Thai bird chilies, 3 stemmed and seeded and 4 stemmed
2 teaspoons palm or brown sugar
2 garlic cloves, crushed and peeled
Juice of 1½ limes
1 teaspoon fish sauce
½ cup fresh Vietnamese mint leaves (rau ram)
1 small red onion, thinly sliced
1 cup fresh cilantro leaves
2 tablespoons olive oil (the best you can afford)

2 shallots, thinly sliced
6 fresh cilantro roots, rinsed, scraped, and rinsed again, or 24 fresh cilantro stems, finely chopped
½ cup beer or white wine
4 pounds cockles, rinsed (discard any that don't snap closed when touched)
Salt if needed

1. Use a mortar and pestle to pound (see page 12) the 3 seeded Thai bird chilies, palm sugar, garlic, lime juice, and fish sauce to a paste, pounding each ingredient thoroughly before adding the next. The resulting paste should be rather liquidy. Set it aside.

2. Tear the mint leaves and combine the onion, cilantro, and mint leaves in a mixing bowl. Add the chili paste and toss.

3. In a straight-sided pan with a tight lid, heat the olive oil over medium-high heat. Add the shallots, cilantro roots, remaining Thai bird chilies, and beer. Stir well and bring to a simmer.

4. Add the cockles to the pot, cover, and cook until they have opened, about 4 minutes. After 5 minutes remove from the heat and discard any that haven't opened.

5. Using a slotted spoon, transfer the cockles to a bowl. Strain the cooking liquid through a fine-mesh sieve and set aside.

6. Remove forty of the cockles from their shells and put them in a mixing bowl, keeping the remaining cockles in their shells.

LISTEN
Lou Reed, *Street Hassle*—it's scary how much I like his shit.

DRINK
Absinthe, touch of water, touch of sugar. Zakary Pelaccio, MD, prescribes at least three of these before using power tools and operating heavy machinery.

7. Add the shucked cockles to the bowl with the mint and cilantro. Toss to combine and season with salt if necessary.

8. Divide the cockles still in their shells between 4 shallow serving bowls and spoon the strained cooking liquid over each one. Top each bowl with a mound of the shucked cockle salad, making sure that a whole Thai chili lands in each bowl. Serve immediately.

TREASURES OF THE SEA WITH DYNAMIC SPICY BROTH

Simply serving tasty soup with seafood in it is not how I get down. Bowls of this spicy, incredibly aromatic broth—made with a little pork fat to round out the mouthfeel and hold the flavors together—provide a hot tub for some sensuous underwater creatures, whose absolute freshness is paramount. Clear, bright flavor. Textural integrity. That's how this simple soup becomes Treasures of the Sea with Dynamic Spicy Broth.

SERVES 4

6 fresh cilantro roots, rinsed, scraped, and rinsed again, or 24 or so fresh cilantro stems

7 fresh Thai bird chilies, 5 stemmed and seeded

6 garlic cloves, 5 crushed and peeled and 1 thinly sliced

2 shallots, 1 peeled and 1 thinly sliced

3 tablespoons rendered pork fat or lardo (page 194)

2 cups Crab Stock (page 329)

2 cups Chicken Stock (page 324)

1 lemongrass stalk, outer layer removed and stalk crushed with a blunt object

3 fresh kaffir lime leaves, 1 whole and 2 torn

Pinch of MSG

Fish sauce to taste

2 tablespoons fresh lime juice, plus more to taste as needed

1 green (unripe) mango, peeled, roughly chopped, and the pit reserved

1 tablespoon fresh ginger, 1 inch thinly sliced

½ cup Shaoxing wine or dry sherry

20 Manila clams, well rinsed and soaked in several changes of icy cold water for at least 30 minutes

12 small shrimp, peeled

4 skin-on red mullet fillets, cut from two ¾-pound fish

A little olive oil (the best you can afford)

Salt and freshly ground black pepper

8 small squid bodies, including tentacles, cleaned and scored in a crosshatch pattern

Fresh Vietnamese mint (rau ram) and Thai basil leaves for garnish

1. Use a mortar and pestle to pound (see page 12) the cilantro roots, 5 Thai bird chilies, crushed garlic, and whole shallot to a paste, pounding each ingredient thoroughly before adding the next.

2. In a large pot over medium-high heat, heat 1 tablespoon of the pork fat until hot but not smoking. Add the chili paste and cook, stirring occasionally, until it's aromatic, about 3 minutes.

3. Add the crab and chicken stocks and bring them to a simmer. Add the lemongrass, the whole kaffir lime leaf, MSG, fish sauce, lime juice, and mango (including the pit). Reduce the heat to low and simmer the broth for 1 hour.

LISTEN
Vetiver, any album. Life flows from it.

DRINK
Campo Vulcano Soave Classico.

4. Strain the broth through a fine-mesh sieve into a large saucepan. Put the pan over medium-low heat and keep the liquid at a low simmer.

5. Wipe the first pot with a paper towel and add the remaining pork fat. Heat it over medium-high heat until hot, then add the sliced garlic, sliced shallot, and ginger and cook, stirring occasionally, until the shallot and garlic are translucent, about 3 minutes.

6. Add the Shaoxing wine and, when it bubbles up, add the clams. Cover the pot and cook for 3 to 4 minutes, until all the shells have opened (peek in; if most of them haven't opened, give the pot a shake and cook for another 30 seconds before peeking again). After 5 minutes remove the pot from the heat and discard any clams that did not open.

7. Add the shrimp, the bruised chilies, the torn lime leaves, and the simmering broth. Reduce the heat to medium-low and stir well. Taste and, if you think it needs it, tweak the flavor with lime juice or fish sauce until it tastes really good.

8. Heat a cast-iron or black steel pan over medium-high heat. Rub the red mullet with olive oil and season with salt and pepper. Cook skin side down, pressing down gently on the fish with a spatula the whole time (this will prevent it from curling and give it an even cook), until the edges of the flesh go from irridescent to opaque, 1½ to 2 minutes. (The fish will fully cook once you set it in the hot broth a bit later.) Transfer the fish to a plate and set it aside.

9. Add the squid tentacles to the clams and shrimp. Cook for 30 seconds and then add the squid bodies. Turn off the heat and season the broth with more fish sauce to taste. Let the soup sit for 1 minute, then ladle it into 4 serving bowls, being sure to distribute the goodies. Lay your mullet, skin side up, on top, like a proud red cap!

10. Garnish with some recently torn or snipped Vietnamese mint and Thai basil. Breathe deeply. Smells good, don't it?

OYSTER LETTUCE CUPS WITH BACON AND KIMCHI

Corwin, my executive chef, Jori, my fiancée, and I went to Seoul a few years back, and besides Soapy Soju, the drunk, bitter, and perverted soju bottle mascot, this dish was one of the great joys we discovered while we ate and drank the hell out of the sprawling city. It's almost as easy to make as it is to throw it down your gullet—you'll have downed five of these lettuce cups before you finish your first glass of soju.

MAKES 20 LETTUCE CUPS, SERVING 4 TO 6 AS A SNACK

5 slices good bacon
1 tablespoon coarsely ground black pepper
¼ cup Aïoli (page 307)
20 small inner Boston lettuce leaves

20 oysters, freshly shucked and held in their liquor
A little Kimchi (page 292 or good-quality store bought), julienned
2 tablespoons minced fresh chives

1. Preheat the oven to 400°F.
2. Cut each slice of bacon into four 1-inch squares. Lay the squares on a parchment-paper-lined baking sheet and cook until the fat has rendered and the bacon is warmed through, about 5 minutes.
3. Stir the black pepper into the aïoli until well combined. Lay the lettuce leaves on a platter. Add ¼ teaspoon of the black pepper aïoli to the center of each leaf. Put a square of warmed bacon on top of the aïoli and then top each with an oyster. Drizzle each oyster with a touch of the oyster liquor.
4. Garnish each with kimchi, chives, pixie dust, and any other special incantations. Eat with your hands.

RIFF ALERT!

Try this instead of the kimchi version: Oyster, squeeze of lemon, piece of bacon, 2 or 3 candied chili threads. To make candied chili threads: Preheat the oven to 200°F. Combine ½ cup sugar and ¼ cup water in a small pan. Bring the liquid to a boil, cook the mixture for 30 seconds, take it off the heat, and let it sit for 5 minutes. Meanwhile, take 5 fresh Thai bird chilies, stem, halve lengthwise, and scrape out the seeds. Julienne lengthwise. Stir the chili threads into the syrup to coat, then use a slotted spoon to transfer the threads to a parchment-paper-lined baking sheet. Put the sheet in the oven for 20 minutes, remove, and let cool, then use right away or store in an airtight container in a cool place for up to three weeks.

LISTEN
Innervisions by the great **Stevie Wonder,** even if your intention is to listen to only one track (or eat only one oyster lettuce cup), you invariably end up listening to it all.

DRINK
Satoh Shochu—watch out, it creeps up on you.

NOODLES

My love for noodles is congenital. For the five years right before I was born, my mom and dad lived in Rome, so I came into a family that was serious about its pasta. Instead of Kraft mac and cheese, there was carbonara; instead of Chef Boyardee, there was bucatini all'amatriciana. Today nothing's quite as comforting to me as a big bowl of pasta (Martelli, Setaro, Latini, or homemade please) tossed with fresh tomatoes, garlic, and butter just warmed together in a pan. Italian noodles, I thought, were as good as it gets.

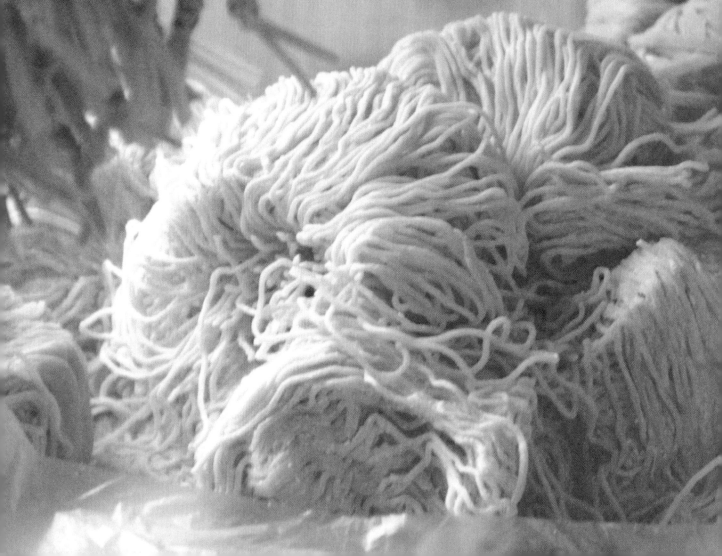

Then I went to Asia and discovered a whole new world of slippery, chewy pleasure: rice noodles, wheat noodles, noodles as thin as vermicelli and as thick as pappardelle. There were bold broths and subtle ones, sauces and stir-fries, and plenty of chili. All that was missing, I thought, was the care Italians put into fresh pasta and achieving the perfect texture. The pan mee vendors on the streets of Malaysia showed me how wrong I was, rolling out noodles to order. Asia even ups the ante by serving noodles for breakfast.

Whether they're tossed with tomato sauce or curry, noodles are stomach-fillingly satisfying in a way few things are. Plus, they almost force you to play with your food, as you attempt to capture them with your hands, trying desperately (and if you're me, futilely) to slurp them without spattering your shirt.

PAN MEE

On Raja Chulan, a street that runs through the major downtown business district of Kuala Lumpur, there was a hawker whose stall was always flooded with customers, and for good reason: his version of pan mee, the homey Chinese-Malay chicken noodle soup, was awesome. I chatted him up, hoping for the secret to his method, and he kindly jotted down a few notes for me. His directions, including "⅓ tapioca flour, ⅔ regular flour, a small glass of peanut oil, and water" for the handmade noodles, left plenty to the imagination. So I started with good chicken stock flavored with ikan bilis, ginger, and garlic and took off from there.

SERVES 4

FOR THE PAN MEE DOUGH
⅓ cup tapioca flour
⅔ cup all-purpose flour, plus more
    for dusting

Sea salt
1 tablespoon peanut oil

FOR THE BROTH
10 cups Chicken Stock (page 324)
1 cup ikan bilis, rinsed
2 inches fresh ginger, peeled and
    chopped

6 garlic cloves, roughly chopped
6 scallions, dark green tops only
A fist-sized chunk cured ham or
    prosciutto rind (about ½ pound)

FOR THE SOUP FIXINGS
Salt
10 ounces snow peas, threads
    removed
1 cup plus 3 tablespoons neutral oil,
    such as grapeseed or canola
1 cup ikan bilis
1½ pounds ground pork shoulder
Fish sauce to taste
12 medium shiitake mushroom caps,
    each cut into 6 triangles

½ cup dried red chilies, such as
    cayenne
2 cups fresh pea or other tender
    leafy greens
5 scallions, thinly sliced on a
    diagonal, whites and greens
Chili Oil (page 318)
Brown rice vinegar to taste

MAKE THE PAN MEE DOUGH

1. Combine the flours with a good pinch of sea salt and form into a mound on a wooden board. Make a well in the center and add the oil and 2 tablespoons water. Use a fork or your fingers to incorporate the oil and water, bit by bit, into the mound of flour, adding up to 2 tablespoons more water as necessary.

2. Bring the dough together and knead for about 15 minutes. The dough should feel firm but not hard. A great way to test whether the dough is ready is to form it into a tight ball and press down on the center of the dough with the tip of your finger, applying enough pressure to dent the dough. If the dough bounces back

LISTEN
Chromeo, "You're So Gangsta"—nerdy hip-hop funk to get your ass movin' and the dough kneadin'.

DRINK
Try a nice dry, hard cider, perhaps from Farnum Hill in New Hampshire, which is crisp, light, and refreshing and shares that homey, familiar quality with the soup.

rather quickly, it's ready; if it stays indented, keep kneading. (As the legendary Italian pasta dough aphorism goes, "If your ass crack isn't sweaty, the dough isn't ready.") Wrap in plastic wrap and keep it at room temperature until you're ready to use it or in the fridge overnight.

MAKE THE BROTH

1. In a stockpot, combine the chicken stock, ikan bilis, ginger, garlic, scallion tops, and ham rind. Warm over low heat, stirring occasionally, and bring to simmer. Simmer for at least 45 minutes and up to 1½ hours.
2. Strain the broth and discard the solids.

MAKE THE SOUP FIXINGS

1. While the broth is simmering, bring a large pot of water to a boil, salt it until it tastes like the ocean, and set up an ice-water bath. Blanch the snow peas in the boiling water for 30 seconds, then transfer to the ice bath with a slotted spoon. Reserve the hot water to boil the noodles. Drain the snow peas and cut each into thirds on the bias.
2. Heat a medium skillet over high heat and add 1 cup of the oil. Let it get hot enough so that a ¼-inch cube of bread sizzles lightly and browns in 30 to 60 seconds when you drop it in (about 300°F on a deep-frying thermometer). When the oil is at the right temperature, scatter the ikan bilis into the oil, reduce the heat to medium, and use a wooden spoon to move them around in the oil from time to time until they begin to turn a light golden color, 2 to 4 minutes. Transfer the ikan bilis to a paper-towel-lined bowl with a slotted spoon. Discard the oil when it has cooled completely.
3. Heat 2 tablespoons of the remaining oil in a large sauté pan over high heat, then add the ground pork. Cook, breaking it up, until it's just barely cooked through (later the ground pork will get sprinkled into hot broth to cook it further). As it cooks, season it with fish sauce. Set a cooling rack on a baking sheet and cover it with a kitchen towel. Transfer the meat with a slotted spoon to the towel-covered cooling rack.
4. Add enough oil to the residual pork fat in the sauté pan to total about 3 tablespoons fat. Heat the fat over medium-high heat and add the shiitakes, sautéing the mushrooms until well browned, 4 to 5 minutes. Spoon the mushrooms onto a paper-towel-lined plate to drain.
5. Meanwhile, in a dry pan over medium heat, toast the dried chilies until they take on a dark color, pressing them down with a wooden spoon to increase contact with the pan, 3 to 4 minutes. Be careful not to inhale over the toasting chilies. Remove from heat and set aside.

CUT THE PAN MEE NOODLES

1. Dust a pasta roller or rolling pin, your work surface, and a cutting board with all-purpose flour. Using the pasta roller or rolling pin, roll the dough to $1/8$-inch thickness. Tear or cut the dough into irregular shapes about 2 inches long and 1 inch wide. (Really, any size will do, because it's your party.) Put the torn noodles on the flour-dusted board as you work.

2. Prepare another ice water bath and bring your pot of salted water back to a boil. Cook the pan mee noodles in the water until slightly before they're al dente, about 3 minutes. Drain the noodles in a colander, then transfer them to the ice bath.

FINISH THE SOUP

1. Bring your strained stock to a boil. Add the parcooked noodles and cook for 2 minutes. Add the pork, mushrooms, pea greens, snow peas, and toasted chilies. Boil for 1 more minute.

2. Ladle the soup into serving bowls. Garnish each bowl with the fried ikan bilis and sliced scallions. Drizzle with chili oil. Serve with fish sauce and brown rice vinegar at the table so your guests can season to taste.

CARAMEL PORK WITH HONG KONG NOODLES

This is my riff on a particularly delicious Chinese-Malay dish I had in Kuala Lumpur's Chinatown. I stayed true to the original—sweet, crispy pork tossed with egg noodles—though I go for a slightly thinner noodle (you can even use vermicelli) and garnish the dish with the Korean dried chili threads called *sil gochu.* You could certainly substitute thinly sliced fresh chilies or crushed dried chili as long as there's some heat to balance the salty sweetness of the sauce. Either way, the chili, scallions, and fried garlic slivers are icing on an already frosted cake.

SERVES 4

FOR THE PORK
1½ inches fresh ginger, peeled and minced
1 tablespoon five-spice powder
¼ cup hoisin sauce
¼ cup soy sauce
¼ cup Shaoxing wine or dry sherry
2 tablespoons honey
1 to 1½ pounds boneless pork shoulder, cut into 1-inch strips

FOR THE FRIED GARLIC GARNISH
5 garlic cloves, peeled
½ cup olive oil (the best you can afford)

FOR THE CARAMEL SAUCE
2 cups sugar
½ cup soy sauce

TO FINISH THE DISH
Salt
1 pound Hong Kong or wonton noodles
1 tablespoon plus 1 splash neutral oil, such as grapeseed or canola
4 scallions, thinly sliced on the bias
2 tablespoons sil gochu

MARINATE THE PORK
1. Pound the ginger to a paste using a mortar and pestle or mince it very finely. Combine it with the five-spice powder.
2. Put the hoisin sauce, soy sauce, Shaoxing wine, honey, and five-spice mixture in a large mixing bowl and whisk well. Add the pork shoulder and toss to coat well. Cover and marinate in the refrigerator for at least 12 hours and up to 2 days.

FRY THE GARLIC
1. Put the garlic cloves in a small saucepan and cover completely with cold water, then bring it to a boil over high heat. As soon as it boils, remove from the heat and pour off the boiling water. Refill with cold water and repeat the process.

LISTEN
Mikey Dread "Warrior Stylee," because he's cool . . . and he's dread.

DRINK
Cold, crisp Tiger beer.

Drain the garlic and run the cloves under cold water to cool them. This process mellows the garlic's flavor.

2. Pat the cloves dry, then thinly slice them lengthwise.

3. Heat the olive oil in a small saucepan over medium heat to about 300°F (measured on a deep-frying thermometer). Sprinkle the garlic into the hot oil, moving the pieces around with a spoon so they don't stick together, and fry evenly on all sides. Fry until they stop sizzling and start to turn golden brown, about 2 minutes.

4. Transfer the garlic slices with a slotted spoon to a paper-towel-lined plate. Set them aside.

COOK THE PORK

1. Preheat the oven to 375°F.

2. Remove the pork from the marinade, strain the marinade into a saucepan, and bring it to a boil. Reduce the heat to maintain a bare simmer.

3. Put the pork on a wire rack set in a roasting pan filled with ½ inch of water. Roast the pork in the oven for 15 minutes. Brush the warm marinade over the pork, then turn the heat up to 400°F and roast for another 10 minutes. Brush with marinade again and cook for about 10 more minutes, or until cooked through and the internal temperature reaches 145°F. Remove the pork from the oven and set it aside until it's cool enough to handle.

MAKE THE CARAMEL SAUCE

1. Pour the sugar into a medium saucepan and cook, stirring with a metal spoon, over medium heat until it has taken on an even, roasty brown color and bubbles menacingly.

2. Add ½ cup water and boil, stirring with the metal spoon, until the caramel dissolves completely. Transfer the syrup to a sauté pan large enough to hold the noodles (but don't add the noodles yet).

3. Turn the heat to high and bring the syrup to a boil. Add the soy sauce and cook, stirring, for a minute or so. Turn off the heat but keep the pan on the stovetop.

FINISH THE DISH

1. Bring a pot of water to a boil, salt it until it tastes like the ocean, and prepare an ice bath. Blanch the noodles in the boiling water for about 2 minutes. Transfer them to the ice bath to stop the cooking. Drain the noodles and drizzle them with a splash of oil to keep them from sticking together. Keep the noodles on a plate at room temperature.

2. Slice the pork against the grain into bite-sized pieces. Add the sliced pork to the caramel sauce, turn the heat back up under the saucepan, and bring to a boil, tossing the pork to coat it in the sauce. Reduce the heat so the sauce simmers and let the liquid reduce a bit.

3. Heat the remaining tablespoon oil in a large sauté pan over high heat, then add the noodles, stirring and tossing a bit.

4. With a slotted spoon, transfer the pork pieces from the caramel sauce to the pan with the noodles. Add a touch of the caramel sauce as well and toss it all together.

5. Plate the sweet, porky noodles on a long platter. Lightly drizzle with the remaining caramel sauce and garnish with the scallions, fried garlic slivers, and sil gochu.

RM		
雞 扒 7.00	BEEF GINGER RICE	牛葱姜
豬 扒 7.00	CHICKEN GINGER RICE	猪姜葱
羊 扒 10.00	PORK GINGER RICE	鱼葱姜
卡 扒 10.00	FISH GINGER RICE	姜姜
魚 扒 9.00	LUM MEE	
魚 9.00	FRIED HOKKIEN MEE	福海广
粥 4.00	FRIED HAILAM MEE	炒炒
粥 4.00	CANTONESE STYLE YEE MEE	炒
粥 4.00	SOUP MEE HOON	
粥 5.00	SOUP MEE SUA	
飯 4.00	FRIED MEE SUA	
飯 4.00	FRIED TOONG FUN	
飯 4.00	BEEF NOODLE /RICE	
飯 4.50	LOH MEE	
飯 5.00	ASSAM FISH	
飯 4.00	PRAWN SAMBAL	
飯 5.50	FRIED VEGETABLE	
飯 4.00	EGG FOO YOONG	
飯 5.50	FRENCH TOAST	
7.00	COFFEE POWDER 咖啡粉	1/2 kg
6.50	BELACHAN 馬來占	

ASSAM LAKSA

This is one of many kinds of laksas or, simply put, noodle soups. Every town in every region of Malaysia has its own special laksa. Multiply the number of variations by a million and you'll come up with the number of people who'd chew me out if they knew I even considered speculating about the origins and cultural nuances of laksa. So I'll just say that the universe of laksa can be broken up into the curry and the noncurry. This one falls into the latter category, and it's named for the dried fruit (assam gelugor) that acts as a souring agent. Connoisseurs intentionally mispronounce this laksa as "awesome laksa," while haters rename it entirely, calling it "funky fish slop." I once read a blog comment by some guy who wrote about how disgusted he was by the soup because it tasted like sardines. He just couldn't believe the fucking soup tasted like sardines! Well, the soup's base and garnish are made from sardines. Go figure.

SERVES 6

FOR THE BROTH
6 cups Chicken Stock (page 324)
6 cups Crab Stock (page 329)
2 tablespoons belacan, toasted (see page 333)
¼ cup neutral oil, such as grapeseed or canola
6 fresh long red chilies, such as Anaheim or Hungarian Wax, stemmed, seeded, and each cut crosswise into 4 pieces
3 shallots, each cut into 3 pieces
4 garlic cloves, sliced
3 lemongrass stalks, woody outer layer removed, stalks halved and crushed

2 inches fresh galangal, peeled and cut crosswise into 3 pieces
1 inch fresh turmeric, halved crosswise
3 pounds fresh whole sardines, scaled, filleted, and rinsed (bones reserved)
½ cup unsweetened tamarind paste
3 galangal flower heads
5 assam gelugor slices, rinsed very well under warm water
7 dried red chilies, such as cayenne
Sea salt
1 tablespoon sugar
Fresh lime juice to taste

TO FINISH THE SOUP
Salt
1 cup neutral oil, such as grapeseed or canola
1 cup ikan bilis
1½ pounds lai fun or laksa noodles
2 cups fresh pineapple in approximately 1-inch-long by ¼-inch-thick pieces
2 English cucumbers, peeled and julienned

5 fresh Thai bird chilies, thinly sliced
¼ cup loosely packed fresh Vietnamese mint leaves (rau ram)
¼ cup loosely packed fresh mint leaves

MAKE THE BROTH

1. Bring the chicken stock and crab stock to a boil in a large pot.

2. Meanwhile, use the back of a spoon to crush the toasted belacan to a tacky powder. Heat the oil in a large saucepan or stockpot over medium heat, then add the long red chilies, shallots, garlic, lemongrass, galangal, turmeric, and crushed toasted belacan. Stir well and cook until the garlic and shallots are translucent but not brown, about 3 minutes.

3. Add the sardine bones and continue to cook for 5 minutes, lowering the heat if the vegetables threaten to brown. Cut the sardine fillets into ½-inch pieces and reserve, chilled.

4. Add the hot stock to the sardine-vegetable mixture and stir to incorporate. Add the tamarind paste, galangal flowers, assam gelugor, and dried chilies. Bring to a simmer and season generously with salt and sugar. Continue to simmer for about 30 minutes.

5. Strain the sardine-vegetable liquid through a fine-mesh sieve, discarding the solids. Return the liquid to a clean saucepan and return it to a gentle simmer. Adjust the seasoning with salt and lime juice. The broth should be sweet, salty, sour, and deliciously fish funky.

6. Add the sardine fillets to the broth, breaking them up with a spoon. Take the broth off the heat and keep it covered.

FINISH THE SOUP

1. While the broth simmers, bring a large pot of water to a boil and salt it until it tastes like the ocean. Heat the oil in a small saucepan over medium-high heat to 300°F (measured on a deep-frying thermometer). Fry the ikan bilis until golden and crunchy, about 5 minutes. Transfer them to a paper-towel-lined plate to drain.

2. Cook the noodles in the boiling water for 2 minutes, then strain the noodles and add the noodles to the sardine broth. Turn the heat under the broth pot to medium and cook until the noodles are al dente, about 3 minutes more.

3. Taste the broth and adjust the seasoning again if necessary. Ladle it into a large bowl. Set the table with a stack of serving bowls and small bowls of the pineapple, cucumbers, sliced chilies, and both kinds of mint leaves to garnish the soup. Slurp it up.

LISTEN
Willie Hutch, "Party Down."
Dig through the vinyl and whip out some funky classics to go hand in hand with the funky flavor.

DRINK
Jurançon Sec, a blend of gros manseng and petit manseng that's always a great foil for sour-spicy good times.

PASTA CON SARDE, p.90

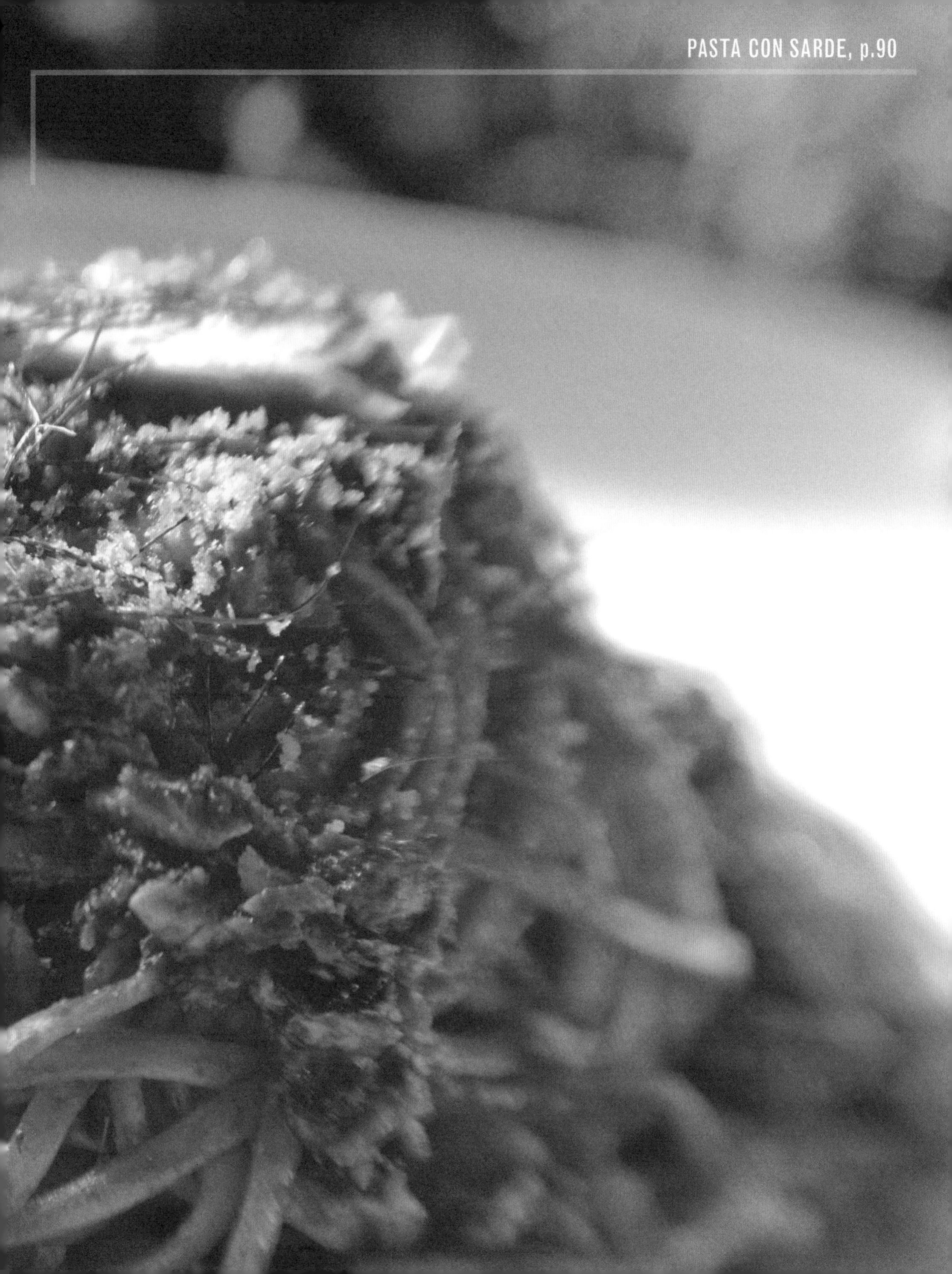

PASTA CON SARDE

Sardines are easily my favorite fish, and I've yet to find a pasta dish using sardines that comes close to this Sicilian classic. The smell of the fennel and the sardines cooking, simmering together along with tomatoes and raisins, is hypnotic. Because it demands fresh sardines, this dish should not be premeditated, but rather the natural result of happening upon glistening, gorgeous, plump fish at the market, so perfect and shiny that you blush and feel compelled to remark on their beauty. When they look like that, this is what you do.

SERVES 4 GOOD EATERS

4 salt- or oil-packed anchovy fillets
2 to 3 slices day-old bread (any kind except whole wheat or brioche)
½ cup finely chopped fennel fronds
½ cup finely chopped flat-leaf parsley
½ cup raisins
¼ cup Pernod or passito di zibibbo (optional)
2 garlic cloves, minced
¼ cup pine nuts
Salt

¼ cup olive oil (the best you can afford)
2 tablespoons tomato paste
2 large ripe tomatoes, cored, peeled, seeded, and diced
2 branches wild fennel or 1 teaspoon fennel pollen or ½ teaspoon of ground fennel seeds
10 fresh sardine fillets
1 pound dried pasta, preferably bucatini, linguine, or spaghetti

1. If you're using salt-packed or oil-poached anchovies, rinse them, then soak them for 20 to 30 minutes, changing the water once halfway through. Drain them, remove and discard their backbones, and set the anchovies aside.

2. Toast the bread in a toaster or a preheated 350°F oven until it's golden brown. When they have cooled a bit, put the toasted slices in a food processor and pulse to make fine crumbs. You'll need ¾ cup.

3. Add half of the fennel fronds and all of the parsley to the crumbs and pulse a few times to combine them well. Set aside.

4. Soak the raisins in the Pernod for 30 minutes to 1 hour (or warm water if you prefer to not use Pernod) in a small bowl. Cover the bowl with plastic wrap and set it aside in a warm spot.

5. On a cutting board, chop the anchovy fillets with the minced garlic, then take the flat part of a chef's knife and smear the ingredients into the board, scraping across the board as you smear. Scoop up the paste with the knife, form it into a blob, and repeat the smearing and scraping until you have a smooth paste.

6. Heat a small sauté pan over medium heat for 1 minute. Add the pine nuts to the dry pan and toast, tossing often (or else they'll burn!), just until they begin to release their aroma and color slightly, about 3 minutes. Spill them onto a plate to cool. Once they've cooled, give them a coarse chop.

LISTEN
Kid Creole & The Coconuts
"Mister Softee"—'cause I got a real soft spot for anything with sardines.

DRINK
If you can find a Sicilian wine made from the zibibbo grape, even a touch of passito, grown on the island of Pantelleria, nothing would be better with this dish.

7. Bring a large pot of water to a boil and salt it until it tastes like the ocean.

8. Meanwhile, heat the olive oil in a straight-sided sauté pan over medium heat. Add the anchovy-garlic paste and cook, stirring often, until you smell the garlic, about 2 minutes. Add the tomato paste, stirring to combine and coat the other ingredients, then add the diced tomato, remaining fennel fronds, and ¼ cup water. Continue to cook, stirring occasionally, to blend the flavors and thicken the sauce slightly, 8 to 10 minutes.

9. Add the wild fennel or fennel pollen and the sardine fillets. Use a fork to roughly mash the fillets into the sauce, leaving the pieces in chunks.

10. Cook the pasta in salted boiling water for 1 minute less than the package instructs. Drain the pasta and add it to the sauce. Drain the raisins (sip on the infused Pernod if you are feeling frisky), give them a coarse chop, and add them to the pasta along with the pine nuts. Toss it all together.

11. Divide the pasta among four big bowls. Sprinkle each with the herbed bread crumbs and eat now.

ANELLI CON RICCI DI MARE

I was in Catania, Sicily, with my friends Paolo and Jeff when a local friend of Paolo's took us to this tiny seafood joint, a real hole in the wall, where we proceeded to feast for hours. At one point a waiter brought out a stainless-steel bowl filled with a frothy orange liquid—it turned out to be whipped uni, also known as . . . sea urchin gonads. Behind him another waiter carried a colander filled with steaming anelli, little ring-shaped pastas that you can eat with a spoon. The second waiter dumped the pasta into the bowl of orange froth, then the first waiter used two metal spoons to vigorously toss the whole concoction. The sweet and briny smell of the urchin mingling with the steamy, starchy pasta was overwhelming and really sexy. Whether you add the theatrical flair of mixing the two at the table is up to you.

SERVES 4 TO 6

Leaves from 6 ramps
½ cup olive oil (the best you can afford), plus another splash
Sea salt and freshly ground black pepper
1 pound anelli pasta
5 garlic cloves, minced
2 teaspoons hot red pepper flakes

¼ cup finely chopped flat-leaf parsley
8 whole, live sea urchins (see Note) or 40 lobes sea urchin roe (aka uni)
4 tablespoons (½ stick) unsalted butter, cubed
Juice of 1 lemon

1. Lightly coat the ramps with a little olive oil and season them with salt and pepper. Heat a grill pan or cast-iron pan over high heat and char (not burn) the leaves, about 30 seconds per side. Cut the leaves crosswise into thirds, transfer them to a plate, and set aside in a warm place.

2. Bring a large pot of water to a boil and salt it until it tastes like the ocean. Cook the pasta in salted boiling water for 1 minute less than the package instructs.

3. While the pasta is cooking, heat 2 tablespoons of the olive oil in a large straight-sided sauté pan over medium heat. Add the garlic and cook, stirring, until fragrant and translucent, about 2 minutes. Add the hot red pepper flakes, stir, and cook until fragrant. Add the remaining oil and, when it's warm but not hot, stir in the parsley.

4. Whisk in half of the sea urchin, breaking it up to make a sauce. Gradually add the butter and whisk to emulsify the sauce. Keep the sauce warm over low heat.

5. Drain the pasta, reserving 1 cup of the pasta water. Add the pasta to the sea urchin sauce and stir well. Raise the heat to medium and cook, tossing constantly, for 1 minute. If the sauce starts to thicken, gradually add a little of the reserved pasta water. The sauce should be thick and creamy and should adhere to the pasta.

6. Transfer the pasta to a large bowl and top it with the remaining raw sea urchin and the ramp leaves. Top off with lemon juice.

NOTE

Buying whole live sea urchin is the best way to get that briny flavor you're after, when you can really taste the ocean. But how to get at those sweet, sweet gonads? Grab your kitchen shears, find the small hole on the underside of each urchin, and insert the smaller blade. Hold the urchin over the sink to catch any liquid and snip the top of the urchin off, like you're giving the spiny guy a Caesar do. (Give the urchin a sniff—if you detect an unpleasant funk, throw that one out and move on to the next one.) Remove the piece and turn the urchin upside down to drain out any liquid in the shell. Using the back of a small spoon handle or a chopstick, delicately remove the yellow-orange lobes (that's uni, baby!), trying your damnedest to keep them intact. Transfer them to an empty bowl as you extract them and use them as soon as possible.

LISTEN
The Rolling Stones, *Tattoo You.* First "Heaven," then "Waiting on a Friend," then "No Use in Crying"—some of the last great work from one of the greatest rock 'n' roll bands.

DRINK
Greco di Tufo (NovaSerra from Mastroberardino), a clean white from Campania that won't overpower the delicate urchin. It's easy to drink. Like three bottles, no prob.

GARGANELLI WITH BRAISED GOAT OR LAMB HEART

When I buy whole animals for my restaurants, the hearts rarely make it onto the menu—they usually end up in my mouth. Sometimes I'll just slice a heart thinly, hit the slices with salt and pepper, and drop them on the griddle. But when one of my farmer friends ended up with a surplus of hearts and asked me if I'd take them off his hands, I braised them, and that treatment became part of the repertoire. Braising hearts requires a delicate hand: because they're all muscle (and therefore not as forgiving as braised pork belly or beef short ribs), they have the potential to dry out if you're not careful. Pay close attention. Touch the heart. Watch it as it cooks. Pull one out, cut a slice, and eat it. There is a fine line between tender and overcooked.

SERVES 4

3 lamb and/or goat hearts (about 1½ pounds)
Sea salt and freshly ground black pepper
4 garlic cloves, sliced
5 ripe tomatoes, cored, peeled, and cut into chunks
1 piece Parmesan rind, about 2 inches square

4 fresh thyme sprigs
5 dried chilies, such as cayenne
1 to 2 cups sangiovese wine
1 cup Chicken Stock (page 324)
1 pound fresh or dried garganelli
Olive oil (the best you can afford)
2 ounces Parmigiano-Reggiano, finely grated (about ½ cup)

1. Preheat the oven to 300°F.
2. Season the hearts generously with salt and pepper. In a medium ovenproof saucepan with a lid, combine the hearts, garlic, tomatoes, Parmesan rind, thyme, dried chilies, and 1½ teaspoons salt. Add enough wine to flood the bottom of the pan by ¼ inch, then add the chicken stock.
3. Heat the saucepan over medium heat until the liquid simmers, then cover with a lid and cook in the oven until the hearts give easily when poked with the tip of a sharp knife, about 2 hours.
4. Take the pan out of the oven, remove the lid, and set the pan to the side until the hearts are cool enough to handle. Remove the hearts from the liquid and slice them about ¼ inch thick against the grain. Put the slices on a plate and cover with plastic wrap.
5. Strain the braising liquid, pushing the solids into the sieve with the back of a spoon to extract their goodness before discarding them. Return the liquid to the pan and bring to a simmer over medium heat, cooking until the liquid has thickened slightly, about 15 minutes.
6. Meanwhile, bring a large pot of water to a boil and salt it until it tastes like the

LISTEN
ESG, *Dance to the Beat of Moody.* It's a pagan ritual in our house to dance to post-punk-era south Bronx funk—with a goat heart on a skewer.

DRINK
An old, mature, luscious Brunello.

ocean. Cook the pasta in the boiling water for 1 minute less than the package instructs and drain the pasta, reserving 1 cup of the pasta water. Dump the cooked pasta back into the pot in which it cooked.

7. Pour the reduced braising liquid into the pasta pot and turn the heat to medium. Stir the pasta and cook for about 1 minute. If the liquid gets too thick, gradually add a bit of the reserved pasta water to the pot.

8. Add the sliced hearts to the pasta pot, along with a generous glug of olive oil. Toss, increase the heat to medium-high, and stir in all but a handful of the grated cheese. Add a little more pasta water if necessary, then taste and add a little more salt if necessary, until it tastes really good. Remove from the heat and transfer the pasta to a large bowl. Sprinkle with the remaining cheese and serve.

POULTRY

I don't understand people who hate chicken, saying it's dull and insipid. It goes well with just about anything. You can roast it, braise it, poach it, sauté it, and fry it. Chicken parties just as well with clams as it does with curry. If all you have in your house is some peppercorns, a couple of lemons, and a chicken, you have the makings of a beautiful meal. That's why chicken figures so big in my at-home repertoire. A roasted chicken with some garlic and good bread to sop up the juices is a staple item of the Good Life to which I aspire daily.

Chicken's entire anatomy is awesome——thighs and necks! hearts and livers!——and despite what some antibreast men might tell you, even that often-dry part can shine if you just give it some love and affection . . . and don't overcook it.

But the fact that chicken is so versatile doesn't mean it can't be brought to the sort of fussed-over, tear-jerking level of deliciousness typically associated with more upmarket proteins. In France, for instance, they revere the bird. During one unforgettable trip there I dropped an amazing amount of cash on poularde de Bresse en vessie, pedigreed poultry that had been cooked slowly in a pig's bladder, the original sous-vide. I'd do it again in a second.

In other words, I like me a chicken. At home, I buy chicken only if I know where it was raised and if that "where" is a place where things are done in a manner with which I'm comfortable. Or at least if the story is persuasive enough. (A little denial helps us all through the day.) Everyone lives near someone who raises chickens. I know people who raise chickens in the city, for chrissakes! Make the effort to find humanely raised chicken or, hell, go to the Agway, buy some chicks, and raise your own. And by the way? This is just my *advice*, which I follow only 88.4 percent of the time. I mean, shit, a guy's gotta eat!

Now, when I go and eat at restaurants—especially inexpensive little ethnic joints where the food is so cheap I try hard not to think about where it's from—I give up control to enjoy my taste experience. (It's like watching a movie and suspending disbelief. You know there's a high level of bullshit going on, but if you can just calm the fuck down for a couple of hours you're bound to have some fun.) Then I return home to find Jori, my fiancée, crafting laundry detergent out of vinegar and making pasta from flour ground in a mill sixty miles away, and I enjoy my natural, holistic home experience as I stream movies on an iPad, text from a smart phone, and watch my son play video games. It's hypocritical—like my friends from childhood who would wolf down cheeseburgers and pork ribs at the diner but then keep kosher at home—but perfection is the enemy of progress. Someone said that once.

TURMERIC-RUBBED CHICKEN WITH CELERY MOSTARDA

I like to think of this as a curry pan sauce. You roast chicken rubbed with garlicky turmeric-and-chili-spiked butter, then add lemongrass and coconut milk to the pan. And boom, an easy currylike sauce that mingles with the juices from the chicken! And for those of you who thought turmeric was a tasteless powder used to give things a yellow color, make the effort and find fresh or even flash-frozen turmeric. You'll be shocked by the aromatic, almost carrotlike flavor.

SERVES 4

1 whole chicken (about 3 pounds)
2 fresh Thai bird chilies, stemmed
2 inches fresh turmeric, peeled
4 garlic cloves, crushed and peeled
Sea salt
4 tablespoons (½ stick) unsalted
    butter, softened

Celery Mostarda (page 299)
½ cup well-shaken coconut milk,
    preferably Aroy-D brand
Juice of 1 lime
6 lemongrass stalks, outer layer
    removed

1. Rinse the chicken very well under cold water. Remove the innards from the cavity and reserve them for chicken stock or make yourself a little liver-heart-neck snack. Place the chicken on a paper-towel-lined plate and let it dry, uncovered, in the fridge for at least 4 hours and up to 2 days.

2. Use a mortar and pestle to pound (see page 12) the chilies, turmeric, garlic, and 1½ teaspoons salt to a paste. Add the softened butter and combine thoroughly with a fork.

3. Rub the chicken all over with the turmeric butter. Wrap the bird in plastic wrap and refrigerate overnight. (I typically make the celery mostarda at this point so that the flavors get to meld overnight. But hey, you're a grown-up—you decide when you want to make the mostarda.)

4. The next day, remove the chicken from the fridge and let it come to room temperature. Preheat the oven to 425°F.

5. Gently warm the coconut milk with the lime juice and a pinch of salt in a small saucepan over low heat.

6. Take the lemongrass stalks and crack them along the stalk, maybe 3 to 4 times from the base to the tip, just to open the layers and expose the insides. Spread the broken lemongrass stalks in a roasting pan or large cast-iron skillet.

7. Put the chicken on the lemongrass stalks and transfer the pan to the oven. Roast the chicken for 20 minutes and then lower the heat to 350°F.

8. Add the coconut milk mixture to the pan and baste the bird every few minutes until the bird is cooked through, about 20 more minutes. (Don't worry if the coconut milk breaks. You're cool either way.) Poke the bird with a metal skewer

LISTEN
13th Floor Elevators, "Splash 1"—Roky Erickson flipped out, but before he did he produced some supercool numbers that are still relevant today.

DRINK
Coulaine Chinon 2006—sturdy enough to stand up to the marinade and the mostarda and good enough to keep drinking through the night.

in a joint of the thigh, leave it there for 20 seconds, then touch it to your lip. Is it hot? Cool, the chicken's done. If you're a sissy about your chicken, cut into the leg. If the juices that spill out are light pink or clear, it's ready.

9. Let the chicken rest in the pan with the juices for 10 minutes before serving. Serve it with the celery mostarda.

TURMERIC-RUBBED CHICKEN WITH CELERY MOSTARDA, p. 98

CHICKEN AND CLAMS WITH AGRETTI

I first encountered agretti, a grassy succulent with a seaweedlike bite, in Rome, where it appears in markets for a short time in the particularly warm months of spring. When I got back to the United States, I asked Nancy Macnamara of Honey Locust Farm House if she could grow some. She did (and well, too); then a few other farmers followed, though none could quite match what Nancy grew. Sadly, agretti never blew up like I thought it would, but you can still find it in the spring at better farmers' markets. If you do come across agretti, all you need to do is warm it in garlicky olive oil and add a little lemon for a true treat. But for this recipe I turned to one of my favorite partnerships, chicken and clams, to make a more substantial agretti salad.

SERVES 4 TO 6

- 4 salt- or oil-packed anchovy fillets, minced
- ½ pound prosciutto or jamón Ibérico fat, chopped
- 6 cups Chicken Stock (page 324)
- 1 whole chicken breast on the bone, 3 pounds
- Sea salt and freshly ground black pepper
- About ¼ cup plus 2 tablespoons olive oil (the best you can afford)
- 8 garlic cloves, 4 crushed and peeled and 4 minced
- 1 pound agretti, woody stems discarded
- 2 lemons
- 3 medium shallots, minced

- 5 fresh thyme sprigs
- ½ cup dry Riesling
- 3 pounds Manila clams (or a mix of different types small to medium clams), soaked in several changes of cold water for at least 1 hour
- ½ cup chopped fresh flat-leaf parsley
- 3 celery stalks, thinly sliced (preferably on a mandoline)
- Skin from 1 Preserved Lemon (page 302), julienned
- 6 thin slices prosciutto di Parma, julienned
- ½ teaspoon hot red pepper flakes

1. If you're using salt-packed anchovies, rinse them, then soak them for 20 to 30 minutes, changing the water once halfway through. Drain them. If using oil-packed, drain the oil. Mince the anchovies and set them aside.

2. In a large, shallow saucepan with a tight lid, combine the prosciutto fat and the chicken stock and bring to a boil over high heat. Reduce the heat and keep the liquid at a gentle simmer.

3. Season the chicken breast generously with salt and pepper. Add the breast to the stock, cook for 5 minutes, then cover the pan and remove it from the heat. Let it sit for 25 minutes, then take the chicken breast out of the stock (reserving it). When it's cool enough to handle, remove the skin from the breast and discard

LISTEN
The Stones, *Sticky Fingers*, especially "Can't You Hear Me Knocking."

DRINK
Austrian Riesling—any one from Alzinger will be beautifully crisp and dry, just right on a sunny but cool spring day.

it, then cut the meat from the bone and discard the bones. Season the chicken with salt.

4. Warm 2 tablespoons of the olive oil in a large sauté pan over medium heat and cook the crushed garlic until aromatic, 1 to 2 minutes. Add the agretti and toss in the pan until just warm, no more than 1 minute. Season with a good sprinkle of salt and a squeeze from one of the lemons, take the pan off the heat, and set aside.

5. Heat a large pot with a lid over medium-high heat. Add enough of the remaining olive oil to cover the bottom, then add the minced garlic, shallots, anchovies, and thyme. Cook, stirring, for 1 minute, add the wine, bring it to a boil, and let it boil for 1 to 2 minutes to cook off the alcohol. Pour in ½ cup of the reserved chicken-cooking liquid and bring back to a boil.

6. Add the clams, cover, and increase the heat to high, shaking from time to time until the clams have opened, 1½ to 5 minutes. Discard any that haven't opened after 5 minutes. Take the pot off the heat, then add the parsley, toss once, and drain the clams over a bowl, reserving the liquid and discarding the thyme sprigs.

7. Cut the chicken breast crosswise into ⅛-inch-thick slices. In a large, warm bowl, gently toss the chicken with the agretti, celery, preserved lemon, and clams. Season the clam liquid with salt and lemon juice to taste and spoon it over the ingredients until they're well dressed. Divide among four to six bowls and garnish with the prosciutto and red pepper flakes. Serve wedges of lemon alongside.

CRISPY CHICKEN SALAD

This salad is more than just salad. Yes, there are crispy pieces of fried chicken tossed with a sensational Southeast Asian dressing and fresh herbs. But next to all that brightness is a little bowl of rice and some budu, a fermented anchovy sauce from southern Thailand that's as awesomely fish-guts-smelly-funky as it gets. Tempered with a little kecap manis and lime, the budu provides a rich mouthful of sea-salty pleasure.

SERVES 4

FOR THE DRESSING
¼ cup plus 2 tablespoons palm sugar
¼ cup fish sauce
2 tablespoons minced scraped, rinsed cilantro roots
1 fresh long red chili, such as Anaheim or Hungarian Wax, seeded and finely chopped

2 garlic cloves, crushed and peeled
¼ teaspoon salt
3 tablespoons rice vinegar
2½ tablespoons fresh lime juice

FOR THE BUDU SAUCE
½ cup budu sauce
1 tablespoon kecap manis

Juice of ½ lime

FOR THE CRISPY CHICKEN
2 cups Chicken Stock (page 324)
1 medium shallot, thinly sliced
1 garlic clove, thinly sliced
1 inch fresh ginger, peeled and thinly sliced
2 boneless, skinless whole chicken breasts (4 pieces, kids)

3 cups neutral oil, such as grapeseed or canola
2 cups all-purpose flour
Sea salt and freshly ground black pepper

TO FINISH THE DISH
Sea salt
5 fresh eggs
Freshly ground black pepper
2 cups cooked jasmine rice
1 cup loosely packed fresh Thai basil leaves

1 cup bean sprouts
Pinch of sil gochu
1 fresh long green chili, such as Anaheim or Hungarian Wax, sliced

MAKE THE DRESSING

In a small bowl, combine the palm sugar with the fish sauce. Use a mortar and pestle to pound (see page 12) the cilantro roots, red chili, garlic, and ¼ teaspoon salt to a paste, pounding each ingredient thoroughly before adding the next. Add the palm sugar mixture, the vinegar, and the lime juice and combine well by pounding and stirring with the pestle.

NOTE

I came up with this recipe for a dinner Jori, Corwin, and I cooked at a big, fancy hotel in Kuala Lumpur. It was a cool experience—Americans invited to Malaysia to cook Malaysian food!—but shockingly, the hotel couldn't get us half the ingredients we asked for . . . Malaysian ingredients! You gotta love a corporate procurement system that manages to find really crappy frozen fish while you're standing on a goddamn peninsula. Anyway, it wasn't so bad. We had the opportunity to hit the markets, which is the best way to cook anyway. Which leads me to this advice: use the best fresh herbs you can get in this salad. If the Thai basil you find is wilted, use cilantro or mint or scallions. It's all about adding a little aroma, freshness, and texture.

MAKE THE BUDU SAUCE

In a small bowl, whisk together the budu sauce, kecap manis, and lime juice. Set aside.

MAKE THE CRISPY CHICKEN

1. In a large saucepan with a tight lid, bring the chicken stock, shallot, garlic, and ginger to a simmer over medium-high heat. Add the chicken breasts and immediately reduce the heat to bring the liquid to a very low simmer. Poach for 5 minutes, then turn off the heat, cover the pan, and let it sit until the chicken is cooked through, about 25 minutes.
2. Remove the meat from the poaching liquid and, when it's cool enough to handle, use your fingers to shred it along the grain into long, thin pieces. Strain the poaching liquid, then cool and store it for the next time you need yummy chicken broth.
3. In a large straight-sided sauté pan, heat the oil to 375°F (measured on a deep-frying thermometer).
4. Put the flour into a medium bowl and season it generously with salt and pepper. Dredge the shredded chicken in the seasoned flour. Shake off any excess flour, then fry the chicken in batches until it's a roasty golden color and crispy, 3 to 4 minutes per batch. Use a slotted spoon to transfer the crispy chicken to a paper-towel-lined plate to drain. Season immediately with salt and pepper.

FINISH THE DISH

1. Bring 4 cups water to a boil in a large straight-sided sauté pan and season with a sprinkle of salt. Have a slotted spoon at the ready. Lower the temperature of the water to a gentle simmer. Gently crack two eggs and carefully pour them from their shells into the water. Cook them until the white is firm but cloudlike, 3 to 4 minutes. Use a slotted spoon to transfer the cooked eggs to a paper-towel-lined plate to drain. Season with salt and pepper. Cook two more eggs, keeping the remaining egg on hand as a spare. Alternatively, a nice 3-minute soft-boiled egg would work for this dish, too.
2. Divide the cooked rice among four serving bowls. Drizzle the rice with the budu sauce. Top the rice with a poached egg. Combine the crispy chicken with the Thai basil, bean sprouts, sil gochu, and chili in a mixing bowl. Add the dressing and toss with your hands. Top the egg with the crispy chicken salad. Serve immediately.

LISTEN
Grand Funk-mutha-fucking Railroad, "Aimless Lady"—It's the Railroad!

DRINK
Southern Thai summer cooler—2 ounces **rye,** 1 tablespoon **gula jawa syrup,** juice from ¼ **lemon,** a few leaves of **holy basil** muddled in there, crushed **ice,** top with **seltzer.**

CURRY LEAF FRIED CHICKEN

At a night market in Langkawi, an island off the northwestern coast of Malaysia, I rolled up to a hawker stall and bought a cone of nasi uduk. It's actually an Indonesian rice dish, and a fairly common street snack, which consists of a banana-leaf cone filled with coconut rice. What made this one stand out was the two pieces of fried chicken that sat on top of the mound of rice. As I watched the women cooking the chicken in a large *kuali*, or wok, I noticed that they would periodically sprinkle curry leaves into the bubbling oil along with the chicken pieces. The complex and warming aroma was unforgettable. When I returned to the States, I got to work trying to re-create that chicken, deciding I wanted to infuse the meat with a rich, savory flavor before frying it with the curry leaves. Maybe it was because I ate that chicken while on an island, but I settled on a cincalok brine. The fermented little shrimp contribute the depth and roundness I was looking for, something intriguing but not inaccessible. In the end, this is still good old fried chicken.

SERVES 4

FOR BRINING THE CHICKEN
One 8-ounce bottle cincalok
2 garlic cloves, crushed and peeled
2 tablespoons black peppercorns
2 tablespoons coriander seeds
1 dried bay leaf
1 whole chicken (about 3 pounds), cut into 8 pieces

FOR THE CHILI VINEGAR
2 cups chopped long green chilies, such as Anaheim or Hungarian Wax
2 cups distilled white vinegar
1 teaspoon sea salt

FOR FRYING THE CHICKEN
2 cups all-purpose flour
¼ cup kosher salt
¼ cup freshly ground black pepper
6 cups neutral oil, such as grapeseed or canola
Coarse sea salt
4 sprigs fresh curry leaves

THE DAY BEFORE

BRINE THE CHICKEN

In a large saucepan, combine the cincalok, garlic, peppercorns, coriander seeds, bay leaf, and 2 cups water. Bring the water to a simmer over medium-high heat and cook for 10 minutes. Remove the pot from the heat and let the solution cool completely. Pour the cooled mixture into a large bowl. Add the chicken pieces, tossing well, then cover the bowl with plastic wrap and refrigerate for 24 hours.

LISTEN
Burning Spear, *Live*, from '77—I'm not so into Malaysian music, and reggae is island music, too!

DRINK
Cold island beer like Red Stripe or cold star fruit juice.

Puree the chilies, vinegar, and 1 teaspoon sea salt together in a blender. Transfer the liquid to a bowl and refrigerate, covered, for at least 24 hours to let the flavors meld. Strain the mixture through a fine-mesh sieve, discarding any solids.

THAT DAY

FRY THE CHICKEN

1. Remove the chicken from the brine and pat it dry. Whisk together the flour, kosher salt, and pepper in a large bowl. Dredge the pieces of chicken in the flour and put them on a cooling rack set over a baking pan. Let sit them for 5 minutes and then repeat the dredging process to make sure you get a perfect coating of flour.

2. Meanwhile, heat the oil in a large, heavy saucepan to 350°F over high heat (measured on a deep-frying thermometer). Once the temperature is reached, reduce the heat to medium-high to maintain it.

3. Working in batches, add the chicken to the oil and fry until the chicken is golden, crispy, and cooked through, about 12 minutes for white meat and 15 to 17 minutes for dark. Remove the chicken pieces with a slotted spoon and place on a cooling rack. Season generously with coarse sea salt.

4. When the chicken has finished cooking, fry the curry leaves in the cooking oil until crispy, about 10 seconds, then transfer them with a slotted spoon to a paper-towel-lined plate to drain.

5. Place the chicken on a large plate and crumble some of the fried curry leaves over it. Pile a few more whole fried curry leaves on the side as a garnish and serve with a little bowl of the chili vinegar.

CURRY LEAF FRIED CHICKEN, p. 106

CHICKEN CLAY POT, p. 112

CHICKEN CLAY POT

This dish has been on Fatty Crab's menu since day one. At first glance it might *look* like nothing more than a clay pot bubbling with a simple potpie-style filling. But those flashes of green aren't peas—they're chilies. And those chunks of white aren't potatoes but cubes of tofu. What looks like cornstarch-thickened broth *is* actually cornstarch-thickened broth, but there are some really thrilling flavors in there (bits of salted fish that provide little electric shocks of salinity and a touch of MSG), which make it a bag-of-chips dish—you know, the kind you just can't seem to stop eating.

SERVES 2

FOR "VELVETING" THE CHICKEN
About 3 cups neutral oil, such as grapeseed or canola

2 boneless, skinless chicken breasts

Sea salt

½ cup cornstarch

TO FINISH THE DISH
1 teaspoon cornstarch

1 cup Chicken Stock (page 324), seasoned with salt to taste

One 2.5-ounce square firm fresh tofu, cut into large dice

1 ounce salt mackerel, cut into small dice

2 long green chilies, such as Anaheim or Hungarian Wax, diced

1 inch fresh ginger, very thinly sliced crosswise (preferably on a mandoline)

4 garlic cloves, very thinly sliced on a mandoline

Sea salt

½ teaspoon MSG

TO GARNISH
1 teaspoon dark sesame oil

1 teaspoon Chili Oil (page 318)

2 tablespoons thinly sliced scallion

"VELVET" THE CHICKEN

In a medium heavy saucepan, heat 1 inch of oil to 350°F (measured on a deep-frying thermometer). Meanwhile, cut the breasts into bite-sized pieces. Season the breast chunks lightly with sea salt, then dredge them in the cornstarch. Fry them until the cornstarch seals around the chicken, about 30 seconds. This is a Chinese technique that gives a uniform appearance and texture to the chicken. Transfer the chicken with a slotted spoon to a paper-towel-lined plate to drain and season again with salt.

NOTE

Clay pots are ideal here because they retain heat evenly, but feel free to make it in a pot and serve in bowls.

LISTEN
Beatles, *Rubber Soul*—I started listening to this album when I was five years old, and it still has yet to be overplayed.

DRINK
2 ounces **Beefeater gin**, 1 ounce **white vermouth**, 4 leaves of **ivy** that grows on the ground (yeah, ivy; it's tasty), 1 **cerignola olive**, pitted. Muddle the olive and the ivy in a rocks glass. Top with two **ice cubes**. Pour gin and vermouth over ice in a shaker, shake, and then strain into the rocks glass. Garnish with a thin strip of **orange peel**.

1. In a small bowl, whisk the cornstarch into 2 tablespoons warm water until well combined to make a slurry.

2. Warm the chicken stock in a small saucepan, then divide it between two 8-inch flameproof clay pots. Divide the tofu, salted mackerel, diced chilies, ginger, garlic, 1 teaspoon salt, and the MSG between the pots. Stir to combine, then add the "velveted" chicken breast. Put the pots over medium-high heat and bring the liquid to a boil. Add 1 tablespoon of the cornstarch slurry to each pot. Cook, stirring gently, just until the chicken is fully cooked, about 2 minutes. Serve immediately with the sesame oil, chili oil, and sliced scallion as garnish.

WHOLE POACHED CHICKEN WITH WHITE FUNGUS AND PRESERVED BLACK BEANS

This dish is all about the delicate flavor and texture of chicken. To me it's always essential to use the highest-quality chicken you can find, but here it's especially important. Floating around among the yielding chicken flesh are frilly clusters of crunchy, snappy white fungus. Also known as "cloud ear mushrooms," they're dried and sold in gift boxes; they bloom beautifully in hot liquid to resemble an intricate loofahesque sea creature. I know, the name "white fungus" isn't really a turn-on, but the textural contrast the mushrooms provide is stunning. (If you can't find white fungus, use fresh maitake mushrooms.) I began cooking this dish years ago, poaching whole milk-fed poulardes from Four Story Hills Farm in a double bouillon with chunks of foie gras, which adds even more richness and a silky mouthfeel, but feel free to omit it if you have some sort of moral (or financial) objection.

SERVES 4

1 whole chicken (about 3 pounds)
2 tablespoons kosher salt
About 4 cups Double Chicken Stock (page 325)
1 inch fresh ginger, peeled and thinly sliced
2 garlic cloves, crushed
1 tablespoon Chinese preserved black beans, rinsed well and soaked in cold water for 1 hour

4 pieces dried white fungus
6 ounces raw foie gras, cut into chunks (optional)
Sea salt and freshly ground black pepper
1 cup fresh cilantro leaves

1. Rub the chicken with the kosher salt all over the body and inside the cavity. Put the chicken in a large Dutch oven or soup pot with a lid.

2. In a separate pot, heat the stock to just below a simmer and pour enough of it over the chicken to submerge three-quarters of the bird. (Add a little water if needed to to reach this level.) Add the ginger, garlic, and preserved black beans. Bring the liquid to a simmer over medium heat, then cook, covered, basting occasionally, 30 minutes.

3. Add the fungus to the broth and continue to cook, covered, for another 15 minutes. Add the foie gras chunks and continue to cook, covered, until the chicken is cooked through, about 15 minutes more. The chicken is done when the legs feel loose at the joints after you give them a little shake and when the juices from the thickest part of the thigh run clear or very light pink when you poke it with a skewer.

BONUS SNACK!

Sauté the liver and heart of the chicken in some good olive oil. Pour the whole mess onto a cutting board and season with salt and a squeeze of lemon. Take an anchovy fillet and a couple parsley leaves and chop everything together. Scrape it all up and slide it into a bowl. Grab a few pieces of pumpernickel bread and give them a shmear.

LISTEN
Beirut, *Gulag Orkestar.* Works with the vodka and won't offend the chicken.

DRINK
Shots of chilled Stoli, please. Goes so well with the bonus snack.

4. Remove the bird from the broth and cut the breast meat from the bone. Remove the thighs and legs from the body. Season all of it with sea salt and pepper. Thinly slice the breast meat against the grain.

5. To serve, put the leg meat into a serving bowl and snuggle a piece or two of white fungus in there. Lay the sliced breast meat over the legs in the bowl. Ladle the broth over the meat and be sure to include any chunks of foie gras. Garnish with the cilantro leaves.

WHOLE POACHED CHICKEN, p. 114

CHICKEN AND LARDO

Years back, after a trip to Italy's Le Marche region, I couldn't stop thinking about chicken *en potacchio*. It's a simple, supersavory dish of fowl braised in an aromatic mixture of garlic, chili, white wine, rosemary, and a little pork fat. And then there's the rather onomatopoeic name—*Potacchio!* you say, as you spit out a branch of rosemary. To add a little contrast to the white wine and pork fat in my version here, I supplement with gooseberries. You could use fresh currants instead of gooseberries because they too add a bright punch to the dish without overwhelming the other delicate flavors.

SERVES 2 TO 4

1 whole chicken (about 3 pounds), cut into 8 pieces
1 tablespoon kosher salt
Freshly ground black pepper
3 ounces lardo (page 194), cut into medium dice
½ cup dry white wine

4 garlic cloves, crushed and peeled
2 tablespoons hot red pepper flakes
Three 1-inch fresh rosemary sprigs
10 cape gooseberries or 20 fresh currants
Coarse sea salt
4 lemon wedges

1. Season the chicken pieces generously with kosher salt and pepper.
2. Heat the lardo in a large, straight-sided sauté pan with a tight lid over medium heat and cook until it has rendered most of its fat and turns into small crispy bits, 5 to 6 minutes. Use a slotted spoon to transfer the crispy bits to a paper-towel-lined plate to drain.
3. Raise the heat under the rendered fat to medium-high. When it's hot but not smoking, add the chicken pieces (in batches if necessary), skin side down, and sear them until perfectly golden and saliva inducing, about 6 minutes.
4. Turn the pieces over in the pan (they should be skin side up) and add the lardo bits, white wine, garlic, pepper flakes, and rosemary sprigs. Bring the liquid to a boil, then reduce the heat and simmer, covered, until the juices of the chicken run clear (or light pink) when poked lightly with a skewer, 20 to 25 minutes. Turn off the heat and add the gooseberries or currants.
5. Transfer the contents of the pan to a serving bowl (or serve the dish from the pot at the table). Season with coarse sea salt and freshly ground black pepper and serve with the lemon wedges.

LISTEN
James White & the Blacks—"Contort Yourself"—that's what I did when I first tried this dish in the hills of Le Marche.

DRINK
Verdicchio, maybe one from the glamorous Angela Velenosi.

SQUAB WITH SICHUAN PEPPER GLAZE AND AMARANTH SALAD

Good squab is seriously gamy and incredibly rich. Such boldly flavored flesh screams out to join forces with an equally ballsy culinary partner. This simple, sweet glaze includes a healthy dose of Sichuan peppercorns; their tingly, citrusy punch, paired with the squab, will start a raucous party in your mouth. The amaranth greens (called "Chinese spinach" in Asian markets and "blood spinach" in places with a flair for the dramatic) further slice into that rich, rich squabbiness. I love amaranth's hearty crunch, but you can substitute any fresh, crisp green that looks good to you.

SERVES 4

FOR THE SQUAB
¼ cup Sichuan peppercorns
2 cups Master Stock (page 322), or Chicken Stock (page 324) with a pinch of MSG
1 tablespoon Chinese rock sugar or palm or brown sugar
4 squabs (1 to 1½ pounds each)

Sea salt
1 tablespoon neutral oil, such as grapeseed or canola
4 garlic cloves, smashed
1 inch fresh ginger, peeled and crushed
½ pound (2 sticks) unsalted butter

FOR THE AMARANTH SALAD DRESSING
1 tablespoon Chinese rock sugar
2 tablespoons rice vinegar

1 tablespoon mirin

FOR THE AMARANTH SALAD
1 tablespoon olive oil (the best you can afford)
½ pound amaranth greens
¼ cup raw chopped almonds

1 tablespoon julienned peeled fresh ginger
1 tablespoon julienned black truffle

MAKE THE SQUAB

1. Preheat the oven to 400°F. Meanwhile, in a dry pan over medium-high heat, toast the Sichuan peppercorns, swirling them until they crackle lightly and release their aroma, about 3 minutes. Scoop half of the peppercorns into a small bowl and set aside. Grind the remaining peppercorns in a spice grinder and set aside.

2. Simmer the stock in a medium saucepan until it has reduced by about half, then stir in the rock sugar until it dissolves. Stir in the whole Sichuan peppercorns. Remove from the heat and set it aside.

3. Season the squabs generously with sea salt and the ground Sichuan peppercorns. Heat a heavy pan, large enough to hold two squabs, over medium-high heat until the pan just begins to smoke. Lightly coat the bottom of the pan with oil and add the squabs to the pan, skin side down. Reduce the heat to

NOTE

Squab is at its best when it rests for a few days to a week before cooking. After five or six days in the fridge, the gamy flavor that makes squab so awesome has adequate time to develop. Resting the squab also dries out the skin, leading to more beautiful color and a crispier bite when you do cook it. I like to buy whole squabs, organs in, and hang them from their necks in the fridge for two days with a plate underneath to catch any digestive by-products. At the end of the two days, I eviscerate the birds, rinse them with cold water and pat dry, and hang them for another two to three days in the fridge. (You can also lay the squabs on a baking rack if you don't have the room or the means to hang them.)

medium. Cook the squabs until the bottoms are golden brown, about 4 minutes, then flip them and continue to cook until the other sides are golden brown, about 4 minutes more.

4. Turn the birds onto their backs, then add half the garlic, ginger, and butter. Let the butter foam and continue to cook the squab, basting frequently with the butter, for 4 minutes. Remove the two squabs and transfer them to a cooling rack set over a plate. Pour the butter from the pan over the squabs. Repeat the process with the remaining two birds, using the remaining garlic, ginger, and butter.

5. When the second batch of squabs is done, place them all on a rack set in a roasting pan or baking pan. Add about ¼ cup water to the bottom of the pan. Put the pan in the oven and cook the squabs until they're medium-rare (when you prod the breasts with a finger, they'll give a little and then spring back slowly), about 10 minutes.

6. Pull the roasting pan out of the oven and set the rack of squabs onto a fresh pan. Reserve the drip pan. Pour half of the master stock–rock sugar mixture over the birds.

MAKE THE DRESSING

In a small saucepan, combine the salad dressing ingredients and cook over medium-high heat, stirring to dissolve the sugar. When the sugar is completely dissolved, transfer the mixture to a medium bowl to cool.

MAKE THE SALAD AND FINISH THE DISH

1. Pour the drippings from the squab drip pan into a large sauté pan, then heat it over high heat. Add the olive oil, then add the amaranth leaves (in batches if necessary to avoid crowding), stirring to coat with the oil-drippings mixture, and cook until just wilted, no more than 30 seconds. Transfer the amaranth to the dressing bowl and toss to combine. Add the remaining salad ingredients and toss again. Serve the salad in a wide shallow bowl alongside the squab.

2. Place the squabs on a large platter and coat with some of the remaining glaze. If there's a lot of extra glaze, serve it alongside the squab in a sauceboat.

LISTEN
Tricky, *Pre-Millennium Tension*—it's heavy at times, but the power of the dark side is very strong . . . give in now and again . . . we'll call it "balance."

DRINK
Jori's Hot Tea-oddy: ½ cup **Darjeeling tea leaves**, 3 tablespoons **chamomile buds,** 2 tablespoons **lavender buds**, 1 large fresh **sage leaf**, ½ inch **lemon peel**, 1 tablespoon local **honey.** Combine everything in a medium pot, and add 4 cups boiling water. Steep for 4 minutes and drain into another pot. Keep the infusion warm over low heat. When you're ready to imbibe, combine 1½ shots **Scotch**, ½ shot **St. Germaine**, and 4 shots of the hot tea in a large mug.

FATTY DUCK

The idea for Fatty Duck, a staple on the Fatty Crab menu, first took shape in my mind while I was driving on the BQE—the birthplace of all great ideas, right? I was gnawing on a greasy, deep-fried piece of salt-and-pepper duck from one of those nameless Chinatown joints as I steered with one hand. The duck was overcooked and kind of skimpy, but still really good. As I swerved violently my thoughts gelled in a rare moment of coherence: this duck would be fucking phenomenal if there was something more to it. My early idea to kick things up a notch with a sweet-spicy, peppery garnish has since been improved upon by the rhythm master Corwin Kave. Plump, a little crispy, sweet and spicy and pickly—shovel this duck into your mouth with both hands.

SERVES 4 TO 6

FOR STEAMING THE DUCK

2 whole Pekin ducks (4 to 5 pounds each), broken down by your butcher into leg quarters and breast pieces, leaving the breast pieces on the rib cage

Sea salt and freshly ground black pepper

Enough liquid, such as pork belly braising liquid (see page 198) or water, to fill the bottom of a large stockpot by an inch (about 4 cups)

5 inches fresh ginger, peeled and sliced

6 garlic cloves, crushed and peeled

5 shallots, sliced

4 fresh Vietnamese mint (rau ram) stems

4 fresh Thai basil stems

¼ cup fresh cilantro roots, rinsed, scraped, and rinsed again, or 32 fresh cilantro stems

2 lemongrass stalks, outer layer removed and stalks crushed with a blunt object

FOR FRYING THE DUCK

4 cups neutral oil, such as grapeseed or canola

½ cup tapioca flour

½ cup rice flour

¼ cup sea salt

¼ cup freshly ground black pepper

TO FINISH THE DISH

¼ cup palm or brown sugar

4 cups steamed Tamaki Gold short-grain rice

2 fresh Thai bird chilies, thinly sliced

¼ cup packaged preserved mustard greens, thinly sliced

½ cup fresh cilantro leaves

STEAM THE DUCK

1. Score the skin on the breasts, then generously season all the duck pieces with salt and pepper.

2. Add the stock or water to a deep pot with a tight lid. Set a large steamer basket

LISTEN
Gil Scott-Heron "The Bottle," definitely the live version from the *It's Your World* album—fuck it; listen to the whole damn album.

DRINK
J. Hofstätter Gewürztraminer Kolbenhof—a gewürz that you can keep on swillin' and that will feel right at home with fatty, spicy fowl.

over the liquid and line the basket with the ginger, garlic, shallots, herbs, and lemongrass. Place half of the duck on top—you have to cook the legs and breast separately since they have different cooking times. Bring the liquid to a boil, then reduce the heat to low. Cover the pot and steam the leg quarters over medium heat until they're fork-tender, about 1 hour. Steam the breasts until they're medium-rare to medium, about 30 minutes.

3. Remove the duck from the steamer. When the pieces are cool enough to handle, cut the leg quarters into three pieces with a cleaver and the breasts into 4 to 6 pieces, depending on their size.

FRY THE DUCK

In a medium heavy saucepan, heat the oil to 375°F (measured on a deep-frying thermometer). Meanwhile, in a large bowl, whisk together the tapioca flour, rice flour, salt, and pepper. Dredge the duck pieces in the flour mixture, shaking off any excess. Gently add the pieces to the oil in batches and fry until they're golden and crispy, about 5 minutes per batch. As they're fried, transfer the pieces to a paper-towel-lined plate to drain.

FINISH THE DISH

1. Combine the palm sugar and 2 tablespoons water in a small saucepan. Cook gently over low heat, stirring and breaking up the sugar with a spoon, until the sugar is completely dissolved.

2. Serve the fried duck over the steamed rice. Drizzle with the palm sugar syrup and sprinkle with the chilies, preserved mustard greens, and cilantro leaves. Eat with your hands and spit out those bones!

BUNNY BUNNY

I love rabbit so much I gave it its own chapter!

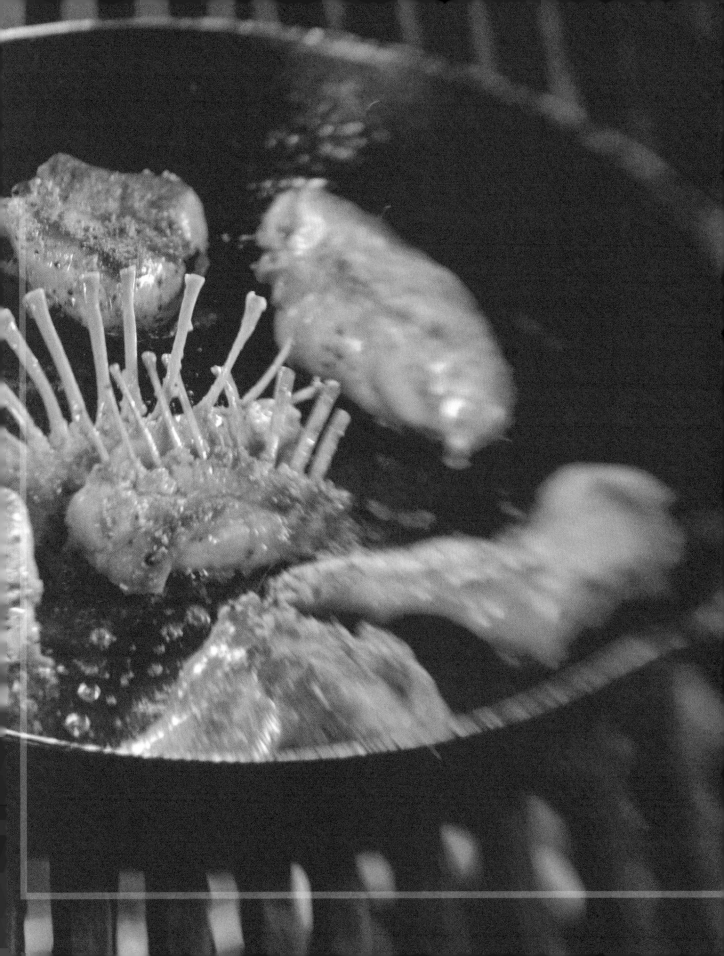

FRIED RABBIT WITH CHILI SHRIMP SAUCE

Zak snack attack! Fried hunks of bunny coated in a light, tempuralike batter. A chili sauce with the mellow, funky depth of dried shrimp. I dare you to resist.

SERVES 4 TO 6

FOR THE CHILI SHRIMP SAUCE
¼ cup neutral oil, such as grapeseed or canola
2 tablespoons dried shrimp
1 teaspoon minced peeled fresh ginger
3 fresh Thai bird chilies, thinly sliced

3 garlic cloves, minced
2 tablespoons olive oil (the best you can afford)
1 teaspoon palm or brown sugar
1 teaspoon sea salt

FOR THE RABBIT
2 rabbits (about 3 pounds each), each cut into 8 pieces—2 front legs, 2 hind legs, 2 rib cages, and 2 cross-cuts of the saddle
Sea salt and freshly ground black pepper
2 cups all-purpose flour

1 cup rice flour
1 egg yolk
About 2 cups sparkling water
4 cups rendered leaf lard (page 196) or vegetable oil
1 lemon, cut into wedges

MAKE THE CHILI SHRIMP SAUCE

1. Heat the neutral oil in a saucepan over medium-high heat to about 325°F (measured on a deep-frying thermometer). Add the dried shrimp and fry, stirring occasionally, until they turn a golden color, about 4 minutes. Use a slotted spoon to transfer the shrimp to a paper-towel-lined plate to drain.

2. When the shrimp are cool enough to handle, add them to a mortar and pound to a coarse powder. Use the pestle to pound (see page 12) them along with the ginger, chilies, garlic, olive oil, palm sugar, and 1 teaspoon salt, pounding each ingredient thoroughly before adding the next, to make a paste. Scrape the paste into a bowl and set it aside.

MAKE THE RABBIT

1. Season the rabbit with enough salt and pepper to lightly coat the pieces. In a medium mixing bowl, combine the flours with 1 tablespoon each salt and pepper. Whisk in the egg yolk and then slowly pour in the sparkling water, whisking all the while, until you have a thin batter, similar to liquidy pancake batter. Add more sparkling water if necessary.

2. Heat 2 inches of the lard or oil in a large heavy pot over medium-high heat to 325°F.

3. Working in batches, dredge the rabbit pieces in the batter, let the excess drip

LISTEN
Seal Cub Clubbing Club, "World of Fashion," followed by "Dawn Lamb" (polka remix). Melodies just right for rabbit.

DRINK
Schioppettino—Ronco del Gnemiz. Full-bodied enough to work with the chili without upstaging the bunny.

off, and gently slip each piece into the hot fat. Cook the rabbit pieces, turning occasionally, until golden and crispy on all sides, 7 to 8 minutes. The larger pieces, like the hind leg, will take longer to cook than the smaller ones. If you want to shorten the cooking time, before you dredge, you can chop the leg into two pieces with one swift motion of a cleaver.

4. Transfer the rabbit to a paper-towel-lined plate to drain. Season the pieces with salt while they're still hot.

5. Serve the rabbit on a big platter with lemon wedges and little bowls of chili-shrimp sauce on the table for guests.

ROASTED RABBIT WITH CREAMED CORN AND DATES, p. 130

ROASTED RABBIT WITH CREAMED CORN AND DATES

Fresh, sweet summer corn always conjures images of the county fair for me. Maybe that's because sweet corn is the only *fresh* vegetable you can consistently find at county fairs, amid a sea of fried dough and Pronto Pups. But this isn't a corn dish you're likely to find within a thousand feet of a Ferris wheel. Maybe one day, in a glorious future, where fresh, natural foods replace processed crap, that won't be the case. But until then ride the coaster, win some stuffed animals for your guy or gal, and throw this together when you get home. Chewy, sweet bits of dates offset by sharp bursts of super thinly minced chili ensure that you won't nod off into a summertime candy-colored sweet corn dream and end up facedown, snoring in your bowl.

SERVES 4 TO 6

FOR THE RABBIT

2 rabbits (about 3 pounds each), each cut into 8 pieces—2 front legs, 2 hind legs, 2 rib pieces, and 2 sides of the saddle

Sea salt and freshly ground black pepper

About ¼ cup neutral oil, such as grapeseed or canola, or more as needed

FOR THE CORN

2½ cups fresh summer corn kernels, cobs reserved

1 to 1½ cups heavy cream

2 garlic cloves, minced

Sea salt

4 dried Medjool dates, pitted and diced

FOR THE GARNISH

1 tablespoon finely minced fresh red chili (Thai bird chili, cayenne—whatever you've got that's hot)

1 tablespoon coarsely chopped fresh summer savory

2 tablespoons chopped fresh fennel fronds

MAKE THE RABBIT

1. Preheat the oven to 375°F. Meanwhile, season the rabbit with enough salt and pepper to lightly coat the pieces.

2. Heat the oil in a large ovenproof sauté pan over medium-high heat until it's smoking. Sear the rabbit, in batches if necessary to avoid crowding the pan, until well browned on all sides, 3 to 4 minutes per side. (Once they're properly seared, they won't stick at all.) If cooking in batches, wipe out the skillet between batches and replenish with fresh oil as necessary.

LISTEN
RJD2, *Since We Last Spoke.* Puts me in a groovy daze.

DRINK
Côtes du Ventoux Domaine de Fenouillet, an inexpensive rosé that should become a staple for those who love life in the summer.

3. Transfer the pan to the oven and roast the bunny pieces until they're just cooked through, 7 to 8 minutes. Then transfer to a paper-towel-lined plate. Repeat for each batch.

MAKE THE CORN

1. Chop the cobs into 1- to 1½-inch pieces. Bring 1 cup of the cream, the garlic, the cob pieces, and ½ teaspoon salt to a boil in a medium saucepan. Reduce the heat to low, simmer for 5 minutes, and take the pan off the heat. Keep it in a warm place and let the cobs steep for at least 30 minutes.

2. Strain the cream mixture into a small saucepan, discarding the solids, and warm it over low heat. Add the corn kernels and dates and let them steep in the cream for 5 minutes. Add a little more cream if you like creamy creamed corn. Add salt to taste and set aside.

GARNISH THE DISH

Divide the creamed corn among four or six serving bowls and sprinkle with the chili, savory, and fennel fronds. Top each bowl with two or three pieces of roasted rabbit.

LAMB AND GOAT

I really got into playing with goat at my restaurant 5 Ninth after I bought a cheap-ass Texas-style smoker on a whim at Home Depot. In the smoker's large chamber I'd make a low hardwood charcoal fire. I'd fill the small, offset chamber with wood chunks. After marinating some tasty goat for a day, I'd smoke it, nice and slow. The thing was, we kept the smoker in the garden of 5 Ninth—and because the smoker didn't retain heat all that well, often the goat would still be smoking at the beginning of service. Great, I thought, the sweet smell will act like the adult version of the ice-cream-truck's siren song: men and women will swarm, crumpled ten-dollar bills in hand. No dice, though. I guess my accidental marketing method was too far ahead of the curve.

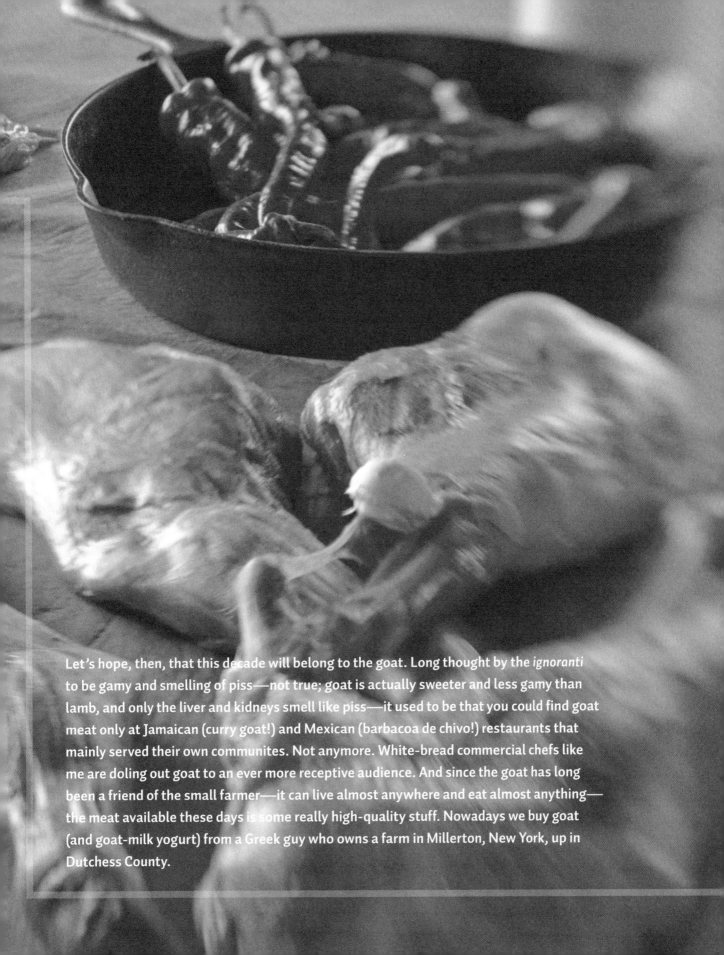

Let's hope, then, that this decade will belong to the goat. Long thought by the *ignoranti* to be gamy and smelling of piss—not true; goat is actually sweeter and less gamy than lamb, and only the liver and kidneys smell like piss—it used to be that you could find goat meat only at Jamaican (curry goat!) and Mexican (barbacoa de chivo!) restaurants that mainly served their own communites. Not anymore. White-bread commercial chefs like me are doling out goat to an ever more receptive audience. And since the goat has long been a friend of the small farmer—it can live almost anywhere and eat almost anything— the meat available these days is some really high-quality stuff. Nowadays we buy goat (and goat-milk yogurt) from a Greek guy who owns a farm in Millerton, New York, up in Dutchess County.

GOAT'S-MILK-BRAISED GOAT PARTS

Great news, everyone! Goat is kosher! You know what's not kosher? This dish. It's a slow, elegant braise that looks prettier while it's cooking than just about any other braise you can think of. The meat, marinated in red chili and seared a roasty brown, is then bathed in sweet white goat's milk and finished with green herbs and pink galangal flowers. Another cool aspect of the dish is that you're braising the legs, shoulder, and the ribs, which gives you an opportunity to taste the different textures of the different cuts. And, OK, I admit that there's the perverse pleasure of cooking a young animal in what might be its mother's milk. It just seems so wrong and so right.

SERVES 6 TO 8

FOR MARINATING THE GOAT

5 inches fresh ginger, peeled and roughly chopped
6 fresh long red chilies, such as Anaheim or Hungarian Wax, roughly chopped
6 garlic cloves, roughly chopped
3 tablespoons sea salt
About ½ cup olive oil (the best you can afford), or more as needed
½ young goat, broken down into leg, shoulder, and ribs (about 14 pounds total)

FOR BRAISING THE GOAT

12 fresh long red chilies, such as Anaheim or Hungarian Wax
Sea salt
3 tablespoons neutral oil, such as grapeseed or canola, plus a little for the chilies
3 cups fresh goat's milk
1 cup Chicken Stock (page 324)
2 white onions, cut into 8 pieces each
6 garlic cloves, crushed and peeled
3 fresh Thai basil sprigs
3 fresh purple basil sprigs
1 lemon

FOR THE GARNISH

1 galangal flower, thinly sliced
¼ cup fresh Thai basil leaves
¼ cup fresh purple basil leaves

MARINATE THE GOAT

1. Use a mortar and pestle to pound (see page 12) the ginger, chopped long red chilies, chopped garlic, salt, and olive oil into a paste with the consistency of loose salsa, pounding each ingredient thoroughly before adding the next. If you feel the marinade has yet to achieve the loosey goosey consistency, add more olive oil.
2. Rub the goat parts with the ginger-chili paste and refrigerate, covered, overnight or up to 48 hours.

LISTEN
Bill Summers and Summers Heat, *Jam the Box*. Yeah, we call it "the box," Bill.

DRINK
Goat's milk with a sprinkle of salt. A toast. And then a floral grappa . . . because there was no booze in the milk, damn it!

BRAISE THE GOAT

1. Preheat the oven to 500°F. Remove the meat from the marinade, wiping some off and reserving the excess.

2. Toss the whole long red chilies with a pinch of salt and a bit of oil to just coat them. Transfer them to a baking sheet and roast, shaking the sheet once or twice, until they're lightly blistered all over, 7 to 10 minutes.

3. Reduce the heat to 250°F.

4. Combine the goat's milk and chicken stock in a medium saucepan and bring it to a bare simmer over medium heat, making sure not to boil the mixture.

5. Heat 1 tablespoon of the oil in a large heavy casserole over medium-high heat. (It might have to straddle two burners.) Add the onions and the crushed garlic to the pan and cook them until translucent but not brown, about 8 minutes. Use a slotted spoon to transfer the vegetables to a plate.

6. Wipe the casserole clean with a paper towel, heat over medium-high heat until smoking, and add the remaining 2 tablespoons of oil. Sear the goat pieces one at a time until they're golden brown on all sides, about 5 minutes per piece, transferring them to a platter as they finish. But pay attention! You don't want to burn the marinade. (Obsessives should cut the loin from the ribs before moving on to braising—the loin will be done before the leg.)

7. Cut a piece of parchment paper to fit the top of the casserole. Return the onion and garlic to the casserole, along with the reserved marinade. Pour in the warm goat's milk mixture and add both types of basil sprigs, the goat pieces, and the roasted chilies. Bring the liquid to a gentle simmer over medium-high heat, cover the casserole with parchment paper and a tight lid or foil, then transfer it to the oven.

8. Cook until the leg meat is tender (sliceable but not falling apart) and barely resists when you tug it from the bones with your hands, about 1 hour and 45 minutes. Remove the leg from the oven and put it on a platter in a warm spot.

9. Continue to cook the rest of the goat for at least another 30 minutes, until the ribs are as tender as the leg was. Remove the ribs from the oven and add them to the platter.

10. Continue to cook the shoulder for 45 to 60 minutes more. Take the casserole out of the oven and transfer the shoulder to the platter to rest.

11. Strain the cooking liquid through a fine-mesh sieve into a bowl. Reserve the roasted chili bits for the garnish. Puree the braising liquid in a blender (or use an immersion blender). Add a little salt and lemon juice until it tastes really good.

SERVING THE MEAT

You can do this one of two ways. The schmancy way is to slice the meat and serve the slices in a shallow bowl in a puddle of the pureed braising liquid. Garnish with some galangal flower, herbs (tear the leaves), and the braised chilies.

Or do it hungry monkey style: Put the meat on a plate in the center of the table. Give everyone a little bowl of pureed braising liquid topped with galangal flower and herbs (tear the leaves). Evenly distribute the roasted chilies onto plates, which have been set in front of your guests, in order to avoid fights. Then let them go at that meat.

SMOKED-CHILI-RUBBED GOAT SHOULDER

I'll barbecue the hell out of a goat: get the whole animal on the grill or do up just the head or maybe the legs—whatever strikes my fancy. But the shoulder is probably my favorite cut to treat to hours and hours of gentle smoky caressing. This is party cooking, because (a) everyone will want some of this tender, spicy action and (b) though it takes a while to cook, you're only *not* sitting on your ass and drinking for, like, 10 minutes. So relax, then eat, and maybe whip up some Pineapple Pickle (page 291), which goes so well with this goaty goat.

The goat shoulder smokes for approximately seven hours. The smoking should be done in an indirect smoker (Texas-style chamber smoker). A temperature of 225°F to 250°F (a big variation, as smokers can be hard to control) should be maintained for 7 to 8 hours. The time variation is big, too, as there are so many smokers, and often backyard versions don't hold heat all that well. At a constant 250°F, it should not take longer than 7 hours, but an understanding of the variable types of equipment should be acknowledged.

SERVES 4

- 4 fresh long red chilies, such as Anaheim or Hungarian Wax, chopped
- 2 fresh Thai bird chilies, chopped
- 3 inches fresh ginger, peeled and chopped
- 8 garlic cloves, crushed and peeled
- 1 bunch of flat-leaf parsley, leaves only
- 2 tablespoons sea salt
- ¼ cup olive oil (the best you can afford)
- 1 bone-in goat shoulder (about 5 pounds)

THE DAY BEFORE

1. Use a mortar and pestle to pound (see page 12) the chilies, ginger, garlic, and parsley with the salt to a coarse paste, pounding each ingredient thoroughly before adding the next. Add the olive oil, pounding again to form a pretty smooth paste.
2. Rub the goat shoulder with the chili paste and refrigerate, covered, for 24 hours.

THAT DAY

1. Preheat a smoker (see Headnote above).
2. Place the goat shoulder in the smoker (reserving any leftover marinade) and let it ride for about 3 hours. Keep an eye on the temperature, stoke your fire, and drink a Scotch. Occasionally baste the goat with the leftover marinade. After 3 hours, periodically jiggle the leg. When it gives you the sense that if you pulled just a bit harder you could tear it from the joint, it's ready, but it'll probably take another 3 to 4 hours. Serve it straight away on a platter and tear into with your hands.

LISTEN
Idris Muhammad, *Boogie to the Top*—a fun, funky album. My favorite tune is "Bread" ("B-R-E-A-D, that's what I said!"). Dance with your goat!

DRINK
Laphroaig, a couple rocks. Goat, chili, and smoky Scotch—there should be a song about this trio.

GOAT OR YOUNG LAMB LEG WITH SALTED CHILIES

The *young* part is not to be ignored here. As the animal ages, it develops a slightly gamy, deep flavor, which is excellent. But for this spartan preparation you must insist on a young animal's meat, which will be delicate and sweet. Then all you need is grilled bread, perhaps rubbed with olive oil and garlic, for a spectacular meal.

SERVES 4 TO 6

1 bone-in leg of goat or young lamb (about 5 pounds)
Sea salt and freshly ground black pepper
½ cup olive oil (the best you can afford)

8 garlic cloves, crushed and peeled
½ cup dry white wine
3 fresh summer savory, marjoram, or rosemary sprigs
Salty Oil-Cured Chilies (page 293)

1. Preheat the oven to 325°F.
2. Season the meat generously with salt and pepper. Heat all but 1 tablespoon of the oil in a roasting pan straddling two burners over medium-high heat. Add the leg and cook for 3 to 4 minutes without turning. Continue to cook, turning to brown it well on all sides, about 10 minutes total. Transfer it to a plate and set it aside.
3. Heat the remaining tablespoon of oil in the pan over medium-high heat. Add the garlic and cook, stirring often, until translucent, about 3 minutes, being careful not to burn. Add the wine, let it bubble, and cook for about 2 minutes, scraping the bottom of the pan with a wooden spoon. Reduce the heat to medium-low, stir in the savory, and cook for 1 minute more. Remove the pan from the heat and add ¼ teaspoon salt, stirring to combine.
4. Put the seared leg back in the roasting pan. Slide the pan into the oven and roast, basting the meat every 15 or 20 minutes, until the internal temperature reads 130°F, 1 to 1½ hours total. The low-tech method for testing doneness is to insert a metal skewer into the meat, hold it there for 15 seconds, then press it to your lips. If it feels noticeably warmer than your body temperature, but not hot, it's done.
5. Remove the meat from the oven and let it rest in a warm spot for 20 to 30 minutes. Serve the leg with the chilies and a basket of grilled bread rubbed with garlic and olive oil.

LISTEN
Hendrix, the old stuff—on vinyl, please. When I say old, I mean before Jimi became Jimi. Like the shit with Curtis Knight, et al.

DRINK
Whatever white you opened to cook the meat, to ensure that you cook with good wine . . . unless you just don't give a damn anymore and, if that's the case, why are you taking time to cook from a book?

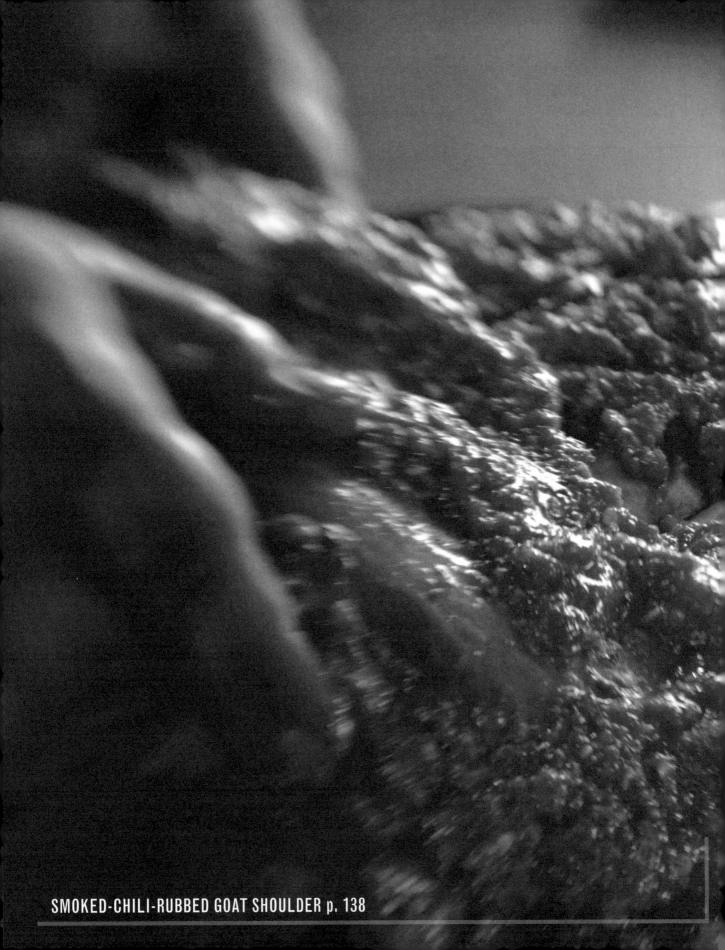

SMOKED-CHILI-RUBBED GOAT SHOULDER p. 138

LAMB RIBS WITH BRAISED ROMAINE AND SHEEP'S MILK CHEESE

In 2003 I called Tom Biggs at Vermont Quality Meats and asked him if he had any lamb breasts available. I wanted to braise them, cut them up, and sell the ribs. He was thrilled—he had been selling the breast along with other "scrap" to a dog food processor nearby. I called Sylvia Pryzant, too, at Four Story Hill Farm, who agreed to sell me lamb ribs for $1 a pound. John Jamison, of Jamison Farm, started giving me lamb ribs along with my other purchases, because he had been using frozen lamb ribs instead of ice to chill the highly coveted lamb parts that he sold to high-end restaurants in town. That was a good run, but as is often the case, I wasn't alone in my fondness for fatty off-cuts that take well to low and slow cooking. The early wave that a few of us rode crested and then came crashing down as the demand for lamb ribs and belly exploded. And exploded for good reason: the shit is real tasty, especially when you make it like this.

SERVES 4 TO 6

- 1 lamb breast (2½ to 3 pounds)
- 3 tablespoons plus 2 cups olive oil (the best you can afford)
- Sea salt and freshly ground black pepper
- 1 head of garlic, unpeeled, halved crosswise
- 2 medium onions, quartered
- 2 fresh long chilies, such as Anaheim or Hungarian Wax, roughly chopped
- 1 cup dry white wine
- 2 dried bay leaves
- 6 fresh thyme sprigs
- 4 cups Chicken Stock (page 324)
- 1½ cups all-purpose flour
- 2 heads of romaine lettuce, outer leaves removed
- ¼ pound hard sheep's milk cheese, such as Ossau-Iraty Vieille or Brebis

1. Preheat the oven to 300°F. Meanwhile, bring the meat to room temperature.
2. Heat 3 tablespoons of the oil in a large ovenproof sauté pan with a lid over medium-high heat. Season the breast generously with salt and pepper and sear, in batches if necessary to avoid crowding the pan, on all sides until golden, 3 to 4 minutes per side. Transfer the breast to a plate.
3. Lower the heat to medium and add the garlic, onions, and chilies. Cook, stirring occasionally, until the onions start to soften, about 3 minutes. Raise the heat to medium-high and add the wine, bay leaves, and thyme. Stir with a wooden spoon as the wine bubbles up and cooks down, about 2 minutes, scraping the bottom of the pan with a wooden spoon.
4. Return the breast to the pan, then add enough chicken stock so three-quarters of the breast is submerged (add a little water if you need to). Bring the liquid to a boil, cover the pan, and stick it in the oven to braise. Cook until the breast is

LISTEN
Junior Kimbrough, *Most Things Haven't Worked Out.* He was without question the most powerful bluesman we were lucky enough to share a few decades with.

DRINK
Pappy Van Winkle 12-year and a cube or two of ice. We know Junior would have approved.

done, about 2½ hours. You'll know the breast is done when it yields to you like the soft inner thigh you've only dreamt of. At this point of heightened arousal, have a swig of Pappy and breathe.

5. Remove the pan from the oven, season the breast with a little salt, and let the braise cool a bit. Transfer the breast to a cutting board and strain the braising liquid through a sieve into a wide, shallow saucepan, discarding the solids.

6. Slice off the belly and cut it into big bite-sized pieces. Cut the ribs into single-bone pieces. Pat them all dry and dredge them in the flour. Heat 1½ inches of the olive oil in a large heavy pan to 325°F. Fry the ribs in batches, turning once, until they are golden and crispy, about 3 minutes on each side. Transfer them as they're fried to a paper-towel-lined plate to drain.

7. Meanwhile, cut the romaine heads lengthwise into quarters and add them to the saucepan with the rib braising liquid. Cook over medium heat until the heads have just wilted but there's still a little crunch left, about 2 minutes.

8. Serve the ribs and belly chunks over the wilted romaine and spoon some of the braising liquid onto the plates. Grate a little of the cheese over each, and finish with freshly ground black pepper.

LAMB SHOULDER WITH AN ARBOIS AND GREEN GARLIC

Early spring. The air is still crisp, the snow only just melted, but there's green in the trees and the garlic has started to grow. If you have a bunch planted in your garden and you're as impatient as I am, you pull some as soon as it looks hearty enough to get out of the ground without tearing. There's a hint of the warm weather to come in those green, vegetal garlic shoots. That garlic, the beautiful shoulder from a young lamb, the nutty, sherry-like savagnin from the Arbois, it's all so sexy together that I, in a romantic tizzy, drink too much and insist on eating outside. I imagine I'm communing with the seasons, but really, my lamb is just getting cold.

SERVES 6 TO 8

FOR THE LAMB
½ cup olive oil (the best you can afford)
1 bone-in shoulder (5 to 7 pounds) from a young lamb
Sea salt and freshly ground black pepper
4 shallots, halved

10 stalks green garlic, sliced
1 cup savagnin wine from the Arbois or ½ cup each dry white wine and dry sherry, or more if necessary
6 fresh thyme sprigs

FOR THE SAUCE
5 salt- or oil-packed anchovy fillets
4 dried red chilies, such as cayenne
1 tablespoon olive oil (the best you can afford)
5 stalks green garlic, thinly sliced

A few fresh thyme sprigs
½ cup savagnin from the Arbois or ¼ cup each dry white wine and dry sherry

BRAISE THE LAMB

1. Preheat the oven to 250°F.
2. Heat ¼ cup of the olive oil in a large roasting pan straddling two burners over medium-high heat. Season the lamb shoulder generously with salt and pepper. Brown the shoulder well on all sides, 3 to 4 minutes per side. Transfer the lamb to a plate.
3. Deglaze the pan with a little bit of water and let it bubble, scraping up the brown bits with a wooden spoon. Add about 1 tablespoon more olive oil to the pan, add the shallots and garlic stalks, and cook, stirring occasionally, until they're slightly soft, about 3 minutes. Return the lamb shoulder to the roasting pan, add the wine, the remaining 3 tablespoons olive oil, and the thyme, and bring the liquid to a simmer.
4. Cover the pan with a lid or parchment and then foil, put it in the oven, and cook for 2 hours. Check the pan and add a little more wine if the pan is dry.

LISTEN
The Allman Brothers, "Mountain Jam," because, like the combination of early spring lamb and garlic, it can make me tear up.

DRINK
Savagnin from the Arbois or good dry sherry.

5. Continue to cook the meat until you're struck by the yielding flesh, giving joints, and total clarity of enlightenment, 1 to 1½ hours longer.

6. Transfer the lamb to a plate, reserving the drippings, and let it hang out in a warm place for 30 minutes.

MAKE THE SAUCE

1. If you're using salt-packed anchovies, rinse them, then soak them for 5 minutes, changing the water once halfway through. Drain them and remove and discard their backbones. Mince the anchovies and set them aside.

2. Meanwhile, in a dry pan over medium heat, toast the dried chilies until they take on a dark color, pressing them down with a wooden spoon to increase contact with the pan, 3 to 4 minutes. Be careful not to inhale over the toasting chilies. Set the toasted chilies to the side.

3. While the lamb rests, heat the olive oil in a medium sauté pan over medium heat, add the garlic stalks, and cook until they have softened, about 5 minutes. Break the chilies into pieces and stir them in along with the anchovies and thyme, then pour in the wine. Bring the wine to a boil and cook until the wine reduces by about half. Stir in any drippings from the roasting pan.

4. Put the lamb shoulder on a platter and sauce it up. Pour on the sauce, reserving some in a bowl to serve at the table. Tear the shoulder apart as you dig in. Serve with some roasted potatoes.

BRAISED LAMB SHOULDER WITH RIGATONI

There I was, at Zuberoa in Spain, crying in the dining room. No one had passed away; no girlfriend had broken up with me. In fact, Jori was sitting beside me, teary-eyed herself but still doing her best to comfort me. We had just finished the most perfect lamb shoulder, a dizzying contrast of melting fat, ropes of tender flesh, and the thin crackle of dark roasted tendon. That was the sad part—that we had *finished*. And I was sad, too, because of what I knew I would do next. Instead of staying and eating the restaurant out of lamb and probably passing out on the floor, I politely paid my bill, thanked the proprietor, and went to my hotel for a rest. I am a sheep.

This dish is my really odd ode to that one—mouth-fillingly fatty chunks of lamb shoulder on a heap of what amounts to macaroni and cheese. Some Pickled Ramps (page 298) go well with this.

SERVES 6 TO 8

FOR BRAISING THE LAMB
5 tablespoons olive oil (the best you can afford)
1 bone-in shoulder (5 to 7 pounds) from a young lamb
Sea salt and freshly ground black pepper
1 cup Armagnac, brandy, or whiskey
2 heads of garlic, halved crosswise
2 medium onions, roughly chopped
2 celery stalks, roughly chopped
2 inches fresh ginger, peeled and minced
5 fresh Thai bird chilies, bruised in a mortar
2 cups dry white wine
4 cups Chicken Stock (page 324)
8 fresh thyme sprigs
2 fresh rosemary sprigs

FOR THE PASTA
Sea salt
1 pound rigatoni pasta, preferably fresh
1 cup heavy cream
½ pound soft sheep's milk cheese, such as Tomme du Berger, cut into pieces
Freshly ground black pepper

TO FINISH THE DISH
½ pound hard sheep's milk cheese, such as Ossau-Iraty Vieille
Chilies (optional)
Lemon juice (optional)

BRAISE THE LAMB

1. Preheat the oven to 250°F.
2. Grab your biggest, heaviest Dutch oven, casserole, or roasting pan with a lid, add 3 tablespoons of the olive oil, and heat it over medium-high heat until hot but not smoking. If you're using a roasting pan, it should straddle two burners.
3. Season the lamb shoulder generously with salt and pepper. Add the lamb shoulder to the pot and brown it well on all sides, 3 to 4 minutes per side. Transfer the lamb to a plate.

LISTEN
Roxy Music, "2HB"—actually, keep rolling Roxy as long as you can.

DRINK
Georges Descombes Régnié—biodynamic and really just dynamite with cheese, chili, and lamb.

4. Over medium-high heat, deglaze the pot with the Armagnac, scraping up any brown bits with a wooden spoon. Add the remaining 2 tablespoons of oil and cook the garlic, onions, celery, ginger, and chilies, stirring occasionally, until lightly browned, about 5 minutes. Pour in the white wine, raise the heat, and boil for 2 minutes to cook off the alcohol. Pour in the chicken stock and add the herbs. Return the lamb to the pot and bring the liquid to a simmer over medium-high heat.

5. Cover the pot and braise the lamb in the oven until the meat is really tender, about 5 hours, but start checking after about 3½ hours and every 30 minutes thereafter.

6. Remove the pot from the oven and let the lamb rest in the pot for about 20 minutes. Start a pot to boil water for the pasta. Transfer the lamb to a platter, then strain the braising liquid through a fine-mesh sieve, discarding any solids, into a pan. Simmer the braising liquid, skimming the top often, until it has reduced by half. Taste and tweak the seasoning until it tastes really good.

MAKE THE PASTA

1. Cook the rigatoni in well-salted boiling water for 1 minute less than the package instructs.

2. While the pasta cooks, bring the cream to a boil in a large pot, then reduce the heat to simmer it. Gradually add the soft cheese, whisking constantly, until all the cheese has been added and the sauce is smooth.

3. Drain the pasta, add it to the cheese sauce, and toss to coat. Taste and add a little salt, pepper, even lemon juice or zest or sliced chilies if you'd like. The sauce should adhere well to the pasta, like a mac 'n' cheese. If it looks too loose, increase the heat and cook, stirring constantly, until the sauce reduces and starts to cling.

4. Cut the lamb shoulder into hefty chunks and add them to the saucepan with the reserved, strained braising liquid to warm them through on medium heat for 10 minutes.

5. Divide the cheesy, creamy pasta among your bowls. Top each with chunks of lamb and spoon on some of the reduced braising liquid. Grate the hard cheese over each plate and serve.

BRAISED LAMB SHOULDER WITH RIGATONI, p. 148

LAMB BURGERS

This is my favorite burger to cook when I'm upstate. That's probably because Berry Farm, the local farmstand, always has fresh, particularly fatty ground lamb. And lamb fat is the shit. There's this Uzbeki kebab place in Rego Park, Queens, that grills straight-up lamb fat kebabs. That's right, just fat, which you take down with pita and onions. (But after the Uzbeks switched from a charcoal to a gas grill, it was never the same for me.) So anyway, back at the upstate ranch, Jori and I buy the Berry Farm ground lamb, some duck eggs, and fat Wolfermann's English muffins, race home, make a drinky, and fire up the charcoal grill.

SERVES 4

2 pounds freshly ground lamb, ideally fatty

Sea salt and freshly ground black pepper

2 duck egg yolks

1 teaspoon Dijon mustard

½ pound (2 sticks) cold unsalted butter, cut into ¼-inch cubes

½ lemon

12 scallions, trimmed

1 teaspoon neutral oil, such as grapeseed or canola

Splash of your favorite vinegar

4 English muffins, split

1. Start a hardwood charcoal fire (or, fine, use a gas grill). Let it get nice and hot.

2. Season the ground lamb well with salt and pepper, using your hands to lightly work in the seasonings. Don't overmix. Divide the meat into four balls and form each ball into a patty about 1 inch thick. Season them again on both sides with salt and pepper. If you're going to grill within 30 minutes, leave the patties out. If not, cover and refrigerate them, then let them come to room temperature before you grill them.

3. Bring water to a simmer in a pot that will accommodate a double boiler or metal mixing bowl. Put the egg yolks in the double boiler or metal mixing bowl, whisk them to incorporate some air until they go from rich, deep yellow to a pale yellow and they've increased in volume. Add the mustard and a teaspoon of cold water and keep whisking.

4. Put the double boiler or bowl over the simmering water and start adding the butter, one piece at a time, whisking to incorporate completely before adding the next one. Once you've added all the butter, finish the sauce with a squeeze or three of the lemon and gradually add salt and pepper until it tastes really good. It should be rich, salty, and slightly acidic. If it is, congratulations, you just made hollandaise. Cover with plastic wrap and put the double boiler or mixing bowl in a large bowl of warm water until you're ready to use it.

5. Grill the burgers, flipping once, until medium-rare, about 8 minutes total. If the

LISTEN
Michael Jackson, *Thriller*, to remind yourself how fucking good that album is.

DRINK
A Manhattan: Stir a two-to-one ratio **rye** to **sweet vermouth** (big surprise, I err slightly heavier on the rye) with **ice**. Strain into a chilled glass and add a couple dashes of **Peychaud's bitters** and a **lemon** twist.

flame flares high around the burgers while you're grilling, move them around a bit. You don't want them to get too much color too quickly.

6. Toss the scallions in the oil and season with salt and pepper. Grill them until they're slightly charred and tender, about 2 minutes a side. When they're nicely charred and you've pulled them off the grill, chop them into big pieces and sprinkle them with some of your favorite vinegar and some more salt.

7. Toast the English muffins on the grill. Bun, burger, scallion. Big bowl o' Mr. Holland's Daze (the egg sauce) on the side for dipping. Get excited, slap someone's buns—anyone, no matter. Now you're ready to eat.

FOR THE LOVE OF FERMENTED TOFU

Corwin and I share an almost romantic love for stinky, funky fermented tofu, and his affection led him to create one of the most fantastic sauces I have ever eaten. It's made from cockles, lardo, chili, and fermented tofu. Ain't that something! Absolutely acceptable eaten all on its own, with spoon or finger. Perhaps a bit better with rice. But he and I and all the boys and girls in the playground agree, it is the bees' knees with some roasted baby lamb—a whole animal, a shoulder, a leg, a saddle, whatever gets you to try the sauce-meat combo. I left the recipe as he wrote it for the cooks, which I thought would be kind of cool, but I added a few clarifications in parentheses for home cooks. You may want to add a squeeze or three of lemon or yuzu and a touch more fresh chili as a garnish. Corwin, bro, thanks for keepin' it funky!

FOR THE COCKLE VINAIGRETTE

For 5 lbs cockles
Yield: 2 qt liquid, 1 qt cooked cockles (shucked)
3 ounces lardo-diced
5 ounces shallot-minced
1¼ ounces garlic, smashed
2 ounces fresh ginger, peeled and minced
¼ ounce dried chilies
3 ounces Shaoxing
12 ounces crab stock
3½ ounces fermented tofu
1 ounce sesame oil

Wash cockles and drain off sand. Sweat lardo in a small amount of oil. When lardo is transparent, add shallot, garlic, ginger, and chilies. Sweat for one minute and add cockles. Cook over medium-high heat until clams start to open. Add Shaoxing and crab stock and cover with parchment paper. Simmer over low heat. Once clams are open they are done. Pour cooked mixture into a 4-inch perforated pan (or a colander over a mixing bowl or pot) placed inside a 6-inch hotel pan. Let mixture cool in walk-in (fridge). Once cooled, shuck clams from shell and set aside. Puree liquid in Vita Prep (blender) with fermented tofu, sesame oil, and ½ of the shallot/garlic/lardo/chili mixture. Cool liquid and reserve. Pour some of cooled cockle vin over shucked clams for storage. Reserve remaining liquid for service. Label, date, and store all in walk-in.

PORK

I've been obsessed with pork for as long as I can remember. As a kid I sucked down prosciutto di Parma like other kids ate fruit roll-ups. Yet until recently pork had a serious image problem in the United States. Its rep got so bad that marketers tried to rebrand it, billing it as "the other white meat," relegating it to the role of mere chicken substitute.

Now you'd have to be living under a rock not to know that pork has blown up. Restaurant menus exalt it. Pig farmers and bacon makers are culinary celebrities. And young cooks are tattooing piggies on their arms, backs, and who knows where else. Evidently, people have figured out how fucking good pork is. And, ironically, a major reason for the pig's rising star (and why it's my nomination for earth's most giving creature) is its particularly delicious fat.

For decades, animal fat played scapegoat, and Americans were persuaded to neurotically avoid it (hence the creation of trans fats and that evil butter stand-in, margarine). Yet, as the pig's popularity increased, people slowly came back to fat. Coincidence? I doubt it.

I can't imagine cooking without poaching fish in pork fat, poaching pork in pork fat, letting hot pig fat imbue vegetables with its silky richness, or tossing a hunk of prosciutto fat into my chicken stock. When I'm dreaming up dishes, the words *pig fat* (along with *mayonnaise, hollandaise, duck fat, lamb fat, butter* . . .) run through my head. You don't need to eat a ton of it to enjoy its lovely effects. So I use it as a condiment even more often than I make it the centerpiece. Perhaps this is why this chapter is the longest by far—because for me a dinner that incorporates the rapture-inducing flavor of pig fat is the rule, not the exception.

And in case you need any more convincing about the joys of fat, I'll quote the brilliant book *Fat* by Jennifer McLagan and Leigh Beisch, which you should buy immediately: "Every cell in our body needs fat, our brain and hormones rely on fat to function, and fat supports our immune system, fights disease, and protects our liver. Fat promotes good skin and healthy hair, and it regulates our digestive system and leaves us feeling sated. . . . Diets low in fat, it turns out, leave people hungry, depressed, and prone to weight gain and illness."

No wonder I'm so goddamn happy all the time!

WHOLE SMOKED PIG (THE GUY)

A whole animal means a party. An animal of this size means a serious party involving serious excess. Divest yourself of inhibition. Have a real good time. Toward that end, serve the pig with some Salty Oil-Cured Chilies (page 293), Pineapple Red Curry (page 314), Chili Sauce # 1 (page 309), or, hell, anything you want. I can't think of one condiment from the condiment chapter (pages 304–319) that would suck with this. Some boiled and grilled fingerling potatoes and maybe some corn too if it's a summer party.

As with most of my cooking, nothing is precisely the same each time I make it, but the marinade here is almost always what I use when I smoke up those fatties. Almost as important as the list of ingredients and description of the method, however, is the list of stuff you need to get through this twenty-four-hour cooking adventure, besides your barbecue and your pig. Here are the bare necessities:

2 cases beer on ice—cans, not bottles
A couple joints
2 bottles Pappy Van Winkle bourbon
Plastic cups
An 8-ball
1 carton smokes
iPod and portable iPod docking station, fully charged
2 head lamps
Batteries, for everything

Foldable tarp tent in case of rain
4 high-quality, portable, foldable chairs
About 40 pieces hardwood (pecan, cherry, post oak, apple, etc.)
3 friends who like to stay up all night and, on a serious note, understand the importance of maintaining a consistent temperature in a smoker and, on another serious note, are funny as fuck

SERVES ABOUT 100 OF YOUR CLOSEST FRIENDS

6 bunches of fresh cilantro with roots, leaves reserved and stems and roots chopped
4 hands of fresh ginger, 3 cups peeled and chopped
6 heads of garlic, cloves separated, peeled, and chopped
10 shallots, chopped
2 cups fish sauce
Ten 14-ounce cans coconut milk, preferably Aroy-D brand, shaken
1½ cups dried red chilies, such as cayenne

6 tablespoons whole white peppercorns
Zest of 7 limes
12 fresh kaffir lime leaves, stems and center veins discarded and leaves chopped
1 whole pig (at least 200 pounds), gutted and singed, scalded, or shaved
2 cups kosher salt

LISTEN
Take all the music suggested throughout the book, put it into one play list, and you're set!

DRINK
I think we covered that in the "necessities" list above.

1. Use a mortar and pestle to pound (see page 12) cilantro stems and roots, ginger, garlic, and shallots, to a paste, pounding each ingredient thoroughly before adding the next. Then add the fish sauce to create a thin paste. You'll probably need to work in batches. Transfer to a large bowl and stir in the coconut milk.

2. Grind the dried chilies and peppercorns together in a spice grinder. Add the lime zest and kaffir leaf pieces, and grind them all together until the mixture is fine and slightly moist. Stir the spice mixture into the coconut milk mixture.

3. Rub the pig down and up (put it in a giant garbage bag or large plastic bin), inside and out with the kosher salt. Then rub the coconut mixture all over the salted pig, inside and out.

4. Put the pig, belly up, in a large heavy-duty trash bag and pour any remaining marinade inside the cavity. Squeeze out as much air as possible from the bag and tie it. Let sit for 2 to 3 days in a large refrigerator.

5. Get a large smoker up to 200°F. Remove the pig from the bag, saving as much of the marinade as possible. Put the pig in the smoker, belly up, and pour the marinade into the belly cavity. While it's cooking, focus on stoking your fire, maintaining the temperature, and drinking. The piggy is ready when the internal temperature of the thickest part of the shoulder is at 170°F. Any pig over 140 pounds or so will take the full 24 hours. If you're working with 50-pounders, though, it'll take closer to 12 hours.

6. Remove the pig from the smoker and transfer it to a large table covered with a plastic tablecloth or tarp. Let it rest for about 20 minutes, but pork-mad people will undoubtedly start ripping into the fatty flesh before you can get it to the table. I know because I'm one of them. Use a heavy-duty, sharp knife to remove the primals, peel the skin, and chop the meat. Be sure to have a catch basin for the juice and fat that will be spilling out from the smoky carcass. Toss the reserved cilantro leaves over the chopped meat.

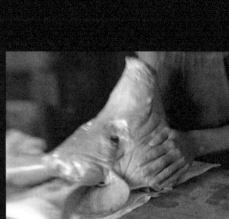

COOKING A WHOLE PIG'S HEAD

If allowed to select only one cut of swine for the rest of my time, I would have no second thought. The pig's head is a culinary trophy for anyone who has fully dedicated himself to true man-on-pig love. The head is the keeper of the greatest and most varied gustatory pleasures—meat, fat, and gelatin—the lovable creature has to offer. All I need for a good time is a whole pig head, simply roasted, my hands, a lot of napkins, a jar of pickled chilies, and a few friends ready to get elbow deep.

Sure, you can buy the component parts—the ears here, the jowls there—but the whole head is an experience that really appeals to a certain type of eater and cook who's willing to take the time to carve, to dig, to get messy. And for those who are patient, the rewards will, simply put, fuck your mouth.

As with a whole pig, a head is best obtained from a farmer friend or butcher (give 'em some advance notice of your needs, though). After a pig is slaughtered, the bristles are shaved or burned off with a torch. If you get a pig that still needs some cleaning up, a razor-sharp knife will do the job. Or an old-fashioned straight razor and your best impersonation of the Barber of Seville.

All this said, some friends of mine like to say that cooking a pig's head is the easy part; it's figuring out how to handle it once it comes out of the oven that's the more intimidating undertaking. Well, first, take a picture. Then, get a knife.

But there are two head-cooking questions I hear often and should address:

Why do you raise the temperature during the cooking process? So the fat renders and the tissue breaks down without the skin browning too much.

How do you know when the head is done? When it's golden, the skin is brittle

and the jowls are yielding. If you poke it from the back, the meat should be so tender that you feel almost dirty touching it.

At this point you can follow any of the recipes that call for pig's head, or you can just dig into the head. As I said, I love it with Pickled Thai Chilies (page 294), but it's also delicious with any sambal, the Fish Sauce and Palm Sugar Syrup (page 315), or Sweet Cilantro Sauce (page 318). Basically anything that's both sweet and spicy or sweet and sour. And anything but mayo. I never thought I'd say it, but this is something for which mayo and aïoli are overkill.

SERVES 4

1 pig's head
½ cup rendered leaf lard (page 196) or olive oil (the best you can afford)

Sea salt and freshly ground black pepper

1. Preheat the oven to 250°F. Put the head in a large roasting pan or on a foil-lined sheet pan. Rub it all over with the leaf lard or oil and season generously with salt and pepper, rubbing it in well to make sure you season all the parts. Wrap the ears in foil.
2. Put the head in the oven and cook for 3 hours, rotating the roasting pan once every hour. After 3 hours, raise the heat to 350°F and continue cooking and turning the pan for 2 more hours.
3. Remove the foil from the ears and continue cooking for 2 more hours.
4. By the 7-hour mark the skin should be brittle, the ears puffy, and the back of the head thrillingly tender. If this is the case, take it out of the oven and let it cool. If the meat's tenderness level fails to make your heart rate quicken, wrap the ears in foil again and continue cooking until it does, checking every ½ hour.

LISTEN
Junior Kimbrough, *You Better Run*—the entire album seven times, since there are about seven hours of cooking ahead of you. I cannot get enough of Junior. And, if you need a default album for every recipe in this book, this is it.

DRINK
Hudson Valley Maple Juleps as made by Miss Jori Jayne Emde. For four juleps, rinse four big handfuls of fresh **mint** in cold water. Pick the leaves from the stems and add the stems to a saucepan. Pour 1 cup **maple syrup** over the stems and bring to a boil over medium heat. Remove the pan from the heat and let the mint stems steep until the syrup reaches room temperature. Divide the mint leaves among four julep cups (preferably metal ones, but glass will suffice), reserving four of the best sprig tops for garnish. Muddle the mint in the bottom of each cup (to bruise it, not to beat it to death). Add ¼ cup of the mint-maple syrup to the cups and squeeze a **lemon wedge** into each one. Add ½ cup **Ancient Ancient Age Kentucky Bourbon** to each one, stir well, and taste, add a little more syrup or lemon until it tastes really good. Add **crushed ice** and a splash of **club soda**. Garnish with the mint springs.

PIG EAR SALAD

People always feel virtuous eating salad. I add a runny egg and fried pig's ears so I can feel virtuous. This salad is a textural marvel, the crispy ears, the soft-boiled egg, those bright, crisp greens. If you have whole ears that are brittle and fantastically crispy, don't even bother slicing them. Just pick them up with your fingers and eat them along with the salad.

SERVES 4

4 fresh eggs
Sea salt
1 cup mixed fresh herbs, such as basil, mint, savory, and parsley
1 big handful of mizuna (about 1½ cups)
1 big handful of arugula (about 1½ cups)

¼ cup plus 3 tablespoons olive oil (the best you can afford)
Juice of 1 lemon
2 fresh Thai bird chilies, minced
2 roasted pig ears, either from a roasted pig's head (page 164) or cooked separately (see Note)
4 lemon wedges, seeded

1. Put the eggs in a small saucepan, cover them with water, and add 1 tablespoon salt. Bring the water to a boil, then reduce the heat and cook at a low simmer for 3 minutes. Drain the eggs and cool them in fresh cold water. Peel and set them aside.

2. Combine the herbs and greens in a mixing bowl. Whisk together ¼ cup of the olive oil, the lemon juice, and the chilies in a small bowl.

3. If you have whole ears that are brittle and fantastically crispy, go to step 5. You can just pick them up with your fingers and eat them along with the salad. Otherwise, cut the ears across the grain into thin strips. Heat a cast-iron pan over medium-high heat. Add the remaining 3 tablespoons olive oil and heat it. Fry the pig ear strips until they're golden and crispy, 3 to 5 minutes. Transfer them with a slotted spoon to a paper-towel-lined tray to drain. Season with salt.

4. Toss the crispy ear slices with the herbs and greens, then dress the salad, tossing with your hands to coat.

5. Divide the salad among four serving bowls. Pull the boiled eggs apart so the yolk spills out over each salad and rest them on top. Serve the lemon wedges alongside.

NOTE

You've got two options for tasty ears, friends. The first and recommended course of action is to roast the whole head and remove the ears. You do that like so: holding the tip of the ear, place the blade of a large, sharp knife at the point where ear meets head. Apply pressure and slice. If you followed the directions for cooking the head, the ears should be puffed and crispy. If, for some reason, they are not, you can put them back in the oven at 375°F or drop in hot oil heated to the same temperature and cook until they're crispy and golden.

Option two: If you want to make this salad, but you didn't tackle the entire head for the reward of the ears, you can easily purchase ears from your butcher and roast them separately. Lightly coat the pig's ears with olive oil, generously season them on both sides with salt and pepper, and roast them on a baking sheet in a 350°F oven until golden, puffed, and crispy, 2 to 2½ hours.

LISTEN
Mose Allison, "Parchman Farm," then the version by John Mayall and the Bluesbreakers with Clapton.

DRINK
Alicia Lini Lambrusco Rosso 2008—red, rich, bright, and low in alcohol, which means buy more bottles.

PIG CHEEKS WITH CHAMPAGNE GRAPES

Warm, lovely pork cheeks deserve a simple, elegant saucing, so pop the champagne . . . grapes. Smashed and seasoned with gula jawa syrup and Thai bird chilies, the pulpy crushed fruit hugs the cheeks, a tight embrace that you'll want to replicate once you've tried this dish. This is the easiest of all pig-face possibilities, a great beginner's recipe.

SERVES 2

¼ cup palm or brown sugar
2 cups champagne grapes or
    quartered red grapes
2 teaspoons fennel pollen
3 fennel flowers (if you can get
    them)
2 fresh Thai bird chilies, thinly sliced
Sea salt

2 cooked pig cheeks, either from
    a whole roasted pig's head
    (page 164) or cooked separately
    (page 169)
Fleur de sel
1 tablespoon freshly ground black
    pepper

1. Simmer the palm sugar and ¼ cup water in a small saucepan, stirring until the sugar is dissolved. Remove from the heat, but keep it warm until you're ready to use it. The syrup can also be stored in an airtight container in the fridge for up to 1 year.

2. Use a mortar and pestle to crush the grapes to a juicy pulp. Stir in the fennel pollen, fennel flowers, chilies, and ¼ cup of the gula jawa syrup. Season with salt to taste.

3. Cut the warm cheeks across the grain into ½-inch-thick slices. Arrange the slices on 2 plates and spoon the grape mixture over the top. Finish with fleur de sel and freshly ground black pepper.

CARVING THE PIG'S JOWLS AND CHEEKS FROM THE HEAD

1. Position the roasty, juicy head so it's staring at you. Stare back, longingly. Notice the jowls, one on each side of the face, which hang low and large. You should remove these before you go at the cheeks, tight, oval knots about the size of a baseball, recessed in their concave bone beds a bit above the jowl.

2. Reach under the left side of the face and take hold of the jowl. Pull it out a bit and make an incision where the top of the head begins, where a crown would rest if he were a king. Following the contours of the hunk of fat and muscle with your knife—as you move it about you'll get an understanding of the anatomy— remove it from the head. If the skin hasn't yet been eaten, it should be now. This is a snack best enjoyed somewhere between warm and hot.

3. Now the cheek muscle will be exposed. Carefully carve it out of its bone pocket with your knife. I admire you, you know. By this time, I've typically destroyed the whole face and I'm drunk, full, and covered in fat. Good work.

LISTEN
Tobacco, *Fucked up Friends*— it's family fun!

DRINK
Champagne—what else? Gaston Chicquet is always a safe bet.

COOKING PIG CHEEKS WITHOUT COOKING THE WHOLE HEAD

If you are cooking cheeks purchased from the butcher and not carved from the whole roasted head, generously season the cheeks with salt and pepper, wrap them in plastic, and refrigerate overnight.

The next day, transfer the cheeks to a small roasting pan and preheat your oven to 200°F. In a small saucepan, heat enough leaf lard, bacon fat, or regular old lard to cover the cheeks to 180° to 200°F and pour the warm fat over the cheeks. Stick the pan in the oven. Four hours later, the cheeks should be fork-tender. Remove them from the oven and let them rest in the lard while you prep the rest of the dish.

COOKING JOWLS WITHOUT COOKING THE WHOLE HEAD

If you've roasted the head, carve the jowls and proceed with Rice Pot Kimchi (recipe follows). If you're making jowls purchased separately, the following brining and braising method softens the meat in a way that is especially pleasant with rice. Serve them with Rice Pot Kimchi or Strawberry Salad (page 174), depending on the season, your mood, or your temperament.

SERVES 2

Enough brine for Braised Pork Belly (page 198) to cover the jowls
2 pig jowls (2 to 3 pounds each) from the butcher
Sea salt and freshly ground black pepper
3 tablespoons rendered leaf lard (page 196) or neutral oil, such as grapeseed or canola

1 onion, cut into chunks
1 large carrot, cut into chunks
4 garlic cloves, crushed and peeled
1 cup Master Stock (page 322), or Chicken Stock (page 324) with a pinch of MSG
10 fresh flat-leaf parsley sprigs
1 orange, quartered
2 jalapeño chilies, halved

1. Pour the brine over the jowls in a large bowl. Refrigerate for at least 24 and up to 48 hours.
2. Preheat the oven to 300°F. Remove the jowls from the brine and give them a light sprinkle of salt and pepper.
3. Heat the lard in a large sauté pan over medium-high heat. Add the jowls and cook until well browned on all sides, 8 to 10 minutes total. Transfer the seared jowls to a plate and add the onion, carrot, and garlic to the pan. Cook, stirring occasionally, until the onions are lightly browned, about 8 minutes. Transfer the vegetables to the jowl plate.
4. Add the stock to the pan and boil, scraping up any browned bits with a wooden spoon, for about 2 minutes. In a separate roasting pan, make a bed of the vegetables. Add the parsley, orange, and jalapeños and put the jowls on top. Pour in the hot stock, cover the pan, and braise in the oven until the meat is meltingly tender, about 2½ hours.

LISTEN
Fatback Band, "Dance Girl.

DRINK
Well, I'm cooking it right now, and I'm drinking an Aloxe-Corton, Savigny-les-Beaune, from '86.

PIG JOWLS WITH RICE POT KIMCHI

What do you want on your big bowl of rice? Me, I'll take a slice of crispy, melting, fat-ilicious jowl and a handful of my homemade kimchi—lightly fermented garden vegetables, like chilies, kale, and scallions that exist somewhere between salad and sauce. The rice soaks up any bits that escape on the way to your mouth.

SERVES 4

1 cup Tamaki Gold short-grain or jasmine rice, rinsed well
2 cooked pig jowls (page 164 or 170)
Sea salt and freshly ground black pepper
3 tablespoons olive oil (the best you can afford)

A big handful of Kimchi (page 292 or quality store-bought)
3 fresh long red chilies, such as Anaheim or Hungarian Wax, thinly sliced

1. Prepare the rice according to your rice cooker's instructions or place it in a medium heavy saucepan and add 1 cup water. Bring the water to a boil, reduce the heat to produce the lowest simmer, cover with a tight lid, and cook for 15 minutes. If the rice isn't tender, add a few tablespoons of water and continue simmering, covered, for a few minutes longer. When the rice is finished cooking, fluff it with a fork.
2. Cut each jowl in half crosswise and season lightly with salt and pepper.
3. Heat the oil in a large sauté pan over medium-high heat. Add the cooked jowls and cook until well browned on all sides, about 4 minutes per side. (If the jowls were cool when you seared them, pop them into a 350°F oven for 5 minutes after searing to warm them through.)
4. Divide the cooked rice among four serving bowls. Top each with some kimchi and seared pig jowl. Garnish with the sliced chilies.

LISTEN
Patti Smith's version of "Gloria" will get you amped up for the fat and spice.

DRINK
A crisp pilsner.

PIG JOWLS WITH STRAWBERRY SALAD

Years ago I started toying with (what was at the time) this weird-sounding but wonderful-tasting pairing. The sweet, slightly acidic berries, with herbs and lots of black pepper, make a fine counterpoint to that fatty, crispy jowl. I'm always tweaking this dish, substituting one fruit for another, experimenting. You should too.

SERVES 4

FOR THE JOWLS
2 cooked pig jowls (page 164 or 170)
¼ cup rendered lard (page 196)
    or neutral oil, such as grapeseed
    or canola

¼ cup all-purpose flour

FOR THE SALAD
1 pound strawberries, trimmed,
    hulled, and halved or quartered
    if large
Top 2 inches of 1 bunch of flowering
    chives (bottoms reserved for
    another use)
2 cups fresh flat-leaf parsley leaves

2 shallots, thinly sliced
3 tablespoons coarsely ground
    black pepper
Zest of 1 lemon, plus 1 tablespoon
    juice
2½ tablespoons mustard oil
Sea salt

FRY THE COOKED JOWLS
1. Cut the jowls against the grain into approximately ⅛-inch-thick slices.
2. Heat the lard in a large sauté pan over medium-high heat until it's good and hot. Dredge the jowl slices in the flour, shaking off any excess, and add them to the lard. Cook until they're golden brown and crispy on both sides, 6 to 8 minutes total. Transfer to a paper-towel-lined plate to drain.

MAKE THE SALAD
In a mixing bowl, combine the strawberries, chives, parsley, shallots, and black pepper. Add the lemon zest, juice, and mustard oil and season with salt to taste. Divide the jowl pieces among four plates and top them with the salad.

LISTEN
Stereolab, *Emperor Tomato Ketchup*—because it's light, like strawberries.

DRINK
White vermouth on the rocks topped with a splash of **gin** and some **lavender flowers**— pretty!

TROTTERS

To understand why I revere the Chinese relationship with food, watch someone from Shanghai, Guangzhou, or Chengdu demolish a foot. Whether it's a chicken foot, duck foot, or part of a pig's foot, the bone, meat, and cartilage go in, but only the bones come out. Anything remotely digestible has been masterfully excised with the tongue. Somehow this skill, and the great pleasure that motivates it, has eluded most Westerners, who unaccountably avoid parts like pig's feet, even though when they're cooked slowly and delicately they offer the perfect balance of soft, fatty skin, tender, tiny muscles, and chewy, sticky, flavor-rich gelatin. Then, as you move close to the tip, there are the tiny knuckle bones, from which you can suck and scrape the most flavorful little bits of meat and then make like the Chinese and spit that bone right back on the plate to the delight of all the others at the table.

This master trotter recipe is delicious on its own—try it on Thanksgiving in addition to turkey and watch your aunts' and uncles' faces for signs of sorrow or ecstasy—or use it to make the next bunch of recipes.

SERVES 4

¼ cup plus 2 tablespoons rendered leaf lard (page 196) or olive oil (the best you can afford)
1 white onion, cut into 4 pieces
1 head of garlic, halved crosswise
3 shallots, cut in half lengthwise
2 inches fresh ginger, peeled and cut into thirds
4 equal-sized pig's trotters (about 1 pound each)
Sea salt and freshly ground black pepper

1 bunch of green onions or scallions, green tops trimmed off and discarded
2 fresh basil stems
2 fresh mint stems
2 fresh cilantro stems
4 cups Master Stock (page 322), or Chicken Stock (page 324) with a pinch of MSG

1. Preheat the oven to 375°F. Cut a piece of parchment paper to fit a 10 x 13-inch roasting pan.
2. In a bowl, toss 2 tablespoons of the lard with the onion, garlic, shallots, and ginger. Spread the vegetables in the roasting pan and roast in the oven until well browned and softened, about 20 minutes. Remove the pan from the oven and set aside. Reduce the oven temperature to 225°F.
3. Season the trotters with salt and pepper. Heat the remaining ¼ cup lard in a large sauté pan over medium-high heat until hot but not smoking. Add the trotters to the pan and brown well on all sides, turning often, about 8 minutes total. Transfer the trotters to the roasting pan with the vegetables. Add the green onions and herb stems.

LISTEN
Allen Toussaint—his whole catalog

DRINK
Sazeracs, especially if you're listening to Monsieur Toussaint.

4. Bring the stock to a boil in a medium pot, then add it to the roasting pan. Press the parchment paper to the surface of the trotters. Cover the roasting pan with foil or a tight lid and transfer it to the oven. Cook the trotters until they are unbelievably tender and yielding, about 3½ hours. Remove the trotters from the pan and strain the braising liquid, reserving it for another use (such as stock). Discard the solids.

SMOKED TROTTERS WITH CURED SHRIMP

This dish crashed into my mind one night (warm, smoky, soft trotter meat!), and I wish I could explain to you (tart spicy shrimp!) or even more so to myself (bitter melon, fresh herbs, and gelatinous broth!) where it came from. Sometimes my path to an idea is perfectly clear to me. But other times it's as if there's a Department of Culinary Eureka housed in a back corner of my subconscious, toiling away at collating influences, associations, and random bits of accumulated stimuli, unbeknown to my conscious mind.

SERVES 4

- 4 cooked trotters (page 176), including 1 cup strained braising liquid
- Sea salt
- ½ Chinese bitter melon, halved lengthwise
- 4 fresh cilantro roots, rinsed, scraped, and rinsed again, or 16 fresh cilantro stems, minced
- ½ inch fresh ginger, peeled and minced
- 4 fresh Thai bird chilies, thinly sliced
- 1 garlic clove, minced
- 1 tablespoon palm or brown sugar
- 2 tablespoons fish sauce
- Juice of 2 limes
- 1 pound medium shrimp, ideally live, shelled, cleaned, and butterflied
- 15 fresh mint leaves
- 30 fresh cilantro leaves
- 1 medium red onion, thinly sliced

SMOKE THE TROTTERS

1. Preheat a smoker to 300°F. Put the trotters in a shallow pan in the smoker with the warm braising liquid. Put the pan in the smoker and cook for 30 minutes, basting the trotters once after 15 minutes.
2. After the trotters have smoked, strain the braising liquid into a small saucepan. Let the trotters cool to room temperature. Pick the meat and soft gelatin from the bones, discarding the bones and gristle.
3. While the pork cooks, bring a pot of water to a boil and salt it until it tastes like the ocean. Prepare an ice bath. Scrape out the seeds and white pith of the bitter melon, then slice crosswise into very thin half-moons. Sprinkle with about 1 teaspoon salt and let it sit in a colander for 15 to 30 minutes. Rinse the melon with cold water, then drop it into the boiling water for 30 seconds. Drain and transfer immediately to the ice bath. Drain and reserve on a paper-towel-lined tray to absorb the excess water.
4. Use a mortar and pestle to pound (see page 12) the cilantro roots, ginger, chilies, garlic, and sugar to a paste, pounding each ingredient thoroughly before adding the next. Stir in the fish sauce and lime juice and stir until the sugar has dissolved.

NOTE

This dish requires fresh shrimp that have never been frozen. If you can get them, buy live shrimp, chill them, and then peel and decapitate while their nervous systems are impaired by the low temperature and they won't wriggle away from you—at least not as much. Keep the peeled product in a plastic container over a bowl of ice in the fridge until you're ready to use the shrimp.

CHINESE BITTER MELON

Not one of the world's prettiest vegetables, bitter melon looks like a sickly cucumber, warty and slightly shrunken. It has a strong, almost chalky flavor that's a bit of an acquired taste for some. Like so many Chinese bitter herbs and vegetables, this one has purported health benefits such as cleaning the kidneys. This dish is actually good for you.

5. Transfer to a bowl and toss the shrimp in the mixture. Let it sit for 10 minutes.
6. Bring the liquid reserved from the smoker to a boil over medium-high heat.
   Remove the pan from the heat and toss the trotter pieces in the liquid. Tear the
   mint leaves. Put the shrimp, bitter melon, herbs, and red onion into a bowl and
   toss well. Use a slotted spoon to transfer the trotters to the bowl and serve
   drizzled with some of the braising liquid.

LISTEN
Brian Eno and David Byrne, *My
Life in the Bush of Ghosts*—
they were clearly turned on
during the production of this
album, and I get turned on by
the flavors in this dish.

DRINK
A Pernand-Vergelesses white
with a joint.

Marine products knife noodles

4 hours above maturing it makes
with the dough which it makes and
extorts the broth with if chewy,
foot and 8 branch marine products
the wall hundred which it does and
the broth taste is know-how of the
love room knife noodles.
Specially Ansong Maj chum is even
in inside explaining of
the habitual drinkers.

King dumpling

About 20 the branch top grade
natural material it puts
in the dumpling blood which
confidential talk it made thinly and
it kneads and the meat vegetable
king dumpling which it puts out
in the large tree steamed dish flag
directness learns with vapor of
high tension and the greasy taste
does wall hundred entirely and
without the taste is the superb article.

SMOKED PORK LOIN WITH MACKEREL MAYO

My take on *vitello tonnato*, the classic Italian dish of sliced veal with a tuna, anchovy, and caper sauce, in which I sub porky pork for the veal and mackerel mayo for the tuna. This awesomely savory dish owes its depth of flavor to the smoker. My obsession with peppery, slightly citrusy daun salam shows up in the pork loin, which is submerged for two days in a brine flavored with this Indonesian bay leaf. Both the pork loin and the mackerel can be made the day before and the dish assembled the next. It's great at room temperature or right out of the fridge.

SERVES 6 TO 8

FOR THE PORK

Brine for Braised Pork Belly (page 198), hot

1 cup finely ground daun salam (Indonesian bay leaf) or 10 Turkish or California bay leaves, finely ground

3 pounds center-cut bone-in pork loin, preferably with the fat cap still attached

FOR THE MACKEREL MAYONNAISE

2 salt- or oil-packed anchovy fillets, minced

2 pounds whole Spanish mackerel cleaned, or 1 pound fillets

1 cup plus 2 tablespoons olive oil (the best you can afford)

Sea salt

2 tablespoons freshly ground green peppercorns

2 egg yolks

1½ teaspoons Dijon mustard

1 garlic clove, very finely minced

1 cup neutral oil, such as grapeseed or canola

Fresh lemon juice to taste

SMOKE THE PORK

1. Combine the hot brine liquid and the daun salam. Let it cool, then submerge the pork loin and refrigerate for at least 24 and up to 48 hours.

2. Preheat a smoker to 200°F, using lighter woods such as pecan, post oak, or cherry.

3. Remove the loin from the fridge and, if you've got a syringe, inject the loin with the brine every 3 inches or so.

4. Smoke the pork loin until the internal temperature reaches 130°F near the bone at the thickest part, about 2½ hours. (Low-tech method: Stick a metal skewer into the thickest part of the loin and leave it there for 15 seconds. Remove the skewer and quickly touch it to your lip. If it is cool or barely warm, continue cooking. If it's very warm but not hot, take the loin out of the oven.) Let the meat rest for 20 minutes at room temperature.

LISTEN
Anything by **The Meters**—they just make you feel good.

DRINK
At the risk of sounding effete, a simple white wine with a few cubes of ice.

WHILE THE PORK COOKS, MAKE THE MACKEREL MAYONNAISE

1. If you're using salt-packed anchovies, rinse them, then soak them for 20 to 30 minutes, changing the water once halfway through. Drain them. If you're using oil-packed anchovies, drain off oil. Mince the anchovies and set them aside.

2. Rub the mackerel with 2 tablespoons of the olive oil and season it inside and out with salt and 1 tablespoon of the ground green peppercorns. Add the mackerel to the smoker (skin side down if using fillets) and cook it until the fish easily falls apart but isn't dry, about 30 minutes for the whole fish and about 15 minutes for the fillets.

3. Remove the flesh from the skin and bones (reserving them for some other purpose) and put it in a bowl. Mash it coarsely with a fork and season lightly with salt and some of the remaining ground green peppercorns.

4. Put the egg yolks in a bowl with the mustard and whisk until they have doubled in volume and turned pale yellow, then stir in the garlic. Slowly pour in the remaining 1 cup olive oil while whisking briskly to create an emulsion. Once you've added all the olive oil, slowly pour in the neutral oil, watching closely. If the mayo seems to be separating, stop, gradually add a few spoonfuls of water, and whisk briskly to bring it back together. Otherwise, add all of the neutral oil and then a few spoonfuls of water to loosen it up a bit. Season with salt, the remaining green peppercorns, and lemon juice. Fold in the mackerel and anchovy. If you find the mayo is a bit tight, gradually add more water until you like the consistency. Transfer the mayo to a bowl, cover with plastic wrap, and refrigerate until you're ready to use.

5. Trim the loin of the fat and bones. Slice the meat as thinly as possible, arrange the slices on a platter, and serve with a bowl of the mackerel mayo. Roll the slices up and start dipping.

SMOKED RIBS WITH FISH SAUCE AND PALM SUGAR SYRUP

Eating a smoked sparerib should be analogous to eating a fresh peach, only instead of juice it's pork fat you want dripping down to your elbow. The seasoning is simple, a salty-sweet syrup to pull the flavor of a great-quality, fatty rib forward. Speaking of fatty, at the uptown Fatty Crab, Corwin has been buying the Big Daddy pork rib, the spare with the skin on and the belly attached. It's a giant, long, and superfatty cut. If you can get this from your local farmer, do so. And either way, keep some extra limes and fresh chilies around to adjust the seasoning and provide a jolt.

SERVES 2 HUNGRY PEOPLE

1 full rack pork spareribs (8 to 10 ribs), membrane removed by your butcher
Sea salt
¼ cup freshly ground Indonesian long pepper or black pepper

4 cups Fish Sauce and Palm Sugar Syrup (page 315)
2 limes, cut into wedges
4 fresh Thai bird chilies, thinly sliced

1. Season the rack generously with salt and pepper and rub it into the meat. Put the ribs in a container large enough to fit the rack with a little room to spare or place in a very large resealable plastic bag. Put them in the refrigerator for at least 4 and up to 24 hours.

2. Meanwhile, get that smoker to 200°F. Use pecan wood if you can. It complements the palm sugar quite well.

3. Put the ribs in the smoker. Keep the syrup near the smoker and ready a pastry brush or meat mop. Cook the ribs, basting with the syrup on both sides every 45 to 60 minutes, until perfectly tender, about 4 hours.

4. Remove the ribs from the smoker and brush them a final time with the syrup. Let the rack rest for about 15 minutes, then cut the ribs between the bones. Serve them on a platter with a bowl of any extra syrup at the table along with the lime wedges, fresh chilies, beer, and lots of napkins.

LISTEN
Hank Williams, to conjure images of the Old South.

DRINK
A six-pack of your favorite brew—and have some Pappy or Booker's on hand for later.

FULL-FAT PORK SHOULDER

I'm pretty sure I could fill a thick-ass book (but a real page turner!) solely with recipes for whole pork shoulder. That's how many ways I've cooked this cut over the years. Working with pig is so rewarding that I will never stop learning from it. I will never stop playing with different ways to eke out that porky essence, the *jus de vie*, but here, now, I'm drawing a line. There is one way to cook a shoulder in this book. One way, folks, and I've given this method a name: Full Fat. I first learned about the "Full Fat" method when I was in college traveling through Mexico. I was in awe of the *carnitas* percolating in its own fat. To this day I long for a giant copper vat in which I can slowly bubble away an entire pig at one time, periodically pulling out gleaming chunks and pressing them quiveringly against my lips.

If you don't eat this shoulder within ten minutes of hauling it from the oven, use it to make the Pork and Cockles (page 189), Pork and Watercress Salad (page 190), or the Cuban (page 192). You can portion out the cooked shoulder and stick it in the fridge for up to a week or the freezer for a few months. Save the lard, too!

THE FULL-FAT SHOULDER COOKING METHOD SHOULD BE USED TO COOK WHOLE BUTTS OR EVEN ENTIRE SHOULDERS, WHICH CAN BE USED TO SERVE 8+ PEOPLE, OR COOLED, WRAPPED, AND REFRIGERATED AND USED FOR MULTIPLE RECIPES.

1 whole pork shoulder (15 to 20 pounds), bone in and skin on
Enough brine for Braised Pork Belly (page 198) to cover the shoulder
Sea salt and freshly ground black pepper

Enough hot rendered leaf lard (ideally 5 pounds, page 196) to cover the shoulder

1. Put the shoulder in a large pot and cover it completely with the brine. Refrigerate for at least 1 and up to 3 days.
2. Preheat the oven to 175°F. (You're not frying the pork, just breaking it down in a *very* warm bath, not a very *hot* bath.) Cut a piece of parchment paper to fit a large deep roasting pan.
3. Drain the shoulder and pat it dry with paper towels. Put it in the deep roasting pan or Dutch oven and sprinkle with salt and pepper.
4. Pour the hot lard over the shoulder. Cover the pan first with the parchment paper and then with foil or a lid if you have one. Slide the whole deal into the oven and let it go for 9 hours, rotating the pan from time to time. (If you have doubts about your oven's calibration, either get it checked or check on the pork a couple hours early.)
5. Pull it out, uncover it, and stab it in a few spots with a skewer. If it's really fucking tender, it's party time. If not, you know what to do.

NOTE

When buying shoulder, you have several choices: the butt, picnic ham, bone in and bone out, skin on and skin off. Ideally, for this recipe, you'd buy a whole bone-in, skin-on shoulder. If you can't, you can still use the method here, just check your pork a few hours before my recommended cooking times.

LISTEN
Lush, *Spooky*—off you go into a dizzy tizzy, which is cool, because you really don't have anything else to do for nine hours.

DRINK
Your face off.

PORK AND COCKLES

I would love to be eating this right now, sitting at the window in a small storefront restaurant near the water, looking out on a gray, windy fall day. The roasty, toasty pork slices wrap me in warmth like a blanket straight out of the dryer. The tender, sweet, briny cockles are like a high five from the nearby ocean. The finishing touch is jamón Ibérico. "Why Ibérico?" a friend asked. The appropriate response was and is "Why not?"

SERVES 4

¼ cup plus 1 tablespoon rendered leaf lard (see page 196) or neutral oil, such as grapeseed or canola
8 fresh Thai bird chilies, slit
6 garlic cloves, crushed and peeled
3 inches fresh ginger, peeled and sliced
6 scallions, sliced
¼ cup dry white wine
2 pounds Full-Fat Pork Shoulder (page 185), cooled and sliced 1 inch thick

Sea salt
¼ cup Master Stock (page 322), or Chicken Stock (page 324) with a pinch of MSG
2 pounds cockles, rinsed
1 tablespoon Chinese fermented black beans, rinsed well and soaked in cold water for 1 hour
12 thin slices jámon Ibérico
1 lemon

1. Heat 3 tablespoons of the lard in a large pot with a lid over high heat. Add the chilies, garlic, ginger, and scallions and cook, stirring, until softened, about 2 minutes. Add the wine, bring to a boil, and let bubble for about 2 minutes to cook off the alcohol. Take the pan off the heat.

2. Heat the remaining 2 tablespoons lard in a large sauté pan over medium-high heat. Lay the slices of pork shoulder in the pan, working in batches if necessary, and cook for a few minutes on the first side. When you can no longer stand the suspense, peak underneath. If it's not roasty brown, keep cooking until it is. Then flip the pieces, reduce the heat a tad, and cook the pieces until they are heated through and have developed a lovely color, another 5 minutes. Transfer the pork to a plate and give the slices a little sprinkling of salt.

3. Pour off the fat from the pork pan, then pour in the stock and bring the liquid to a simmer, scraping up the goodness with a wooden spoon. Return the large pot with the wine and aromatics to high heat, pour in the stock, then add the cockles and the black beans. Cover and cook, shaking from time to time and resisting the urge to peek until at least 90 seconds have passed. When the cockles pop open (discard any that don't open after 3 minutes), pull the pan from the heat. Spoon the cockles and their bathing partners into four serving bowls. Top with the pork slices and jámon Ibérico. Give the bowl a squeeze of lemon and dig in.

LISTEN
Bob Dylan, "Baby, Let Me Follow You Down." With Dylan, the earlier the better.

DRINK
Dogfish Head 60 minute IPA—clean and hoppy, it bounces off the briny saltiness.

PORK AND WATERCRESS SALAD WITH EGG AND CAPER VINAIGRETTE

Yet another way to use your leftover pork shoulder.

SERVES 4 TO 6

FOR THE DRESSING
3 eggs
Sea salt
1 tablespoon Dijon mustard
2 tablespoons sherry vinegar

2 tablespoons capers, drained
½ cup olive oil (the best you can
    afford)

TO FINISH THE DISH
2 pounds Full-Fat Pork Shoulder
    (page 185)
2 bunches of watercress, tough
    bottom stems discarded

1 tablespoon capers
1 fresh Thai bird chili, thinly sliced

MAKE THE DRESSING

1. Place the eggs in a small saucepan and cover with cool water. Bring the water to a boil, then reduce the boil to a gentle simmer. Cook for 3 minutes, drain the eggs, and immediately rinse them under cold water to cool them. Peel.
2. In a blender, combine the boiled eggs, 1 teaspoon salt, the mustard, the sherry vinegar, and the drained capers. Blend on medium, slowly adding all but 1 tablespoon of the olive oil, until the dressing has emulsified. The dressing is meant to be thick but should still be pourable. Add a little water if it's too tight.

FINISH THE DISH

1. Cut the pork into even slices, about ¼ inch thick, against the grain. Heat the remaining tablespoon of olive oil in a cast-iron pan or heavy skillet over medium-high heat until it's hot but not smoking. Add the pork to the pan, working in batches if necessary, and cook until golden on both sides, about 3 minutes.
2. Dress the watercress, put the pork on plates, and top it with watercress, capers, and chili.

LISTEN
The Clientele, *Bonfires on the Heath*—soft, mellow, and easy to enjoy, like this recipe.

DRINK
The Balkan—it'll make you feel cuter. Pour 1 ounce each **vodka, Pernod,** and **raki** over **ice** in a shaker, add a dash of **angostura bitters,** and shake like you mean it. Strain it into a cocktail glass. Repeat and repeat and repeat with more booze.

THE CUBAN

Stoned and at home one night in 2003, I grew hungry. It was around midnight, but I decided to bike back to the Chickenbone Café, where I had been earlier that evening. Brian, a musician who I trained to cook at the restaurant, was working the sandwich press. Cory, my friend and the manager, made me a drink. And I set to work making myself a snack. I pulled out a little of this from here and a little of that from there, unaware that I was building a Cuban sandwich. It ended up tasting really fucking good. Yeah, I was high, but not a removed-from-my-taste-buds-and-critical-thinking high, just pleasantly high. I made one for Brian and one for Cory, and they loved them. They were probably high too, you may argue. Oh yeah? Well, I remembered exactly how I made it when I went in to work the next day. And it stuck. Here it is. So there.

MAKES 4 SANDWICHES

FOR THE PICKLED JALAPEÑOS
5 jalapeño chilies, halved
½ cup distilled white vinegar
½ small white onion, thinly sliced
1 teaspoon sea salt, or more to taste

FOR THE SANDWICHES
¼ cup rendered leaf lard (page 196)
    or neutral oil, such as grapeseed
    or canola
¾ pound Full-Fat Pork Shoulder
    (page 185), shredded
2 baguettes, ends trimmed, halved
    crosswise and lengthwise
¼ cup Aïoli (page 307)
1 cup shaved aged Gouda, such as
    Boerenkaas
12 thin slices prosciutto di Parma

AT LEAST 2 DAYS AHEAD

PICKLE THE JALAPEÑOS
Put the chilies in a heatproof bowl. Warm the vinegar, onion, and salt in a small saucepan over medium-low heat for 5 minutes, stirring to dissolve the salt. Pour the liquid over the jalapeños and let them cool to room temperature. Cover and refrigerate for at least 2 days and up to 2 weeks.

MAKE THE SANDWICHES
1. Cut the jalapeños into strips.
2. Heat the lard in a medium saucepan over medium-high heat, then add the shredded pork, stirring to heat it through.
3. Spread each baguette piece with 1 tablespoon aïoli and divide the remaining ingredients among the four pieces of baguette, layering the cheese, jalapeños,

NOTE

Your plan of attack should be thus: 2 days before you plan to serve these, pickle the jalapeños. The day before, you can make the aïoli and roast the shoulder. Unless you're going to make Cubans for twenty-eight of your pork-loving best friends, portion out enough shoulder for the sandwiches and use the remaining meat to make Pork and Cockles (page 189) or Pork and Watercress Salad (page 190).

LISTEN
The Yeah Yeah Yeahs—their first album, whatever it was called, which was playing all the time back in '03.

DRINK
El Floridita Daiquiri à la Wondrich at Chickenbone, also a cocktail guru! In a shaker filled with **ice**, pour 2 ounces **white rum** (such as Matusalem Platino, Appleton White, or Brugal White), 1 ounce fresh **lime juice**, 1 ounce fresh **pink grapefruit juice**, ¾ ounce **maraschino liqueur**, and 1 teaspoon **superfine sugar**. Shake it like a motherfucker. Strain it into a cocktail glass and garnish with a **lime wheel**.

and prosciutto. Transfer the shredded pork with a slotted spoon to each one before covering with the remaining baguette halves.

4. Heat a large skillet over high heat. Put a second, slightly smaller heavy skillet, preferably cast iron, over high heat at the same time. When the pans are very hot, add some of the lard from the pork pot to the larger skillet. Add each sandwich to the skillet with the lard (cut them in half if they don't fit), and press the second skillet on top, weighing it down with a heavy item. Cook until the bread is golden on both sides and the cheese is melted, 1 to 2 minutes a side.

LARDO

Fatback is a thick cap of almost pure white delight from the back of the pig between the skin and flesh. You can render it to make lard, drape it over or stuff it into lean cuts of meat to help them stay moist as they roast or smoke, or cure it to make lardo, which is one of the most valuable seasonings in my kitchen. Cut thick or thin, rendered and used for sautéing or as a finishing touch, added to sauces, braises, delicate fish dishes, and roasts, lardo, for me, has become a way of life. I discovered the wonders of lardo while living in Florence in the early nineties. A pale, translucent slice of aromatic porkiness slowly melting onto warm bread was as close to a religious experience as I'd come. And the Tuscan cooks who worked with this divine slab of savory, edible statuary marble became, to me, as revered as Renaissance artists.

Lardo deserves grandiose analogies. But for all its grandeur, it's quite easy to make and, covered in the back corner of the refrigerator, keeps almost indefinitely, only improving with age. There are endless combinations of spices to use when curing anything, so as always, the recipe here is only a reference point. In fact, I don't think that I've cured a big batch of lardo the same way twice.

Find a container that will accommodate the fatback as it cures, with just a little room to breathe. Then make yourself a drink and put on some tunes.

YIELD WILL DEPEND ON USE

½ cup black peppercorns
½ cup coriander seeds
5 tablespoons Sichuan peppercorns
2½ cups coarse sea salt or kosher
    salt
10 dried bay leaves, broken into
    small pieces, either Turkish or
    California

One 5-pound piece fatback, at least
    ½ inch thick (1 to 1½ inches thick
    is even better)

1. Toast the peppercorns, coriander, and Sichuan peppercorns in a dry pan over medium-high heat, swirling and shaking them until they crackle lightly and release their aromas, about 3 minutes. Lay the toasted spices between two paper towels and crack them by smashing them with the bottom of a heavy pan. You want them really coarse. No grinding for this one!
2. Mix the salt and spices in a large bowl. Lay the fatback on your work surface and rub a few tablespoons of the spice mix all over it. Add half of the remaining spice mixture to the curing container in an even layer and set the fatback on top. Pour the rest of the mixture evenly over the top of the fatback and cover with a lid or with several layers of plastic wrap.

LISTEN
Canned Heat, "Fried Hockey Boogie"—fat song, fat man, fatback.

DRINK
A spicy Bloody Maria as it's a necessary aid for starting the lardo-making process before noon.

3. Let it sit in the refrigerator for 1 week. Then flip it and rub it again and make sure it's covered in the seasonings and let it sit for another week. If you are using a thin piece of fatback, clean off the salt-spice mixture at this point and wrap the fatback in plastic and keep it in the fridge for at least another 2 weeks before using. If you are using a thicker piece, continue flipping and rubbing it for another 2 weeks before taking it off the salt mixture. Then wait another 2 weeks before using it. That's 4 to 6 weeks of total sitting time, but the wait is worth it. Ideally, you'd let the fatback cure in the salt mix for at least 2 months before using it, but after just 1 month, especially if you started with a thinner piece, it'll be ready to add flavor to roasted potatoes or fish. Take it out of the salt, wrap it in plastic, and reserve it until ready to use. When ready, cut the amount you want to use and rinse the chunks lightly or brush off excess salt and seasoning and slice according to recipe. If eating on its own, toast or grill some bread, slice as thin as possible, and drape thin slices on warm bread.

LEAF LARD

When you slowly heat fat, it melts into lovely, lovely lard. The fat you start with
might be fatback. Or it might be the fat that develops around the kidneys and loin,
which melts into what's known as *leaf lard* and is officially the jam. Ask your butcher
for it, then render it at home and use it to fry, sauté, and bake such traditional joys
as piecrusts and biscuits.

    Of the two main types of lard, leaf lard has the less porky flavor. It's great
for high-heat cooking and, believe it or not, is healthier than standard vegetable
oils. In many recipes throughout this book, I call for rendered leaf lard. If you
are in receipt of this fat in its raw state, you'll need to render it before you cook
with it. You should chop it, put it in a pot, and cover it with cold water. Put the
pot over medium heat and cook the fat until the pieces have almost completely
dissolved and the water has cooked off. It can take hours, depending on how
much fat you have. Strain the rendered fat through a fine-mesh sieve, cool it to
room temperature, then cover and refrigerate. Divide it between the fridge for
immediate use and the freezer for later use. Well stored, it will keep for a month
in the fridge and months in the freezer.

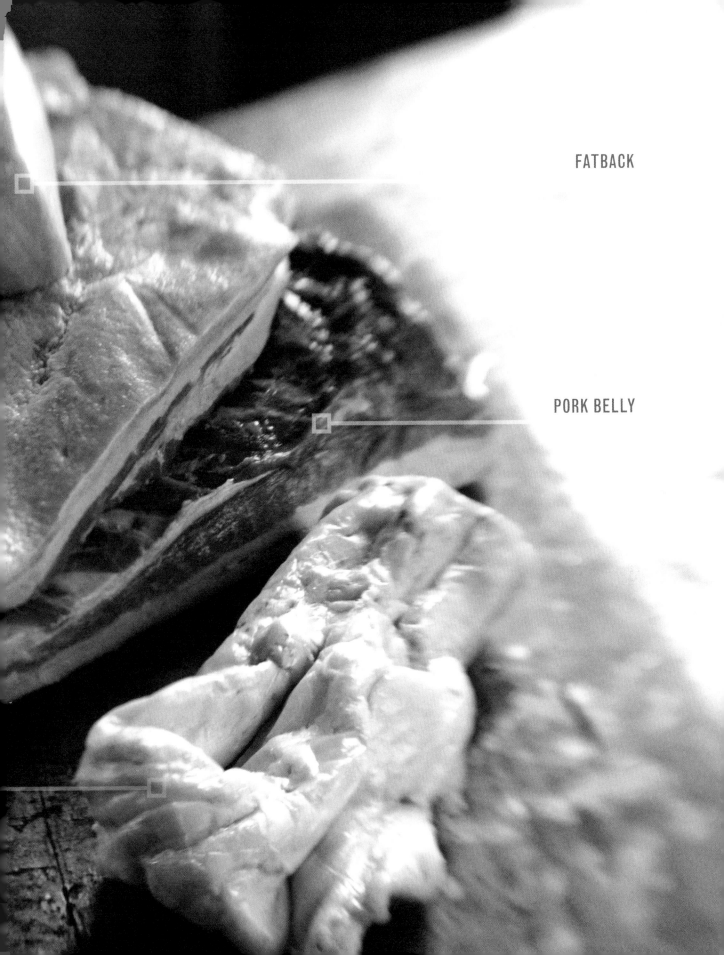

FATBACK

PORK BELLY

BRAISED PORK BELLY

You might wonder why I would brine an already fatty, juicy cut of meat. Simple: to give it flavor. Pork is a dynamite flavor receptor, its clean, mild fat a magnet for whatever seasonings with which it's been anointed. The brine travels deep within the meat, ensuring that every bit, even the very center, is as flavorful as the rest. You might also ask yourself, "Why the heck is this guy asking me to compress the braised belly?" Fine, then, you don't have to, but doing so guarantees neat, pretty portions that cook evenly. I recommend always having some of this pork belly in your fridge (where it will keep for up to two weeks) or freezer (where it'll last for about six months!), in case the mood strikes. Or if you want to make any of the next six recipes.

ABOUT 2 POUNDS PORK BELLY AND 2½ CUPS LIQUID

FOR THE BRINE
¼ cup coriander seeds
2 tablespoons fennel seeds
4 cups sea salt
2 cups sugar
10 garlic cloves, crushed and peeled
10 fresh long red chilies, such as
   Anaheim or Hungarian Wax,
   thinly sliced

5 medium shallots, sliced
3 tablespoons black peppercorns
1 cup packed daun salam
   (Indonesian bay leaves)
2 to 3 pounds fresh pork belly

FOR THE BRAISE
2 tablespoons rendered leaf lard
   (page 196) or olive oil (the best
   you can afford)
1 yellow onion, cut into sixths

1 head of garlic, halved crosswise
2 shallots, halved lengthwise
2½ cups Master Stock (page 322)
   or Chicken Stock (page 324)

BRINE THE PORK BELLY

1. Toast the coriander and fennel seeds in a dry pan over medium heat, swirling and shaking them until they crackle lightly and release their aroma, about 3 minutes. Set aside.

2. Combine the toasted seeds with the salt, sugar, garlic, chilies, shallots, peppercorns, daun salam, and 3 gallons water in a stockpot and bring to a boil over high heat. Reduce the heat and allow the brine to simmer for about 20 minutes. Remove the brine from the heat and let it come to room temperature, then refrigerate it. When it's completely cool, pour it over the belly and refrigerate, covered, for at least 24 and up to 48 hours.

BRAISE THE PORK BELLY

1. Preheat the oven to 225°F. Cut a piece of parchment paper to fit your roasting pan.
2. Remove the belly from the brine, rinse with cold water, and pat dry. Set aside.
3. In the roasting pan straddling two burners over medium-high, heat the leaf lard until hot but not smoking. Add the onion, garlic, and shallots, and cook, stirring occasionally, until golden and tender, 5 to 6 minutes. Add the stock to the pan and deglaze, scraping up any bits with a wooden spoon.
4. When the stock comes to a boil, add the belly to the roasting pan and remove it from the heat. Top the pan with the parchment paper and cover with a tight lid or foil.
5. Braise the belly in the oven until it is tender (when you press the tip of a pairing knife into it, there should be no resistance). Start checking it after 2½ hours, though it could take up to 4 hours.
6. Remove the pan from the oven and let it sit at room temperature for 30 minutes. Using two big spatulas or your hands, transfer the belly from the pan to a large plate or sheet tray and let it cool to room temperature. Strain the braising liquid and reserve for future use. The liquid can be stored in the fridge for up to 5 days or in the freezer for up to 3 months.
7. Wrap the belly tightly in plastic wrap. Press it between two flat pans (such as sheet trays) and put a weight on the top (a few cans of tomatoes will do the trick). Refrigerate, pressed, for at least 12 hours and up to 2 days.
8. After the belly has been cooked and pressed, it's ready for any of the following recipes or any other culinary purpose. It keeps in the fridge, wrapped tightly, for about 2 weeks or in the freezer for up to 6 months. To use frozen belly in a recipe, thaw it completely in the fridge first. Also, I like to cut my belly into portions prior to freezing so I don't have to thaw the whole megillah at once.

PORK FRIES

Ryan Skeen has made quite a name for himself as a champion of charcuterie and delicious things affiliated with animal fat. In 2004, when we were kids, he was my sous-chef at 5 Ninth, and we came up with the pork fry (braised pork belly cut like thick-cut French fries, breaded, and fried) after an impassioned discussion about how best to get a swift, clean kick-in-the-face of pork fat from a finger food. It quickly became a favorite, particularly with the staff. Over time, we've served pork fries with a ton of different condiments, but I think my favorite is an egg-white aïoli, with a Bone Shot alongside.

SERVES 1 TO 6

FOR THE AÏOLI

2 egg whites
3 garlic cloves, minced
Sea salt

1 cup olive oil (the best you can afford)
Fresh lemon juice to taste

FOR THE PORK FRIES

2 pounds Braised Pork Belly (page 198)
2 cups all-purpose flour
Sea salt and freshly ground black pepper

3 eggs, whisked
2 cups panko bread crumbs, pulverized in a food processor
About 5 cups rendered leaf lard (see page 196) or neutral oil

MAKE THE AÏOLI

In a stand mixer or food processor, whip the egg whites with the garlic and a generous pinch of salt. Once they begin to take on volume, slowly add the oil. Once the oil has been incorporated and you have a white cloud of mayo, add lemon juice and salt to taste. Pour the aïoli into a bowl and set it aside in a cool place.

MAKE THE PORK FRIES

1. Cut the skin from the belly and reserve it for another use. Cut the belly crosswise into ½-inch-thick strips. From those strips, cut 2-inch-long pieces that resemble thick-cut French fries.
2. Put the flour in a shallow bowl and season it well with salt and pepper. Put the beaten eggs and panko each in separate bowls. Dredge the pork rectangles in the flour, then dip them into the egg, letting the excess drip off, and finally, gently toss them in the panko. Bread all the pork pieces before cooking. Try to designate one hand as the "egg hand"—this will make your life easier and a lot less goopy.

WHAT'S A BONE SHOT?

Dave Wondrich developed this fantastic shot years ago for the Chickenbone Café. This drink has it all: brown booze, acid, sweetness, spice. I try not to think how many of these I've had in the last eight years—and how many are still in my future. Like the cocktail, Dave is strong and to the point, a remarkable cat who is truly no bullshit. We used to talk about our fantasy projects, and I'll always remember the little bar he saw so clearly. It was an old fashioned bar—not old-fashioned in style (though perhaps that as well) but rather a bar devoted exclusively to the old fashioned cocktail. Well, that and lemonade made from the lemons he'd have to zest to make all those old fashioneds. I loved the idea: make what you enjoy, don't try to do too much, and don't pander. If people don't like old fashioneds, they can fuck off and find another bar. That kind of grit is rare.

FRY THE PORK

1. Heat enough rendered leaf lard (about 5 cups) to reach 2 inches high in a medium shallow saucepan to 350°F. Working in batches of about six pieces, delicately add the breaded pork and fry, turning occasionally, until golden brown on all sides, 3 to 5 minutes total.

2. Transfer the pork as it's done to a paper-towel-lined plate to drain and salt. Serve this ascetic snack with the aïoli.

LISTEN
Captain Beefheart, "Nowadays a Woman's Gotta Hit a Man."

DRINK
The Bone Shot: 2 ounces **Wild Turkey rye** (or your choice), ¾ teaspoon **superfine sugar**, 1 teaspoon fresh **lime juice**, 3 dashes **Tabasco sauce**. Pour all the cocktail ingredients into a shaker over **ice**. Shake well and strain into a chilled shot glass. It's important to take at least two bone shots before getting started. Shoot it; don't sip.

PORK FRIES p. 200

FRIED PORK BELLY WITH CHILI LIME SAUCE

Sweet, sticky, spicy sauce coating fried hunks of pork. If that doesn't generate an irresistible desire in you, then avoid reading the next sentences . . . if you can! When you bite into these golden, saucy morsels, your teeth punch through a crispy shell and the hot, delicious molten fat inside surges into your mouth. Kind of like that gum with the liquid center. But porkier.

SERVES 4

4 cups rendered leaf lard (see page 196) or neutral oil, such as grapeseed or canola
1 cup cornstarch
2 to 3 pounds Braised Pork Belly (page 198), cut into 1½-inch by ½-inch pieces while still cold (see Note)

Sea salt
Chili Sauce #2 (page 309), at room temperature
1 fresh long green chili, such as Anaheim or Hungarian Wax, thinly sliced
2 fresh Thai bird chilies, thinly sliced
3 scallions, thinly sliced

1. Heat the lard to 350°F in a large heavy saucepan.
2. Meanwhile, put the cornstarch into a large bowl, then toss in the pieces of pork belly to coat them. Shake off any excess and fry the belly pieces in the lard until they're golden brown and crispy, about 5 minutes. Using a slotted spoon, transfer the fried pork belly to a paper-towel-lined tray to drain and season with salt.
3. Transfer the fried belly to a bowl and toss it in just enough chili sauce to coat each piece. Sprinkle with the sliced chilies and scallions. Eat.

NOTE

After the pork belly has been cooked, chilled, and pressed, you can easily run a knife under the skin of the belly with the skin facing up. Grab on to the skin once you've cut 1 inch in and, slightly tilting your knife upward, run it under the skin until it has been completely removed from the belly. It is OK if you don't accomplish this in one motion or even one piece. It is most important to take it slow and ensure that you are only removing the skin and not the fat.

LISTEN
Stan Getz and Charlie Byrd, *Desafinado*—smoooooooooth.

DRINK
Straits Sling—à la Singapore. Muddle three **lime wedges** in a sling glass. Into a shaker filled with **ice**, pour 1½ ounces **gin**, ½ ounce **Benedictine**, ½ ounce **Kirsch**, 1 dash **Peychaud's bitters**. Stir very well, drop a few cubes of ice into the sling glass, strain in the liquor, and top with a fine **ginger beer**.

BRAISED BELLY WITH CRISPY SHRIMP

This time you're not frying the braised pork belly. I know, weird. But fear not: I haven't forgotten the fry! It's just that it's reserved for the sweet, delicate rock shrimp, which provide a wonderful balance of textures along with the braised belly. In fact, this is a different role for our friend the belly, who instead of stealing the spotlight is content to be the supporting player, a plush cushion for the more texturally compelling and flavorful fried shrimp.

SERVES 4 TO 6

2 to 3 pounds Braised Pork Belly (page 198), sliced against the grain into pieces no more than $\frac{1}{6}$ inch thick while still cold (see Note on page 204)
$\frac{1}{2}$ cup pork belly braising liquid, Chicken Stock (page 324), or Master Stock (page 322)
3 cups peanut oil
$\frac{1}{2}$ cup rice flour
$\frac{1}{2}$ cup cornstarch

$\frac{1}{4}$ cup sesame seeds, plus 2 teaspoons for garnish
3 tablespoons kosher salt
10 ounces rock shrimp
Sea salt
2 medium shallots, thinly sliced
2 cups loosely packed fresh cilantro leaves
Olive oil (the best you can afford)
1 cup Chili Sauce #1 (page 309)

1. Preheat the oven to warm or your oven's lowest setting.
2. Lay the pieces of pork belly flat on a serving plate, slightly overlapping one another.
3. Bring the braising liquid or stock to a boil and lightly brush the pieces of pork to moisten them with the stock. Don't let any liquid pool in the plate.
4. Put the plate in the warm oven to slightly warm the pork.
5. Meanwhile, heat the peanut oil to 375°F (measured on a deep-frying thermometer) in a medium saucepan.
6. In a mixing bowl, combine the rice flour, cornstarch, the $\frac{1}{4}$ cup sesame seeds, and the kosher salt. Stir well. Dredge the shrimp in the mixture, shake off any excess, and fry until golden and crispy, about 4 minutes. Transfer them to a paper-towel-lined plate to drain and season with sea salt.
7. While the shrimp are frying, toss the shallots and cilantro together in a bowl and season with a touch of olive oil and sea salt.
8. Remove the plate from the oven and spoon some of the chili sauce over the center of the plate of pork, then top the pork with the crispy shrimp. Sprinkle the scallion-cilantro mix over the shrimp and drizzle with more chili sauce and a blessing of sesame seeds.

LISTEN
Fila Brazillia, "Pollo de Palo," then "Heat Death of the Universe"—groovy and weird, like a guy I know.

DRINK
Rock the Chatham Hotel Flyer—a bit of boozy elegance. Muddle 4 fresh **mint leaves**, $\frac{1}{2}$ teaspoon **sugar**, and 1 teaspoon **lemon juice** in a shaker. Add **ice**, then $1\frac{1}{2}$ ounces **white rum**, and shake vigorously. Pour it into a champagne glass and top it off with fine **French bubbly**.

PORK BUNS

A forever resident at Fatty Crab, pork buns are certainly more Chinese than Southeast Asian. Good thing our culinary parameters are loose. This version is actually a riff on a dish I served at Chickenbone Café: scrap pork shoulder topped with whimsical garnish—pickled lychee or marinated mango—that I'd send out to regulars and VIPs. Now we do it with braised belly, and once you've made it, you just buy those pillowy Chinese "bao buns" (page 333), whip up the glaze, and make the sauce—a mixture of kecap manis and sriracha. The garnishes, including pickled radishes and charred green chilies, make it even better.

SERVES 4

FOR THE PORK BUN GLAZE
6 dried red chilies, such as cayenne
¼ cup dried shrimp
1 tablespoon fish sauce
3 tablespoons black vinegar
Juice of ½ lime
3 ounces palm sugar (2 rounds gula jawa) or ¼ cup brown sugar

TO ASSEMBLE THE BUNS
4 fresh long green chilies, such as Anaheim or Hungarian Wax, or jalapeños, stemmed
About 2 teaspoons neutral oil, such as grapeseed or canola
Sea salt
1 pound Braised Pork Belly (page 198)
8 Chinese bao buns
3 cups loosely packed fresh cilantro leaves
8 pickled radishes (page 296), quartered
4 shallots, thinly sliced
Olive oil (the best you can afford)
1 cup kecap manis
Sriracha sauce to taste
2 hard-boiled eggs, quartered

MAKE THE PORK BUN GLAZE

1. In a dry pan over medium heat, toast the dried chilies until they take on a dark color, pressing them down with a wooden spoon to increase contact with the pan, 3 to 4 minutes. Be careful not to inhale over the toasting chilies. Spill them onto a plate, then add the dried shrimp to the pan and toast, shaking the pan and tossing often, until they're a roasty brown. Spill them onto the plate with the chilies and set aside.

2. Bring the fish sauce, black vinegar, lime juice, and 1½ teaspoons water to a boil in a small saucepan over medium heat. Add the palm sugar and stir until the sugar has dissolved, then stir in the toasted chilies and dried shrimp. Remove the pan from the heat and let steep for 10 minutes. Strain the liquid through a fine-mesh sieve, discarding the dried shrimp and chilies.

LISTEN
Can, "Mushroom" and "Oh Yeah" off the *Tago Mago* album—raw, odd, jammin'.

DRINK
A Fatty Crab staple—Singha Beer in a can. Before opening the can, top the rim with yuzu juice, a pinch of salt, and dry ground chili.

ASSEMBLE THE BUNS

1. Preheat the oven to 325°F. Toss the fresh chilies with a little neutral oil and a pinch of salt. Heat a cast-iron pan over high heat until it begins to smoke, then add the chilies and let them blister, spit, and sizzle. Don't cremate them, but make sure you've got some serious blistering on more than half their surface. Dump them into a bowl, cover the bowl with plastic wrap, and let them sit there for at least 10 minutes. When they're cool enough to handle, slice them into ¼-inch rounds. While the chilies steam, cut the skin from the belly (see Note, page 204) and reserve it for another use. Then cut the belly while it's still cold into 2½ x ½-inch pieces.

2. Set a large steamer basket over a few inches of water in a large pot, cover it with a lid, and get the water steaming. Cut a piece of parchment paper the size of the steamer insert and lightly coat it with a small amount of neutral oil. Lay the buns on the oiled paper, place in the steamer basket, cover, and steam until very soft and fluffy, about 5 minutes.

3. Meanwhile, gently rewarm the glaze. Lay the belly slices on a baking sheet and coat with the glaze. Bake in the oven until heated through, about 6 minutes. Remove the pan from the oven and baste the slices with more glaze.

4. Pull the steamed buns from the steamer and fill them with the pork belly.

5. Toss the sliced chilies, cilantro, radishes, and shallots together with a little olive oil and a pinch of salt.

6. Add the kecap manis to two of the smallest bowls you have and squirt a generous dollop of sriracha right in the center. Serve two buns per person on a small plate with a little mix of the radish salad and the hard-boiled egg on the side.

CRISPY PORK AND WATERMELON SALAD

The elements are Southeast Asian—kaffir lime leaf and Thai basil, palm sugar and lime, the incredibly gratifying combo of fruit and fat—but you'd never find anything quite like this in that part of the world. Instead, it's a great example of American cuisine: the flavors of somewhere else converging with local ingredients to make a new, delicious reality. I thought of it while cooking one summer on Long Island, where I was surrounded by watermelon. Pickled watermelon rind, with its tart crunch, is an awesome foil for the sweet red flesh and the crisp-edged chunks of almost-molten belly. It has become a signature dish at Fatty Crab. Oh, and giving it the salad moniker is misleading—at least if you think of salads as light.

SERVES 4 TO 6

FOR THE WATERMELON SALAD

2 cups rice vinegar
3 shallots, thinly sliced
2 fresh Thai bird chilies, thinly sliced
2 fresh kaffir lime leaves
2 inches fresh ginger, peeled and sliced

1½ ounces palm sugar (1 round gula jawa) or 2 tablespoons light brown sugar
1 tablespoon kosher salt
One 5-pound watermelon

FOR THE DRESSING

3 ounces palm sugar (2 rounds gula jawa) or ¼ cup light brown sugar
1 cup rice vinegar
½ cup fresh lime juice
4 inches fresh ginger, peeled and sliced

6 fresh cilantro roots with 1 inch of stems, rinsed, scraped, and rinsed again, or 24 cilantro stems
2 garlic cloves, chopped
¾ teaspoon kosher salt

FOR THE PORK

About 3 cups rendered leaf lard (see page 196) or neutral oil, such as grapeseed or canola
2 pounds Braised Pork Belly (page 198), cut into 1-inch chunks while still cold (see Note on page 204)

1 cup all-purpose flour
Sea salt

TO FINISH THE DISH

1 cup fresh Vietnamese mint (rou ram) leaves
1 cup fresh Thai basil leaves

3 scallions, sliced
¼ cup sesame seeds

MAKE THE WATERMELON SALAD

1. Combine everything for the salad except the watermelon in a small saucepan. Add 1 cup water, bring the liquid to a boil over medium heat, and cook, stirring, until the sugar dissolves.

LISTEN
Coltrane, *Blue Train*—the whole album; it never gets old.

DRINK
Selbach-Oster Riesling Auslese 2005.

2. Meanwhile, cut the rind from the watermelon flesh, reserving both the rind and the flesh. Use a sharp knife to pare away the outer, darker green skin, leaving the inner, whiter fleshy rind. Discard the darker green peel. Cut the white rind into ¼-inch cubes and put them in a bowl. Strain the seasoned rice vinegar liquid over the diced rind. Let the mixture cool, then chill for at least 1 hour and up to 2 days.

3. Cut the flesh of the watermelon into 1-inch pieces (discarding whatever seeds you can). Chill it until you're ready to use it.

MAKE THE DRESSING

Roughly crush the palm sugar using a mortar and pestle or a plastic bag and a rolling pin. Pulse the sugar with the vinegar, lime juice, ginger, cilantro roots, garlic, and salt in a food processor until smooth and well combined.

FRY THE PORK

1. In a large, straight-sided sauté pan or wok, heat 3 inches of lard to 375°F (measured on a deep-frying thermometer).

2. Toss the cubed pork belly in the flour and shake off any excess. Working in batches, fry the pork belly until very crisp and a deep golden brown, 6 to 7 minutes. Transfer the pork with a slotted spoon to a paper-towel-lined tray to drain and season with salt. Return the fat to 375°F between batches.

FINISH THE SALAD

Tear the mint and basil leaves. In a mixing bowl, toss the pickled watermelon rind and the chilled watermelon flesh with the sliced scallions, mint, and basil. Add just enough dressing to coat. Divide the pork among the plates. Top with the salad and garnish each dish with a sprinkle of sesame seeds. Serve immediately.

CRISPY PORK AND WATERMELON SALAD, p. 208

PORK TEA SANDWICHES

High tea, an enduring (and endearing) British tradition, made its way around the world thanks to the Brits' penchant for colonization. Wherever they hung their hats, the tea cart followed. Parts of Asia and Africa maintain the custom, down to finger sandwiches, cakes, and gentility. When I opened Fatty Crab, I really wanted to serve high tea but in a kind of rock 'n' roll style. So I created this sandwich (and the sardine version, page 28) and replaced the tea with booze.

MAKES 12 TEA SANDWICHES TO SERVE 6

¾ cup rice vinegar
Sea salt
1 bunch of scallions, sliced
1 pound Braised Pork Belly (page 200), at room temperature

8 slices Pepperidge Farm Original White Bread
⅓ cup Sambal Aïoli (page 307)
½ cup loosely packed fresh cilantro leaves

1. Pour the vinegar and ½ teaspoon salt over the scallions and let them sit for at least 1 hour. Drain the scallions before you use them.
2. Cut the skin from the belly and reserve it for another use.
3. Spread each slice of bread with 1 heaping teaspoon of the sambal aïoli. Put about 8 leaves of cilantro on half of the slices of bread. Lay 3 or 4 slices cut into ¼ inch thick strips, of the pork belly on top. Add 1 tablespoon drained pickled scallions. Top with the remaining slices of bread, aïoli down, to close the sandwiches. Cut off the crusts and discard. Cut each sandwich into 3 rectangles.

NOTE

Tea sandwiches are all about the white bread: moist, sweet, slightly dense, and very square, like a pain de mie, or French sandwich bread. My favorite is Pepperidge Farm Original White. To keep this lovely bread from drying out, cover the finished sandwiches with damp paper towels and assemble the sandwiches no more than an hour before serving them.

LISTEN
Isaac Hayes, "Hyperbolic-syllabicsesquedalymistic" off *Hot Buttered Soul.* He was a big, bald, bad motherfucker.

DRINK
The Golden Dawn from the Grosvenor House, London, in lieu of tea. Pour ½ ounce **dry gin**, ½ ounce **apricot brandy**, ½ ounce **Calvados**, and ½ ounce fresh **orange juice** over **ice** in a shaker. Shake and feel your rear a-jigglin'. Strain into a coupe and give it a dash of **grenadine.**

CURING AND SMOKING BACON

Andrew Pressler, who used to cook at Fatty Crab, loves bacon almost as much as—OK, maybe more than—I do. (If I had my way, I'd throw some bacon into just about every dish I cook.) One afternoon at the Crab, Andrew was playing around with some house-cured Sichuan pepper bacon. I looked up from whatever I had been working on and saw him walking toward me, managing a huge smile even though his mouth was visibly stuffed. As he got closer, I saw that he was holding a hot dog bun piled with what looked like seven slices of bacon, garnished with a few pickled ramps, some fresh sambal belacan, and aïoli. It was a Sichuan-pepper-bacon sandwich, and it was really fucking good! So we put it on the brunch menu.

I've included two different bacon cures in this book, one for that Sichuan pepper bacon and one for coriander bacon, as I find them both absolutely delicious. The coriander cure was inspired by coriander-seed-laden bacon chunks I found at the M&I Market in the Eastern European stronghold of Brighton Beach, Brooklyn. I have an infatuation with cilantro leaf, stem, root, and seed, so it was only a matter of course that it would end up on my cured pork belly. You'll notice that the ingredients are listed by weight, not volume—it's a bit more precise, which is a good thing when you're curing stuff.

Once you've rubbed the meat with your curing mix and let it rest, the method for making both types of bacon is the same: Lightly rinse off the cure, pat the meat dry, then let the belly sit, uncovered, in the refrigerator for at least one night and up to three. Then smoke that shit.

Or don't. If you want to, you can follow the recipes, stopping before the smoking step, then simply slice and cook. In that case, you're making a kind of pancetta. You can even eat the cured belly unsmoked and uncooked if you hang it in your refrigerator (you'll have to cut it into pieces and brush off excess cure before hanging it) for about seven days. I recommend slicing it very thin when eating in this fashion. A translucent slice or two on a nice, warm piece of bread is an addictive snack. Another great way to serve the uncooked, unsmoked bacon is to lay those slices over warm potatoes that have been crushed with olive oil and sea salt.

As for storing your bacon, it can be refrigerated for weeks upon weeks if it's well wrapped, but if it's not all to be used within a few weeks, I would portion it and freeze some, thawing as needed.

SMOKING BACON

I can't teach you how to smoke meat in a few pages. But I will say that even if you just have a standard Weber grill, you can smoke stuff. Just build a fire on one side of the cooker, let the coals ash over so they're not blazing hot, and throw on some wood chips. Then add your bacon to the other side of the cooker so it gets gentle, indirect heat. I like to smoke the bacon at 180°F until the internal temperature reaches 175°F. This means you need a meat thermometer of some sort. If you're the kind of person who likes to party while his meat's cooking, you might want to purchase a nice remote thermometer, which you can leave in the belly as it cooks and will sound an alarm when the belly has reached the desired temperature. Either way, you don't want to forget about it and let all the fat render out.

The wood and type of smoker you choose is entirely up to you and your surroundings. We've been testing these methods in Ole Hickory Smokers using Texas post oak and cherry woods. Go ahead and try pecan wood, apple wood, or hickory if you want really big smoke or use any untreated wood that you can get your hands on.

It's also fun to experiment with smoking temperatures. I haven't run enough tests to determine which method I like more, but I've smoked bacon at even lower temperatures for longer periods of time with great results. If you have the time and resources, I encourage playing around, as long as you always stay lower than 180°F. Smoking at a higher temperature will produce a yielding, tender texture similar to braised pork belly, which is not what you want from your bacon. Bacon should be toothsome, should have some pull to it.

GULA JAWA AND SICHUAN PEPPERCORN CURED BACON

YIELD WILL DEPEND ON USE (CUT INTO CHUNKS; FREEZE SOME AND HOLD SOME IN FRIDGE)

6 ounces Sichuan peppercorns
2½ ounces whole black peppercorns
½ pound kosher salt
5 ounces palm sugar (3⅓ rounds gula jawa) or 6⅔ tablespoons brown sugar

One 12-pound Berkshire pork belly, skin removed

1. Working in batches, toast both types of peppercorns in a dry pan over medium-high heat, swirling them until they crackle lightly and release their mysterious aromas, about 3 minutes. Cool slightly, then grind them, in batches if necessary, and set the mixture aside.
2. Pound the salt with the gula jawa, then mix them thoroughly with the ground toasted spices. Rub the mixture evenly all over the pork belly. Wrap the belly tightly in plastic and let it cure for 5 days in the refrigerator.
3. Rinse the cure off the belly, pat it dry, and let it stand, uncovered, in the refrigerator overnight.
4. Smoke according to the method on page 215.

LISTEN
Laurie Anderson, *Big Science*—it's suggestive and deep at times but probaby won't get you laid (your bacon might, though).

DRINK
A shot of organic cider vinegar—we all need to cleanse from time to time.

CORIANDER-CURED BACON

4 ounces coriander seeds
1 ounce fennel seeds
2 ounces black peppercorns
5 ounces fresh cilantro root, rinsed, scraped, and rinsed again
3 ounces fresh Thai bird chilies, thinly sliced

½ pound kosher salt
5 ounces palm sugar (3⅓ rounds gula jawa) or 6⅔ tablespoons brown sugar
12 pounds Berkshire pork belly, skin removed

1. Working in batches, toast the coriander seeds, fennel seeds, and peppercorns in a dry pan over medium-high heat, swirling and shaking them until they crackle lightly and release their aroma, about 3 minutes. Cool slightly, then grind in batches and set the mixture aside.
2. Puree the cilantro root and chilies in a food processor, and pound the salt and sugar in a mortar. Then combine with the ground toasted spices in a small bowl and stir thoroughly to mix. Rub the mixture evenly all over the pork belly.
3. Wrap the belly tightly in plastic wrap and let it cure in the refrigerator for 5 days.
4. Rinse the cure off the belly, pat it dry, and let it sit, uncovered, in the refrigerator overnight.
5. Smoke according to the method on page 215.

LISTEN
Eric B. & Rakim, "I Know You Got Soul"—and so does your bacon!

DRINK
La Chouffe blonde ale (add a little to the bacon cure)

BACON AND BEETS

Roasted beets are sweet, deeply colored, and earthy. Dressed in a vinaigrette made with bacon fat and freshened with a little greenery (purslane rocks in this dish), the beets surrender their healthy status and become ballsy. But not as ballsy as that braised bacon.

SERVES 4

FOR BRAISING THE BACON
1 tablespoon rendered leaf lard (page 196) or neutral oil, such as grapeseed or canola
1 white onion, quartered
5 garlic cloves, crushed and peeled
2 shallots, halved
2 pounds unsliced cured and smoked bacon, such as Coriander-Cured Bacon (page 217) or good-quality store-bought slab bacon
½ cup Master Stock (page 322), or Chicken Stock (page 324) with a pinch of MSG
⅓ cup kecap manis

FOR THE BEETS
8 to 10 medium beets, scrubbed and trimmed
About 2 tablespoons rendered leaf lard (page 196) or olive oil (the best you can afford)
Sea salt
1½ teaspoons good balsamic vinegar
2 cups loosely packed fresh parsley, celery leaves, or purslane
2 fresh Thai bird chilies, very thinly sliced

BRAISE THE BACON

1. Preheat the oven to 225°F. Cut a piece of parchment paper to fit a straight-sided ovenproof sauté pan large enough to fit the slab of bacon. Heat the lard in the pan over medium heat. Add the onion, garlic, and shallots and cook, stirring occasionally, until they're translucent, about 5 minutes.

2. Add the bacon, stock, kecap manis, and ½ cup water. Bring the liquid to a boil, top the pan with a piece of parchment paper, then cover with a lid or foil and transfer to the oven. Braise the bacon until the tip of a pairing knife enters the bacon without resistance, 2 to 2½ hours.

3. Transfer the bacon to a platter. Strain the braising liquid, discarding the solids, and reserve it. (This can be done up to 3 days in advance. Wrap the braised bacon in plastic wrap and store the strained braising liquid in a bowl covered with plastic wrap.)

ROAST THE BEETS

1. Turn up the oven to 325°F. Rub the beets with leaf lard and salt and wrap each in foil. Put them on a baking sheet and roast until they are tender, about 1 hour.

LISTEN
The Lounge Lizards, *No Pain for Cakes*—because John Lurie is fucking cool and so is braised bacon.

DRINK
Audrey Saunders's "Little Italy" made with Cynar instead of Angostura bitters or Peychaud's. How good it is with sweet and salty warm pork fat on your chinny chin chin. Pour 2 ounces **rye**, ½ ounce **Cynar**, and ¾ ounce **sweet vermouth** into an **ice**-filled mixing glass and stir until it's very cold. Strain into a coupe and garnish with two skewered **brandied cherries** and a flamed **orange twist** on the top.

2. Remove the foil and let the beets stand at room temperature until they're cool enough to handle, then peel them (wear gloves if you're not down with stained fingers) and cut them into bite-sized pieces.

FINISH THE DISH

1. Slice the bacon crosswise into ½-inch-thick slices. Lay the slices in a baking dish, pour ⅓ cup of the reserved braising liquid over the slices, and bake them in the oven until the bacon has a wonderful sheen and the liquid has reduced a little bit, 5 to 7 minutes.

2. Lay four slices of bacon on each of four serving plates. Pour the liquid from the baked bacon into a bowl and combine it with the balsamic vinegar. Toss the beets in the mixture, then toss in the parsley leaves and sliced chilies. Season with salt to taste and stir.

3. Top each plate with the dressed beets and enjoy.

BEEF

Is it weird to begin a chapter on beef by admitting that I rarely eat beef? In terms of versatility, nothing beats the pig. And when I start craving red meat, I typically look to lambs and goats, because the good stuff is cheaper than beef and the animals are easier for farmers to raise than cows.

But don't get me wrong; there's a tremendous amount of love between me and the rib-eye. I mean, me and the spinalis dorsi muscle are practically a couple. And when you're jonesing for a steak or a braised short rib, there's no substitute for cow flesh. Oh, and brisket! I cook a ton of brisket. I eat a ton of brisket. Beef makes me think of winter, because it's so damn hearty, but also of anchovy and red wine, of grilled onions and scallions and hunks of garlic, of buttered noodles and polenta.

So I got to thinking: because I eat beef so infrequently, the stuff I do make with it must be really special. So here you are, the beefy beef greatest hits.

HANGER STEAK SALAD

If you have a well-stocked Asian pantry, this is the kind of thing you can make last-minute. If not, then go buy yourself the makings of a well-stocked Asian pantry! Your salad-dressing-of-sorts takes the form of a pan sauce that you pour over the steak right before serving. The only question is, what cut of steak? Hanger is a wonderful cut; it's a strip of muscle that more or less holds the internal organs in place, and its proximity to the organs gives it a rich, liverlike depth of flavor. The problem with hanger is there is very little of it on each animal. If there's none available at your local butcher, substituting skirt or flank is better than fine. Oh, and in the spirit of full disclosure? This dish is a salad in Southeast Asian name only—unlike an American salad, it's missing, well, the vegetables. Call it what you will, it's great stuffed into a crispy baguette, though it was made for white rice.

SERVES 2

3 tablespoons palm or brown sugar, or more to taste

3 to 4 tablespoons fish sauce, or more to taste

2 to 3 tablespoons fresh lime juice, or more to taste

Two 1-inch-thick hanger steaks (about 7 ounces each)

Sea salt and freshly ground black pepper

About 1 tablespoon neutral oil, such as grapeseed or canola

2 tablespoons Shaoxing wine or dry sherry, or more to taste

4 garlic cloves, thinly sliced

1½ inches fresh ginger, peeled and thinly sliced

6 fresh Thai bird chilies, thinly sliced

2 fresh long red or green chilies, such as Anaheim or Hungarian Wax, thinly sliced

1 medium red onion, halved lengthwise and thinly sliced

½ cup fresh Thai basil leaves

½ cup fresh cilantro leaves

1. In a small bowl, stir together the palm sugar, fish sauce, and lime juice. Taste the mixture. Do you want it sweeter, saltier, or more acidic? It's up to you.

2. Generously season the steaks with salt and pepper. Heat a large cast-iron skillet or sauté pan over medium-high heat until it's smoking. Add just enough oil to coat the bottom of the pan and add the steaks. Cook until beautifully brown on one side, about 6 minutes, then flip and cook for 4 more minutes more for medium-rare. Transfer the steaks to a cutting board and let them rest for 5 minutes.

3. Reduce the heat to medium and add the Shaoxing wine, scraping up any brown bits with a wooden spoon. Add the garlic, ginger, and chilies, cook for 30 seconds, and remove the skillet from the heat.

4. Slice the steaks against the grain. Add them to a bowl and top with the pan liquid. Then add the fish-sauce-lime dressing, the onion, and the herbs. Toss and serve.

LISTEN
How about some chill-wave—that is, the new psychedelia of **Tame Impala**, *Innerspeaker*?

DRINK
Beer, whatever you got, icy cold.

GRILLED RIB-EYE STEAK

Is there any other steak? I don't think so. I will not argue the merits of grass-fed versus grain-finished. They both have their merits. But two things are certain: Rib-eye is king, and wet aging is bullshit. Dry aging *is* all that and a whole lot more. When buying a rib-eye steak, shoot for one closer to the shoulder (the wider end, where there is more of the prized spinalis dorsi muscle; ideally, ask your butcher for steaks from ribs 7, 8, and 9 and about 1¾ inches thick).

I've given you two of my favorite partners for the king—Red Wine, Farro, and Grapes (page 227) and Anchovy Butter, Arugula, and Roasted Chilies (page 228)—which you can make while the steak is marinating. But does it really matter what you serve with it as long as you have some salt to sprinkle and lemon to squeeze? Buttered fresh or dried pasta is also a welcome accompaniment. And make sure you have plenty of red wine nearby.

SERVES 2

One 20-ounce dry-aged rib-eye
    steak, 1½ to 2 inches thick
Olive oil (the best you can afford)
Kosher salt and freshly ground
    black pepper
Crushed and peeled garlic

Chopped fresh herbs, such as
    rosemary and thyme
Neutral oil, such as grapeseed or
    canola
Lemon juice

IN ADDITION TO TOP-QUALITY MEAT

A charcoal grill (duh)
Hardwood charcoal (I use Cowboy
    Charcoal at home)
2 chimney starters
Grill brush

2 rags
Long-handled meat fork
Tongs
A big plate for the meat once it
    comes off the heat

1. Some of my buddies like to soak the steak for a day or two in seasoned olive oil. That's fine, but to me it's a waste of good olive oil. A rib-eye already has plenty of fat, so just rub the outside with olive oil, salt, pepper or chili, lots of crushed garlic, and herbs (my favorites are rosemary and thyme) about an hour before cooking.

2. Let the steak rest at room temperature for at least 1 and up to 5 hours. Yes, 5 hours—there's no bacteria that will begin to grow on the surface of that steak that won't be torched as soon as it hits the hot grill, and this allows the salt to penetrate the meat and season it throughout.

3. Use the chimney starters with newspaper in the bottom to light the charcoal. (Do not use lighter fluid under any circumstances. That stuff is nasty.) Once the fire dies down and the coals are glowing red, pour them into your grill. Make a mound on one side of the grill with the coals from one chimney starter; on the

Thickness: Anywhere from 1½ to 2 inches is, in my book, a perfect thickness for a rib-eye. But go forth and cook a monster 3-incher if you wish. Just note that it'll require lower heat than the one I call for. The idea is that by the time the inside is cooked the way you like it, the outside should be charred the way you like it, and that won't happen with a hot, hot fire.

Dry Aging: When steak is stored in a cold environment with high humidity (about 38°F with anywhere from 50 to 75 percent humidity), magic happens. The muscle fibers break down (mmm, tender) and the flavors concentrate as moisture evaporates. Wet-aging attempts to have all this happen within the confines of a Cryovac bag, and the results aren't even close.

You've hit the jackpot if you find the guy who is humanely raising cattle locally and dry-aging the meat for weeks himself. Or a good butcher who does it. If you can't find a dry-aged product, approximate it yourself by putting the meat, unwrapped, on a rack on top of a bed of herbs in the back of your refrigerator, swapping out the herbs for a fresh bunch every day. Make sure to put a plate underneath the rack to catch the juices. Five days later the meat should be a little more tender, more intense, and funky.

other side, add the coals from the other chimney starter in one even layer. This creates a range of temperatures for you to grill with, from high heat directly above the highest point of the mound with gradually lower, less direct heat as the mound slopes down and then becomes that even layer. It'll allow you to respond to your steak, giving it great char over high heat but letting you find refuge in a lower heat zone where the flames can't reach if they try to take over and torch the steak.

4. Put the grill grates (you've already cleaned them with your grill brush, right?) over the hot coals and let them get really hot.

5. When the coals are glowing red and have a hint of white ash, they're hot as shit—and it's time to cook. Hold your hand over the grill and familiarize yourself with the range of temperatures; it should be impossible to hold your hand over the hottest part for more than a second.

6. Fold one of the rags into a small square and saturate one side of the rag with the neutral oil. Latch on to it with tongs and use it to rub down all the grates, coating them with oil. (Don't be alarmed by the flare-ups.) Give the oil-rubbed steak a final salt-and-peppering and put it on the part of the grill that's the hottest but out of reach of the flare-up. Grill the steak, turning once, for 10 to 15 minutes total for medium-rare. Though I love rare, bloody meat, cooking a rib-eye a bit beyond rare actually bastes the meat in its own fat (of which it has a ton), and it will be more tender and enjoyable as a result. Save bloody for the sirloin. If flare-ups occur—and they will, because this is a marblicious rib-eye with a fatty, fatty fat cap—move the steaks with the meat fork to an area of lower heat (that is, with a shorter stack of charcoal underneath), then back to the higher heat. This takes some finesse, but you'll get the hang of it. The end game is this: a steak that has a beautiful dark brown, almost black crust but still gives when you prod the center with your finger.

7. Transfer the steak to a cutting board, season it again (salt, a squeeze of lemon, and maybe even a glug of olive oil), then exercise your patience. Let it rest for 15 minutes so when you slice it the juices will stay in the meat rather than spilling out onto the cutting board.

8. Starting at the inside top part of the bone, run a sharp, sharp knife along the bone all the way to the end. Save the bone for someone special—seriously, this is not a bone for your dog. Slice off the eye using the tip of your knife. Slice the eye and the steak against the grain into ½-inch-thick slices.

9. Put the slices on a serving platter and top with all the run-off juices, another squeeze of lemon, and some more olive oil (or the Anchovy Butter, page 228). Fill some glasses with red wine and have yourself a party!

...WITH RED WINE, FARRO, AND GRAPES

Farro is an ancient grain that in this case you cook as you would rice for risotto. I love this dish in the early fall, when you can still grill outside and grapes (Muscats, Champagnes, Niagras) are flooding the market. I serve the grapes by the bunch alongside. A few slices of steak, farro, crunchy sea salt, grapes—I've found my god, and it sure as shit ain't no bearded white dude.

SERVES 4 TO 6

About 5 cups Chicken Stock
(page 324)
¼ cup plus 2 tablespoons olive oil
(the best you can afford)
1 pound (2 cups) farro
1 medium onion, minced
3 garlic cloves, minced
1 cup red wine (cook with good wine;
drink the great stuff)

Sea salt
½ cup minced fresh flat-leaf parsley
½ lemon
Freshly ground black pepper
A couple bunches of grapes,
whatever kind looks lovely

1. Bring the stock to a bare simmer in a medium saucepan over medium heat.
2. Heat 2 tablespoons of the olive oil in a pot over medium-high heat. Add the farro and toast, stirring frequently, until slightly translucent, about 5 minutes. Add the onion and garlic and cook for another 2 minutes. Don't let the garlic brown, so reduce the heat if necessary. That's why your stovetop has knobs.
3. Add the wine to the farro, bring to a boil, and cook, stirring often, until it's completely evaporated.
4. Reduce the heat to medium and add enough hot stock to just cover the farro (about 1 cup) and a generous sprinkling of salt. Stir, stir, and don't stop stirring for more than 30 seconds at a time. This allows the farro to release some of its starch and develop a creamy, voluptuous sauciness.
5. Once the liquid has dropped below the top of the farro, add more stock. Repeat this process until the grains are just tender with the slightest bite (maybe three, four, or five times), 20 to 25 minutes. Taste frequently and adjust the salt as you do so. And for god's sake, don't stop stirring.
6. Once you're satisfied with the farro's texture, turn off the heat and keep stirring. Add the remaining ¼ cup olive oil, the parsley, and some squeezes from the lemon, then season with salt and pepper until it tastes really good. Spoon the farro onto plates and serve with the grapes and slices of the steak.

...WITH ANCHOVY BUTTER, ARUGULA, AND ROASTED CHILIES

This represents a slightly more savory pairing than the red-wine-cooked farro with grapes (preceding recipe) and includes three items I simply cannot live without. The anchovy becomes a compound butter; the arugula is dressed simply with good olive oil and lemon. And the chilies are roasted beside your steak on the grill.

SERVES 2, WITH LEFTOVER BUTTER

FOR THE ANCHOVY BUTTER
12 Sicilian salt-packed anchovies
1 pound high-fat unsalted butter
    such as Vermont Creamery
    cultured butter, at room
    temperature

1 garlic clove, minced (optional)
1 tablespoon minced fresh flat-leaf
    parsley (optional)

FOR THE CHILIES
20 fresh long red chilies, such as
    Anaheim or Hungarian Wax, or
    cubanelle chilies

2 teaspoons olive oil (the best you
    can afford)
Sea salt

FOR THE SALAD
1 pound arugula or several large
    handfuls
Olive oil (the best you can afford)

Coarse sea salt
Sliced crusty bread
Lemon, cut into wedges

MAKE THE ANCHOVY BUTTER

1. Rinse the anchovies, then soak them for 20 minutes, changing the water once halfway through. Drain them and remove and discard their backbones and chop finely.

2. Add the anchovies and butter (and garlic and parsley, if you're using them) to a stand mixer fitted with the paddle attachment and mix until well blended. Or do this in a bowl with your hands or a wooden spoon.

3. Dump the lump of butter (be sure to use a spatula to get all the salty, fatty fun out of the mixing bowl) into the center of a large square of plastic wrap. Fold one side of the plastic over the butter. Using your hands, sculpt the butter into a log and roll it up tightly in the plastic wrap. Twist the ends and put the log on a plate in the fridge for a few hours or up to 2 weeks.

ROAST THE CHILIES

Toss the chilies with the olive oil and a pinch of salt. Add them to the grill alongside your steak, turning occasionally, until they're lightly charred on all sides. Put them in a serving bowl or plate and sprinkle with some crunchy sea salt.

ASSEMBLE THE SALAD

Put the arugula into a large serving bowl. Serve with lemon wedges, really flavorful olive oil, and salt on the side. You can figure out what to do with them.

FINISH THE DISH

When the steak comes off the grill, top it with two ½-inch-thick pats of anchovy butter. Cut up the remaining butter and serve it on the side along with the chilies and dressed arugula. Oh, and grill those bread slices, won't you?

SHORT RIBS WITH PANZANELLA

Just thinking about this dish makes me crave good red wine. Be sure to have plenty on hand for friends and family when you serve this dish. It's a classic European braise (with a sriracha party crasher): savory, tender, sweet beef with a salad of crispy bread and heady, salty blue cheese.

SERVES 4 TO 6

FOR THE SHORT RIBS

6 pounds bone-in beef short ribs, cut across the rack into 3 pieces by your butcher

Sea salt and freshly ground black pepper

1 cup neutral oil, such as grapeseed or canola

2 cups all-purpose flour

1 large carrot, cut into 4 pieces

2 white onions, quartered

1 leek, halved lengthwise, rinsed, and halved crosswise

1 head of garlic, halved crosswise

2 bottles dry red wine

1 bottle ruby port

1 tablespoon black peppercorns

1 tablespoon coriander seeds

1 tablespoon yellow mustard seeds

1 bunch of flat-leaf parsley

10 fresh thyme sprigs

¼ cup sriracha sauce

2 cups Master Stock (page 322), or Chicken Stock (page 324) with a pinch of MSG

FOR THE PANZANELLA

4 medium red onions, cut lengthwise into 8 wedges

7 fresh thyme sprigs, plus 1 tablespoon thyme leaves

¼ cup plus 1 tablespoon olive oil (the best you can afford)

Sea salt and freshly ground black pepper

Splash of sherry vinegar

3 cups 1-inch bread cubes, from a ciabatta, Pugliese, or crusty peasant loaf

8 ounces Bayley Hazen Blue cheese (or your favorite local blue cheese), crumbled

1 cup loosely packed fresh flat-leaf parsley leaves

3 fresh Thai bird chilies, seeded and thinly sliced crosswise

MAKE THE SHORT RIBS

1. Season the meat very well with salt and pepper. Heat 3 tablespoons of the oil in a large skillet or Dutch oven over medium-high heat. In a mixing bowl, combine the seasoned meat with the flour and toss to coat evenly, shaking off any excess.

2. Working in batches to avoid crowding the pan, add the ribs to the oil and cook until they're deep brown all over, about 4 minutes per side. Transfer the meat to a large heatproof bowl or casserole dish as it's browned.

LISTEN

James Pants, *Welcome*—it's hard to listen to just one song off this album, just like it's really hard to have just one bite of this panzanella.

DRINK

You take your pick within the following parameters: aged, rich, and red.

3. Add 2 tablespoons of the remaining oil to the pot and sauté the carrot, onions, leek, and garlic until the vegetables have colored and softened, about 10 minutes. (If the bits on the bottom of the pan begin to burn, add a little water and stir them up.) Pour in the wine and port, increase the heat to high, and bring to a boil, scraping up the brown bits with a wooden spoon. Cook until the liquid is reduced by a quarter, about 10 minutes.

4. Reduce the heat to low, maintaining the liquid at a simmer, then make a sachet by wrapping the peppercorns, coriander, and mustard seeds in a square of cheesecloth tied closed with kitchen twine. Add the sachet, herbs, and sriracha and stir to incorporate. Simmer for 20 minutes, then pour the liquid over the ribs.

5. Let the ribs sit at room temperature until the liquid has cooled, then transfer to the fridge and let the ribs marinate at least overnight and for up to 3 days.

6. Preheat the oven to 300°F. Cut a piece of parchment paper to fit inside a deep roasting pan. Use a slotted spoon to scoop the short ribs and veggies into the roasting pan in a single, even layer.

7. Pour the marinating liquid into a pot, add the stock, bring it to a boil, then pour it over the ribs. Top the roasting pan with the parchment, cover tightly with foil or a lid, and braise in the oven until the meat is incredibly tender and falling off the bone, 4 to 5 hours.

8. Use a slotted spoon to transfer the braised ribs to a baking sheet and set them aside at room temperature. Strain the braising liquid through a fine sieve into a saucepan, discarding the solids. Let the liquid cool at room temperature. As it cools, the fat will rise to the surface. Skim off as much of it as possible. Bring the liquid to a simmer over medium-high heat and cook until it has reduced by half. Taste it as it's reducing and season it with salt, keeping in mind it'll get saltier as the liquid evaporates. This is where a cook earns his or her stripes. Salt lifts the flavor but can easily outstrip flavor as well.

MAKE THE PANZANELLA

1. About 40 minutes before the ribs are done, toss the red onion wedges with the thyme sprigs, a tablespoon of the olive oil, and some salt and pepper. Put them on a sheet of foil and cook them in the oven along with the ribs until the onions are bright and tender, about 30 minutes. Transfer them to a salad bowl, discarding the thyme sprigs, and let them cool to room temperature. Toss them with a splash of sherry vinegar and the tablespoon of thyme leaves.

2. When the ribs are out of the oven, raise the oven temperature to 425°F. In a large bowl, toss the bread cubes with the ¼ cup olive oil and a light sprinkle of salt.

Put the cubes in an even layer on a parchment-lined baking sheet and toast in the oven, stirring the cubes and rotating the pan occasionally, until the bread is golden on all sides, about 10 minutes. Cool to room temperature.

3. Toss the onions with the blue cheese, parsley, and chilies. Add the cooled bread and toss to combine. Add salt to taste.

FINISH THE DISH

1. Add the ribs to the pot of perfect sauce and stir gently to warm the ribs and coat them with the sauce.
2. Divide the panzanella among four to six wide, shallow bowls, put two ribs on top, and drizzle with sauce.

BEEF RENDANG

Rendang is a big spicy braise, one of those traditional Malaysian dishes for which there are as many recipes as there are the small villages called *kampungs*. The one constant across all the rendang variations is that the chicken, lamb, beef, goat, or whatever is simmered in a wok with coconut milk until the liquid has either cooked off or been absorbed by the protein and the pan is dry. This method helps preserve proteins and is especially useful if you don't have any means of refrigeration. Since I assume that you do, I've altered the traditional recipe, using a Western method of braising while maintaining the fantastic Malaysian flavor profile, to produce something I love even more than the original.

SERVES ABOUT 10 PEOPLE

TO MARINATE THE BEEF

1 dried red chili, such as cayenne, soaked in warm water for 20 minutes

2 fresh Thai bird chilies, stemmed, seeded, and sliced

2 inches fresh galangal, peeled and sliced

2½ inches fresh young ginger, peeled and sliced

3 inches fresh turmeric, sliced

5 lemongrass stalks, woody outer layers and bottom 1½ inches removed, tender inner stalk thinly sliced

15 pounds bone-in short ribs, cut 1½ inches long across the bone by your butcher

FOR THE SHALLOT PASTE

8 shallots, roughly chopped

4½ ounces palm sugar (3 rounds gula jawa), roughly chopped, or ¼ cup plus 2⅔ tablespoons brown sugar

4 heads of garlic, cloves separated, peeled, and roughly chopped

FOR THE BRAISE

¼ cup kosher salt

5 cups well-stirred coconut milk (from three 14-ounce cans), preferably Aroy-D brand

6 slices assam gelugor, rinsed very well under warm water

TO FINISH THE DISH

1 cup Kerisik (page 319)

½ cup Gula Jawa Syrup (page 341)

10 fresh kaffir lime leaves, stems and center veins discarded and leaves very thinly sliced lengthwise

3 limes, cut into wedges

It's creamy and delicious, fatty and frothy. And, typically here in our decidedly untropical climate, we get it out of a can. Sad, but true. You should totally make it yourself, though I have to admit, it's a bit of a challenge here in the Northeast.

First, you need impeccably fresh coconuts. I've found that for every four fresh, mature coconuts I've purchased in New York, cracked open, and sniffed, at least one of them smells sour. Can't use those. And, just in case you were wondering, you can't use the young, green coconuts to produce coconut milk. (But you can drink the water, or for a real good time, mix it with a little rum and lime juice.)

Second, it's a huge labor drain. You have to clean the mature coconuts, grate them, and then steep the grated coconut in hot water (about one cup per coconut will do it) before pressing it through a sieve lined with cheesecloth. (See the Kerisik note for more details; page 319.) The first pressing gives you thicker, richer coconut cream. Adding more water and pressing twice more gives you two lovely liquids that when mixed together can be used as standard coconut milk.

What's that you say? Now that you know all that, you want to use canned coconut milk? All right, babies, buy the Aroy-D brand from Thailand. It's what we use at Fatty Crab, and it's the best I've found.

MARINATE THE BEEF

Drain the dried chili, reserving the soaking water. In a food processor, pulse the chilies, galangal, young ginger, turmeric, and lemongrass to make a puree; use some of the chili soaking water if necessary to get the blender going. The puree should be as smooth as you can possibly get it, but don't stress out if there are some chunky bits. Put the short ribs in a container and rub them thoroughly with the puree (wear gloves, because the turmeric will stain your hands). Let the ribs marinate in the fridge for 48 hours.

MAKE THE SHALLOT PASTE

Puree the shallots, garlic, and palm sugar in a food processor until it's as smooth as possible.

BRAISE THE SHORT RIBS

Preheat the oven to 225°F. Cut pieces of parchment paper to fit inside two deep roasting pans. Toss the marinated short ribs (don't wash off that marinade—that's tasty paste!) with the kosher salt and put them in a single layer in the two roasting pans. Divide the coconut milk, shallot paste, and assam gelugor slices evenly between the roasting pans. Toss the ribs to incorporate all the ingredients. Cover the pans with parchment and cover with a tight-fitting lid or foil. Braise the ribs in the oven until they're fork-tender, 5 to 6 hours.

SERVE THE RENDANG

1. Sprinkle the kerisik over the ribs. It will absorb some of the fat and adhere to the meat, thus increasing the splendiferous flavor.

2. Spoon the ribs into a large serving bowl or platter. Top with the braising liquid, oil and all. (If you're planning to reserve some ribs for another day, keep some of the liquid too.) Drizzle the gula jawa syrup over the meat and sprinkle the kaffir lime leaves on top. Serve the ribs with a bowl of lime wedges and a large bowl of steamed coconut rice.

Chaokoh is a quality brand as well. Please, please don't use the Coco Lopez brand, which is sweetened cream and not what you're after.

LISTEN
Some borderline-cheesy seventies groove, like **Herbie Mann's** *Push Push*, **Grover Washington**'s *Mister Magic*, or, if you want to go contemporary, stuff from **Shawn Lee** or **Luke Vibert.** Silly music that you almost forget is there until you realize you've been bobbing your head for the last hour.

DRINK
Tecate with a rim of lime and salt. Yeah, it's Mexican and this dish is Malaysian, but it's acidic and it's beer! What are you going to do, drink bourbon? You'll get too drunk and fuck the dish up.

BEEF RENDANG p. 234

FATTY BRISKET

Three kindred spirits—pitmaster Robbie Richter, Jori, and I—came up with this profound merging of Southeast Asia and the American South. So profound that it could be both mascot and metaphor for Fatty 'Cue. This brisket is perfection all by itself, but you'll be a happy carnivorous creature if you eat it with Sweet Cilantro Sauce (page 318) and some steamed rice, soft steamed bao, or white bread.

SERVES 12 TO 14

FOR THE DRY RUB
2 cups dried red chilies, such as cayenne

2 cups black peppercorns

Zest of 4 limes

1½ cups kosher salt

FOR THE PASTE
2 tablespoons palm or brown sugar

¼ cup fish sauce

20 garlic cloves, peeled

10 small shallots, peeled

2 inches young fresh ginger, peeled

¼ cup well-stirred coconut milk, preferably Aroy-D brand

FOR THE BRISKET
1 whole untrimmed brisket (about 12 pounds)

MAKE THE DRY RUB
1. In a dry pan over medium heat, toast the dried chilies until they take on a dark color, pressing them down with a wooden spoon to increase contact with the pan, 3 to 4 minutes. Be careful not to inhale over the toasting chilies. Transfer them to a plate, then toast the peppercorns, swirling and shaking them until they crackle lightly and release their aromas, about 3 minutes.
2. Working in batches, grind the dried chilies and black peppercorns to a fine powder in a spice grinder. Stir in the lime zest. Transfer the mixture to a bowl, mix in the salt, and set it aside.

MAKE THE PASTE
In a food processor, combine the palm sugar, fish sauce, garlic, shallots, and young ginger. Pulse to a paste, then add the coconut milk and pulse more to smooth it out. Transfer the paste to a bowl and set it aside.

MARINATE THE BRISKET
1. Put the brisket in a deep container and rub on the dry rub. Make sure to coat it thoroughly.

Whole, untrimmed brisket means don't let anyone cut off the fatty deckle and leave you with only the anorexic lean (or flat). Shank any fool who tries to pull that shit on you.

THE WOOD

You should be using a nice hardwood that's local. Don't use pine, cedar, hickory, or mesquite as the brisket will be in the smoker for a long time and the scents from those woods are so strong that they will overpower the flavor of the meat and seasonings.

2. Next rub all of the paste on every part of the seasoned brisket. Cover the container and refrigerate for at least 24 and up to 48 hours.

COOK THE BRISKET

1. Preheat a smoker to 190°F. Remember, you're using a nice local hardwood but no pine, cedar, hickory, or mesquite, which will overpower the flavors in this dish.

2. Smoke the brisket for 12 to 14 hours, monitoring the temperature the whole time and doing what you can to keep it within 10 degrees of the target temp of 190°F. At 10 hours, and every hour thereafter, check the beef with a skewer. The brisket is done as soon as the skewer goes in and out easily and when you get a jiggle that's borderline erotic upon poking the brisket with a finger. Or, fine, when it's around 150°F in the lean, flat part of the brisket. This is not your Jewish grandma's brisket, so don't expect it to fall apart.

3. Using some large, flat spatulas, remove the brisket from the smoker. Let the meat sit untouched for at least 20 minutes before carving and devouring in order to give the brisket some time to reabsorb its juicy juices.

LISTEN
Hours of southern soul while you drink southern beer and dream of southern girls—that is, if you don't have one of your own.

DRINK
Lone Star. We're smoking brisket here, and that's Texas style.

AND NOW A WORD FROM OUR GUEST COMMENTATOR, ROBBIE RICHTER

"And, now the first-place trophy for brisket, considered by many to be the most difficult meat to cook, goes to . . ." is something you'll often hear at BBQ competitions. If you attended a Kansas City Barbecue Society–sanctioned contest in the Northeast in the early twenty-first century, you've probably heard my team's name called. So listen up.

We'll address the intricacies of cooking, slicing, and serving brisket, but first an anatomy lesson. Brisket (North American Meat Processors Association NAMPS 120) comes from the chest or "roping end" of the cow. Each brisket consists of two muscles, separated by a thick band of fat: the pectoralis major (NAMPS 120A), also known as *the first cut, the lean, or the flat*, and the pectoralis minor (NAMPS 120B), better known as *the second cut, the moist, the point, the nose, or the deckle*. That the smaller, well-marbled, juicier NAMPS 120B, which lies at a 45-degree angle to the flat, is not technically the deckle is not something I'll take a stand on at this particular brisket briefing. Just know that, for me, this is the most important cut of beef.

So how does one choose a brisket? First, don't waste your money on prime. America's most hallowed BBQ joints have been using the select grade for decades. Choose a thick, flexible brisket of no less than 12 pounds. Don't trim it; that knife will come in handy soon enough. As for rubs, I'll leave you to your own devices. Before you put the brisket in the smoker, cut a notch in the thinnest end of the flat, perpendicular to the grain. When you take that brown-crusted fucker out of the pit, it'll serve as an important slicing guide.

Some barbecuers cook 15-pound briskets at 400°F for five hours. Others take the opposite approach: 180°F for 18 hours. I prefer 200°F for approximately 14 to 16 hours. That said, a brisket can't tell time. When it's done, it's done. Briskets have usually finished cooking when the internal temperature hits the high 170s. Be sure to insert your thermometer into the center of the flat. When cooking at such low temps, don't count on the meat to get any more done once it's out of the smoker. There isn't much carryover.

Now that the steaming hot, brown-crusted brisket is oozing beef fat all over your cutting board, let it rest for a bit while you put our morphology lesson to work. Remember that fat seam between the flat and the deckle? Run the back edge of a knife, or for that matter a gloved index finger, along it. The two cuts should separate easily. The flat's now ready for slicing.

Use long, steady strokes to carve sexy slices against the grain—do not saw. The KCBS instructs judges to look for slices as thick as a No. 2 pencil, or approximately ¼ inch. That's a good starting point. Now to further your brisket education, grab one of those slices to see how your brisket turned out. Hold both ends of the slice and gently stretch it. If it breaks too easily, it's overdone; if it snaps back like a rubber band, it's underdone. Ideally, it'll resist with slight tension, then break. If it doesn't, that's what you'll shoot for next time. Or try my favorite method of brisket evaluation, aka the Dougie test, named for a fellow pitmaster who has chosen to remain anonymous. Fold the slice over: if it breaks apart, you've made pot roast; if it snaps back, she needed more time in the cooker.

Now slice the deckle into $7/8$-inch-thick ribbons (surely you have calipers on hand) and then cube them. Judiciously reseason the surface of each cube and place them back in the smoker. Soon the rub and fat will marry, creating a rich crust encasing an inner core of beefy goodness. These meaty chunks of beefy goodness are known as *burnt ends.* Back in the day, they were the crusty scraps that the brisket carvers reserved for themselves. Follow this program and you'll see why I consider burnt ends to be the be all and end all of beef barbecue.

Sweetly and fattily yours,
RR

BRAISED BEEF CHEEKS

Braised beef cheeks have really deep flavor, as though the Beef Fairy had cooked each strand of muscle separately in rich beef stock until supermoist and tender before reassembling them into the original elliptical shape. So, needless to say, I went through an intense period of beef cheek braising. This recipe is an amalgamation of the many twists and turns that my obsession has taken over the years. Once the cheeks have cooked, and your braising liquid is there to act as gravy, you don't need much else, maybe some soft polenta or buttered fresh noodles. I occasionally serve fun garnishes like braised Belgian endive. So rock it if you want to go the extra mile, but as the intense flavor of the cheek will prove, there is really only one star of this meal.

SERVES 6

FOR THE BEEF AND MARINADE

6 dried red chilies, such as cayenne

¼ cup neutral oil, such as grapeseed or canola

6 beef cheeks (about 5 pounds total), trimmed by your butcher of all glands and peripheral connective tissue

Sea salt

Peppermill filled with 2 parts black peppercorns, 1 part Sichuan peppercorns, and 1 part coriander seed

1 cup all-purpose flour

¼ cup Scotch

¼ cup olive oil (the best you can afford)

2 medium yellow onions, quartered

1 large carrot, chopped

1½ heads of garlic, cloves separated and crushed (but left unpeeled)

12 fresh flat-leaf parsley sprigs

1 bottle red wine (not nebbiolo, unless you've got the bread)

2 tablespoons yellow mustard seeds

2 tablespoons sriracha sauce

1 tablespoon tomato paste

2 tablespoons fish sauce

½ pound dried Medjool dates, halved and pitted

FOR THE BRAISING

1 tablespoon fresh roasted coffee beans

1 teaspoon cumin seeds

3 black cardamon pods

4 cups Master Stock (page 322)

Sea salt and freshly ground black pepper

2 tablespoons unsalted butter

Splash of aged balsamic vinegar

BROWN AND MARINATE THE MEAT

1. In a dry pan over medium heat, toast the dried chilies until they take on a dark color, pressing them down with a wooden spoon to increase contact with the pan, 3 to 4 minutes. Be careful not to inhale over the pan while toasting the chilies. Set them aside.

LISTEN
Dinky, "American Guy," just as a jumping-off point.

DRINK
When braising beef of such intensity, drink wine made from the noblest grape, nebbiolo.

2. Heat the neutral oil in a large heavy skillet over medium-high heat.
3. Pat the cheeks dry and season them with salt and a generous grinding of the peppermill mixture. Dredge the cheeks in the flour, shaking off any excess, then add the cheeks, in batches if necessary, to the oil. Cook, turning once, until they're brown and crusty on both sides, about 8 minutes total. Transfer the cheeks to a paper-towel-lined plate to drain.
4. Pour off the excess oil from the pan. Increase the heat to high and deglaze the pan with the Scotch, scraping the brown bits from the bottom of the pan with a wooden spoon as the Scotch bubbles away. When most of the Scotch has evaporated, lower the heat slightly, add the olive oil, and swirl it around the pan to coat the bottom. Add the onions, carrot, garlic, and parsley and cook until the veggies begin to soften, about 6 minutes.
5. Add the red wine and bring it to a boil. Light a match, tilt the pan to pool the wine, and ignite. (In lieu of igniting, one can boil out booze.) After the flame subsides, stir in the mustard seeds, sriracha, tomato paste, fish sauce, dates, and toasted chilies, reduce the heat, and simmer for 15 minutes.
6. Transfer the seared cheeks to a deep platter or bowl. Pour the wine mixture over the cheeks and let it all cool to room temperature, then refrigerate for 48 hours.

BRAISE THE CHEEKS

1. Preheat the oven to 300°F. Remove the submerged cheeks from the fridge and let it all come to room temperature.
2. Make a sachet by wrapping the coffee beans, cumin seeds, and cardamom pods in cheesecloth and tying it closed with kitchen twine. Transfer the cheeks and their liquid to a Dutch oven or an ovenproof stockpot. Add the stock and the sachet to the pot and bring the liquid to a simmer. Cover the pot with a tight fitting lid and then transfer the pot to the oven and braise until the meat is fork-tender, about 3½ hours, though start checking after 2½ hours.
3. Remove the cheeks from the braising liquid and set them aside, then strain the liquid into a saucepan, discarding the solids, and simmer the liquid over medium-high heat until it has reduced by half. Season it with salt and pepper. Warm the cheeks in the saucepan with the reduced liquid, then gently swirl in a couple tablespoons of butter and some aged, gorgeous balsamic vinegar. Serve the cheeks with red wine and chicory salad, such as puntarelle (page 249).

JORI JAYNE BURGER

During our rare bouts of exercise, Jori and I often play a game inadvertently designed to distract us from the task at hand: one-upping each other with ideas for delicious treats. In one particularly memorable episode, on a long hike in upstate New York, she pretty much swept the competition (me) with this concoction, a beef burger that's actually made mostly of smoked pork fatback. It seems so wrong, but you can't help digging in. In the steel cage match between biological desires and intellectual prudence, the biological wins every time.

MAKES ABOUT 6 BURGERS

FOR THE BURGERS
1¾ pounds beef brisket, cut into 1- or 2-inch cubes or ask your butcher to grind it
¾ pound hanger steak, cut into 1- or 2-inch cubes

½ pound smoked fatback (see Note)
Sea salt and freshly ground black pepper

FOR THE KIMCHI SLAW
1 cup Kimchi (page 292), julienned
¼ cup Sambal Aïoli (page 307)

4 scallions, very thinly sliced on the bias

TO FINISH THE BURGERS
Sea salt and freshly ground black pepper
6 Martin's Potato Rolls with sesame seeds

Aïoli (page 307)

MAKE THE PATTIES

1. Using a meat grinder with a medium-coarse disk, grind the brisket and hanger together into a stainless-steel bowl set in a larger bowl filled with ice. As soon as you've completed grinding the beef, put the bowl into the fridge. Next, take the smoked fatback from the fridge and grind it into a separate bowl. Refrigerate it, too, to chill before proceeding.

2. Combine the ground meat and the fat in a large stainless-steel bowl with 2 tablespoons salt and a whole lot of pepper. Using your cold clean hands, mix the fat and the beef together thoroughly but without overmixing. Work quickly. If the fatback begins to melt in your hands as you mix, refrigerate the mixture and resume a little later. Cover the bowl with plastic wrap and stick it in the fridge.

NOTE

Because of the extra-fatty deliciousness of these burgers, they require special skill at the grill. If you lack the confidence to cook something this fatty directly over the coals, use a griddle or cast-iron pan on your grill.

SMOKING THE FAT

As this is a time-consuming process, I recommend smoking 5 pounds of fatback even though you'll need only about ½ pound for the burger mix. Wrapped well in plastic wrap or in a freezer bag, the smoked fatback can hang out in your fridge for up to 1 month and in the freezer for up to 3 months. Preheat your smoker to 150°F and keep it there. Rub the fatback with enough salt and pepper to coat and smoke it for 1½ hours. Transfer the fatback from the smoker (leave the smoker on) to a plate and pop it into the fridge to cool completely. Once it's chilled, return the fatback to the smoker and smoke for another 1½ hours. Transfer it to the fridge once more and let it cool completely.

MAKE THE KIMCHI SLAW

Squeeze the kimchi to remove as much liquid as possible, then transfer it to a bowl and stir in the aïoli and scallions.

FINISH THE BURGERS

1. Start a charcoal fire (or, fine, use a gas grill) and heat clean grill grates over it.
2. Form the meat into about 6 patties, packing them tightly together without handling them too much and melting the fatback with your hands. Season them lightly with salt and pepper, and put them on the grill in a hot spot but not directly over the flame. Remember, these are special high-fat, high-deliciousness patties, which will flare violently if they get too close to burning hot wood or charcoal. (If the previous sentence scared the hell out of you, you should heat a griddle or cast-iron pan on your grill and cook the burgers on it.)
3. Grill the burgers, flipping once, until the fat is sizzling and they are about medium-rare, about 8 minutes total. Be forewarned, my darlings, once all that fat begins to sizzle on the inside, the burgers will cook especially quickly, going from medium-rare to medium before you can finish your first bone shot.
4. Lightly toast the inside of the burger buns, and put a dollop of aïoli on each side. Put a fatty patty onto each bun bottom and top with the kimchi slaw. Close her up and chow down.

LISTEN
Lou Reed, *Transformer*—he gets you ready for a party and can't judge your indulgences.

DRINK:
Bone Shots (page 201)!

SALADS AND VEGETABLES

I eat salad with my hands. This has been true for as long as I can remember—it used to exhaust my mother's patience. I don't think she had an issue with my manual consumption method per se—she, too, is an enthusiastic eater. Rather, her endless "Zakary-use-your-fork!" protests came from an unarticulated guilt-driven devotion to grooming me for successful sleepovers and dinners at friends' tables. As if she couldn't quite bring herself to say, "If you can't learn to eat with your fork, how will you ever make it in this world?"

My rejoinder, almost thirty years later, is that while I might have been uncouth, at least I ate my greens. Now, as a parent myself, I see greater value in my son's appreciation of salad than in his use of the salad fork. Oh, and I still eat salad—whether it's at home or in a rare uptown four-star situation—with my hands, and so does my fiancée, Jori. It seems I made it through childhood, adolescence, and early manhood, and finally found a kindred spirit who understands that metal and delicate greens have no business hanging out together. Drop the fork and see if your salad experience improves. Feel your food. After all, you pick vegetables with your hands, so why not eat them the same way?

RADISH SALAD WITH BOTTARGA AND POACHED EGG

This is the sort of typical home-style salad I'll eat as a late-night supper with some grilled bread or as a first course followed by a roasted fish. What makes it special is the complex salinity of the bottarga di muggine (salted, dried, and pressed mullet roe), which makes simple stuff like radish salad or buttered pasta instantly more exciting. There's also tuna bottarga, but I prefer the texture—a slight waxiness, like caramel—and lower price of the mullet. Whatever egg you choose to use, be it duck or chicken or wild turkey, it should be very fresh and poached so that the white holds its shape and offers a little protein-rich bite while the yolk becomes a thickened version of itself, one that will ooze languorously over your greens. At the restaurant, I achieve this precise balance by using a laboratory-grade immersion circulator. At home I rely on strict attention to my pot of water.

SERVES 4

Sea salt
5 eggs
Freshly ground black pepper
16 French breakfast radishes
Juice of 1 lemon
About 3 tablespoons olive oil (the best you can afford)

3 cups loosely packed baby watercress or any highly flavored, delicate smaller green
Fleur de sel
One 2-inch piece mullet bottarga

1. Bring 4 cups water to a boil in a large straight-sided sauté pan and season with a sprinkle of salt. Have a slotted spoon at the ready. Lower the temperature of the water to produce a gentle simmer. Gently crack 2 eggs and carefully pour them from their shells into the water. Cook them until the white is firm but cloudlike, 3 to 4 minutes. Use a slotted spoon to transfer the cooked eggs to a paper-towel-lined plate to drain. Season with salt and pepper. Cook 2 more eggs, keeping the remaining egg on hand as a spare in case a yolk breaks. Alternatively, a nice 3-minute soft-boiled egg would work for this dish, too.

2. Slice the radishes as thin as possible using a mandoline or a paring knife. Put them in a colander, toss them with a little sea salt, and let them sit for about 5 minutes. Toss the radishes with lemon juice to taste and 2 tablespoons of the olive oil. Set aside.

3. Toss the watercress with just a touch of the remaining olive oil and a light sprinkle of fleur de sel. Divide half of the watercress among four bowls and top with a poached egg. Use the mandoline or a Microplane rasp to thinly shave some of the bottarga over each egg.

4. Distribute the radishes evenly over the eggs, then top them with the remaining watercress and another shaving of bottarga. Finish with the remaining olive oil and a squeeze of lemon juice. Grilled country bread drizzled with olive oil makes it a meal.

LISTEN
Maybe **Stan Getz**'s work with **João Gilberto** and **Astrud Gilberto**—so pretty and so smooth.

DRINK
Leth Gruner Veltliner "Steinagrund"—a little effervescent on the finish, it's easy to drink while you're prepping and works well with the spicy radish.

PUNTARELLE WITH A GOOD BASIC DRESSING

Even though puntarelle (which is a member of the chicory family) is sold in abundance in the greenmarkets of New York—and elsewhere too, I'm sure—too often you can find only the leaves. Don't get me wrong, puntarelle leaves warmed with a little bacon, garlic, olive oil, lemon juice, and salt, and served with some roasted fish or a yummy chicken are great. But what you really want are puntarelle hearts, the tender, pale, dense network of shoots prized by Italians. When you find the hearts, you dress them using the simple sort-of-recipe here. That's right, no amounts given. Cook by taste. Or as I tell my son, "Use the force." *Star Wars* analogies always work on kids.

A few good anchovy fillets
As much puntarelle as you can get
   your hands on
A few cloves of garlic, peeled

Coarse gray sea salt
The best olive oil you can afford
Fresh lemon juice

1. If you're using salt-packed anchovies, rinse them, then soak them for 20 to 30 minutes, changing the water once halfway through. Then drain them. If you're using oil-packed anchovies, drain the oil. Mince the anchovies and set them aside.

2. Remove any damaged outer leaves from the puntarelle and split the head of puntarelle lengthwise. Remove the leaves, reserving them for another use. Cut the hearts into long thin strips and soak them in a bowl of ice water for 30 to 60 minutes. The puntarelle will begin to curl—that's good! Drain it into a colander.

3. Use a mortar and pestle to pound the garlic and anchovies to a paste with some gray sea salt. (You can also chop and then mash the ingredients to a paste on a cutting board with a chef's knife, then scrape it into a bowl.) Stir in a bit of olive oil and fresh lemon juice. Taste. Do you like it? Does it need a little more of this or that? Adjust, then toss it with the puntarelle. Taste again and adjust. Dig in—with your hands.

LISTEN
The Band, "We Can Talk" (and why not the whole *Stage Fright* album?).

DRINK
Like my folks taught me, Frascati on ice! They were broke and living in Italy in the sixties, when, so I'm told, the white wine available really needed that ice.

RADISH SALAD WITH BOTTARGA AND POACHED EGG, p. 248

BRUSSELS SPROUTS WITH HORSERADISH CREAM

Brussels sprouts are one of the highlights of early fall. So is knobby fresh horseradish root. When I start to raid my garden, to make sure I cook or pickle anything that would otherwise croak, I make this gutsy side dish. It's a great way to keep the love alive when you're on your third day of leftovers from some gargantuan piece of pork you cooked a few days earlier.

SERVES 6

3 tablespoons olive oil (the best you can afford)

2 pounds baby Brussels sprouts, stem ends trimmed, any damaged outer leaves removed

Kosher salt and freshly ground black pepper

3 garlic cloves, crushed and peeled

5 fresh thyme sprigs

1½ cups heavy cream

3 tablespoons freshly grated horseradish root

1. Heat the oil in a large straight-sided sauté pan over medium-high heat. Add the Brussels sprouts and cook, stirring occasionally, until well browned but not yet tender, 5 to 7 minutes. Season with salt and pepper. Add the garlic and thyme and cook until the garlic is translucent, about 3 more minutes.
2. Add the cream and horseradish and simmer until the sprouts are tender and the cream has thickened, about 3 minutes more. Season with additional salt and pepper to taste and serve.

LISTEN
The Soft Pack, "Pull Out"— surf punk.

DRINK
Movia's Veliko Bianco— lingering and lovely but equipped with enough acidity to cut through the cream and whatever flavor of fat is attached to your meat.

KERABU MANGO (MANGO SALAD)

Adzmah, my colleague-slash-mentor at Seri Melayu restaurant in Kuala Lumpur, taught me to prepare this traditional salad that's often served as a condiment for a simple fried or steamed fish. One key to its unbelievable tastiness is semiripe mango, when they're pale yellow, still firm, and their sweetness is just beginning to win out over sourness. Another is the small but essential quantity of stock, which gives the salad its satisfying savory quality. If you've got a commitment to authenticity, go on a hunt for small sweet limes, such as the ones called *calamansi* or *limau kasturi*.

SERVES 4

½ cup neutral oil, such as
  grapeseed or canola
1½ tablespoons small dried shrimp
Juice of 1 lime or 2 calamansi or
  limau kasturi if you can find
  them
½ teaspoon sugar
Sea salt
2 semiripe mangoes, peeled and
  coarsely grated on a box grater
1 stalk lemongrass, woody outer
  layers and bottom 1½ inches
  removed, tender inner stalk very
  thinly sliced

½ medium red onion, thinly sliced
½ inch fresh ginger, peeled and
  julienned
2 fresh Thai bird chilies, thinly sliced
  crosswise
2 tablespoons Simple Fish Stock
  (page 326) or Chicken Stock
  (page 324)

1. Heat the oil in a small saucepan over medium-high heat to 350°F (measured on a deep-frying thermometer). Add the dried shrimp and fry them, stirring occasionally, until they're golden and crispy, about 5 minutes. Transfer them to a paper-towel-lined plate to drain.

2. Stir together the lime juice, sugar, and salt to taste in a small bowl until the sugar and salt dissolve. Taste and tweak the seasoning until it tastes really good. Toss the mangoes, lemongrass, onion, ginger, chilies, and shrimp together, then add the lime juice mixture and the fish stock. Taste, adjust the seasoning, and transfer the salad to a serving bowl.

SLICING LEMONGRASS

Lemongrass is very woody, plus it tends to be even tougher in temperate climates (if you live closer to the equator, congratulations!). Those of us who can find only tough, woody stalks have to peel down a few layers to reach the softer inner core. Slice the peeled lemongrass as thin as you possibly can—a Japanese mandoline is the best way to get the job done. When I worked for Daniel Boulud at his eponymous restaurant, the legendary chef Raymond Blanc from Le Manoir Quatre Saisons in England came in to put on a special dinner. He wanted to marinate rabbit in shallots, red wine, and lemongrass. Among other things, I had to slice the lemongrass. While I did, he was constantly walking by, red wine glass in hand, telling me it was too thick, too thick, too thick! I cut my fingers three times on the mandoline trying to achieve the transparency for which he longed. Just keep in mind as you're slicing that, at least according to Monsieur Blanc, your lemongrass can always be thinner.

LISTEN
John Lee Hooker, *Detroit Special*—he was beyond cool.

DRINK
Sighardt Donabaum 2007 Gewürztraminer—a perfect dish for gewürz and perfect gewürz for the dish.

MY GREEN PAPAYA SALAD

Every Southeast Asian country has some variation of green papaya or mango salad. Since it doesn't taste like much (nice texture, though), it's all about the supporting cast as far as delivering flavor goes. And in this version there's such a big cast that you can lose one or two items and the salad will still taste real good. You can even lose the papaya (shhhh) and make it with all the other goodies. Just don't lose the fish sauce, palm sugar, lime juice, or chili—deal?

SERVES 4 TO 6

FOR THE DRESSING
1 tablespoon fresh cilantro root (4 roots), rinsed, scraped, and rinsed again
1 tablespoon minced peeled fresh ginger
1 fresh Thai bird chili, or more to taste

½ teaspoon minced garlic
½ teaspoon minced shallot
2 tablespoons palm or brown sugar, or more to taste
1 tablespoon fish sauce, or more to taste
Juice of 3 limes, or more to taste

FOR THE SALAD
4 Chinese long beans, trimmed
1 cup loosely packed fresh Thai basil leaves
1 cup loosely packed fresh Vietnamese mint (rau ram) leaves
2 cups julienned peeled green (unripe) papaya
2 cups julienned peeled cucumber
1 cup julienned peeled green (unripe) mango

2 cups julienned peeled ripe mango
¾ cup ½-inch-thick pineapple batons (size of a lady's pinkie)
¾ cup julienned fresh long red chilies, such as Anaheim or Hungarian Wax
¾ cup lightly crushed salted roasted peanuts

MAKE THE DRESSING
Use a mortar and pestle to pound (see page 12) all the dressing ingredients until smooth, pounding each ingredient thoroughly before adding the next. Taste and add more fish sauce, lime juice, chili, and/or palm sugar if you want. The flavor's up to you.

MAKE THE SALAD
1. Heat a grill pan, cast-iron skillet, or grill until very hot. Cut the long beans into a manageable size for your pan, if necessary, then char the beans well on all sides, about 4 minutes total. Transfer them to a bowl, cover it tightly with plastic wrap, and let them steam for about 10 minutes. Cut the beans into ½-inch pieces and return them to the bowl.

LISTEN
Mayafra Combo, "Iffilah Ha-Ha"—Sonnie Taylor from Trinidad backed up by some Italian musicians. Beautiful vocals and a moving jazz-funk vibe to keep you dancing and cooking.

DRINK
A tall glass of water a little cooler than room temp. Seriously.

2. Tear the basil and mint leaves. Toss together the long beans with the papaya, cucumber, mango, pineapple, long red chilies, herbs, and the dressing. If you have a large enough mortar or want to work in batches and take the time to make the salad even better, pound the ingredients with the dressing just to bruise them and further infuse the ingredients with the flavor of the dressing. Transfer the dressed salad to a serving bowl and sprinkle with the crushed peanuts.

KERABU TIMUN (CUCUMBER SALAD)

This is another salad taught to me by the generous Adzmah of Seri Melayu restaurant in Kuala Lumpur. She would take me to the market early in the morning, toting her five-year-old son, whom she called Man. I have no idea why. (Did he wish, I always wondered, that she'd called him Boy, at least until his fifth birthday?) When the cucumbers looked especially awesome, she'd buy a heap of them and later grate them and hit them with this liquidy, flavor-packed dressing. I think it's just dandy with grilled goat or lamb.

SERVES 2 AS A SIDE SALAD

½ cup neutral oil, such as
    grapeseed or canola
1 tablespoon dried shrimp
2 tablespoons well-stirred coconut
    milk, preferably Aroy-D brand
1 teaspoon Sambal Belacan (page
    306)
1 English cucumber, coarsely grated
    on a box grater
½ medium red onion, very thinly
    sliced

1 garlic clove, minced
1 tablespoon fish sauce
1 teaspoon freshly ground black
    pepper
Juice of 1 lime
2 tablespoons Chicken Stock (page
    324) or Simple Fish Stock (page
    326), depending on what protein
    you serve this with

1. Heat the oil in a small saucepan over medium-high heat to 350°F (measured on a deep-frying thermometer). Add the dried shrimp and fry them, stirring occasionally, until they're golden and crispy, about 5 minutes. Transfer them to a paper-towel-lined plate to drain. Once the shrimp have cooled, mince them.
2. In a large bowl, mix the coconut milk and sambal belacan. Stir in the cucumber, onion, and garlic, then add the fish sauce, pepper, and lime juice to taste. Add the chicken stock. The salad should be good and moist. Lastly, add the dried shrimp, broken up in a mortar—roughly.

LISTEN
The Stones, *Beggars Banquet*, because it must be played.

DRINK
Assuming you're eating this with goat or lamb, Massolino Barbera d'Alba 2007, which I can drink through a hot day right on into a cool night.

BOK CHOY WITH CLAMS

This is one of my favorite dishes of greens. Briny and sweet bits of clams, tender young bok choy. Even my son, Hudson, eats this up. Fortunately, he likes clams. And I told him the oyster sauce blend is soy sauce.

SERVES 4

Sea salt
1 pound baby bok choy, leaves separated from stalks
2 tablespoons neutral oil, such as grapeseed or canola
2 shallots, thinly sliced
4 garlic cloves, thinly sliced

¼ cup Chicken Stock (page 324)
2 pounds Manila clams, soaked, rinsed, and scrubbed
1 tablespoon soy sauce
2 tablespoons oyster sauce
1 tablespoon dark sesame oil

1. Bring a large pot of water to a boil, salt it until it tastes like the ocean, and set up an ice bath. Add the bok choy leaves to the boiling water and blanch for 1 minute. Use a slotted spoon to transfer the bok choy to the ice bath to stop the cooking. Transfer the bok choy to a paper-towel-lined tray to drain and dry the leaves well.

2. Heat the neutral oil in a large straight-sided sauté pan with a lid over medium heat. Add the shallots, cook for 1 minute, then add the garlic. Cook, stirring occasionally, until both are translucent, about 3 minutes.

3. Add the stock, increase the heat, and bring to a boil. Add the clams, cover the pan, and cook, shaking the pan once, just until the clams open, discarding any that haven't opened after 5 minutes. Remove the clams, reserving the cooking liquid, and remove the clams from the shells, discarding the shells.

4. Roughly chop the clams on a cutting board and transfer them to a bowl. Add a couple of spoonfuls of the reserved cooking liquid to keep them moist.

5. In a small bowl, whisk together the soy sauce, oyster sauce, and sesame oil. Set aside.

6. Return the pan to the stove and heat it over medium heat. Add the blanched bok choy leaves to the stock mixture, toss to coat, and cook until the leaves are heated through. Add the clams and toss a few times to combine. Pour onto a serving platter, season with a little salt, and drizzle with the oyster sauce mixture.

LISTEN
Lee "Scratch" Perry & the Upsetters. A nappy, dreaded, white hippy who worked as the sound engineer at the Metronome in Burlington, Vermont, turned me on to Lee Perry. White dudes with dreads . . . Right?

DRINK
2008 Heidi Schrock Weissburgunder 2008—its mineral depth just rocks it with the clams and oyster sauce.

SMOKY EGGPLANT AND CHICKEN SALAD

This earthy salad of silky eggplant flesh and tender, toothsome chicken was recently voted the best of the many that Jori and I made at my uncle Jim's house in Steamboat Springs, Colorado. The eggplant tastes best cooked in a smoker or, as Jim does it, on a standard backyard grill decked out with a tray of wet hickory chips. Neither frosty temperatures nor snow deters him from blazing up the grill. They shouldn't deter you either.

SERVES 4

2 medium Italian eggplants
Sea salt
1 whole bone-in, skin-on chicken breast
Freshly ground black pepper
2 tablespoons neutral oil, such as grapeseed or canola
3 jalapeño chilies, finely diced
4 garlic cloves, finely diced
1 tablespoon rice vinegar, or more to taste

2 tablespoons Gula Jawa Syrup (page 341), or more to taste
1 tablespoon dark sesame oil, or more to taste
2 tablespoons fish sauce, or more to taste
6 scallions, white parts only, sliced on the diagonal into ¼-inch pieces
¼ cup celery leaves
1 tablespoon sesame seeds

1. Prepare a charcoal fire, keeping the coals toward one side of the grill. Once they burn down to embers, throw a few hickory chips on top. Wash and dry the eggplants and use a fork to pierce them several times. Put the eggplants on the grill over the side with no coals, close the lid, and let them take in the flavorful smoke for about 5 minutes. Then move them over the heat to char, turning them every 3 to 4 minutes, until they have softened, about 20 minutes total.

2. Remove the eggplants from the heat and let them cool. Then split them lengthwise and scrape their flesh into a bowl with a fork, discarding the skins.

3. Meanwhile, bring water to a boil in a medium saucepan. Add 1 tablespoon salt (and anything that you think will improve the flavor of the chicken you'll poach in the liquid, like garlic, ginger, scallion tops, onions, chilies, etc.). Reduce the heat so the water is at a simmer and add the chicken breast. Simmer for 5 minutes and then turn off the heat, cover the pot, and let the chicken sit in the water until it's cooked through, about 20 more minutes. Remove the chicken from the braising liquid and let the breast cool at room temperature (and save that tasty broth for some other use!). When cool enough to handle, shred the chicken from the bone into the bowl with the eggplant and season with salt and pepper.

LISTEN
Robin Trower, *Bridge of Sighs*. The tune "Too Rolling Stoned" has become a guitar rock anthem for me.

DRINK
Les Crêtes, Torrette 2006. An obscure grape, petite rouge, that's lean and perfect with smoke, whether it's meat or veg.

4. Heat the neutral oil in a medium sauté pan over medium-high heat. Add the jalapeños and garlic and cook until they're just soft, about 3 minutes. Reduce the heat to low, then add the vinegar, gula jawa syrup, sesame oil, and fish sauce. Cook, stirring, for 1 minute and remove from the heat.

5. Add the scallions and celery leaves to the eggplant and chicken and toss to coat. Add the sesame seeds and season to taste with more fish sauce, rice vinegar, and gula jawa syrup. The salad should taste smoky, salty, sweet, and slightly acidic.

ASPARAGUS KERABU, p. 262

ASPARAGUS KERABU (ASPARAGUS SALAD)

Not an authentic *kerabu* (a category of Malaysian salads), this does, however, include *kerisik*, the dry toasted coconut that's a hallmark of *kerabu* authenticity. Its unmistakable fragrance and texture really add to the ribbons of raw asparagus plus charred tips. I came up with this dish specifically for Squab with Sichuan Pepper (page 120), but it goes well with any roasted or grilled meat.

SERVES 4 TO 6

28 green asparagus stalks, trimmed
Juice of 1 lime, or more to taste
2 tablespoons fish sauce, or more
   to taste
½ cup roughly chopped fresh
   Vietnamese mint (rau ram)
   leaves

1 cup bean sprouts
1 small red onion, very thinly sliced
2 fresh Thai bird chilies, julienned
1 tablespoon julienned peeled
   young fresh ginger
1 cup Kerisik (page 319)
1 cup fresh cilantro leaves

1. Cut off the tops of the asparagus approximately ½ inch below the tip and set the tips aside. Using a mandoline or vegetable peeler, slice the asparagus stems lengthwise into long, thin ribbons. Toss them in a bowl with the lime juice and fish sauce and set the mixture aside for at least 15 minutes.

2. Heat a dry cast-iron pan or griddle over high heat and char the asparagus tips on all sides, stirring, 2 to 3 minutes. Then transfer them to a large mixing bowl.

3. Once the tips have cooled, add the mint, bean sprouts, onion, chilies, and ginger and toss well. Then add the asparagus stems with their liquid and the kerisik, toss well, and season to taste with more lime juice and fish sauce. Transfer the salad to a bowl and sprinkle on the cilantro leaves.

LISTEN
Marvin Gaye, "What's Going On?"—the melancholy soul vibe that moves you in more ways than a naked chiropractor.

DRINK
Ezio Voyat Chambave "La Gazzella" 2004—a unique moscato that I can't seem to drink enough of.

KANG KONG BELACAN

Kang kong (also called *Chinese water spinach* and, less appetizingly, *water convolvulus*) is a quirky, hollow-stemmed green. Seasoned with the Malay supercondiment sambal belacan, it's one of the most popular dishes in Malaysia, served with all sorts of rice and chicken dishes. This is the version I serve at Fatty Crab, which is nearly identical to what I remember from the shops in Malaysia. The only difference is that I've muted the heat, something I do for nearly every dish at Fatty Crab, against my will, adjusting it down to suit the local tolerance.

The Sambal Belacan is the most time-consuming element of this dish. If I were you, I'd make a batch to keep in your pantry so you can add a spoonful here, a pinch there. In that case, this dish becomes a quick, perfect lunch with rice.

SERVES 2 TO 4 AS A SIDE

- 2 tablespoons neutral oil, such as grapeseed or canola
- 2 tablespoons Sambal Belacan, toasted (page 306)
- 1 pound kang kong (Chinese water spinach), trimmed (see Note)

Heat a wok over high heat. Add the oil, wait 20 seconds, and then add the sambal. Let it sizzle for 30 seconds, then add the kang kong. Cook, stirring, until nearly all of the kang kong is wilted, about 3 minutes. Turn off the heat and continue tossing. Lift the kang kong out of the wok using tongs or chopsticks, leaving any excess oil behind. Enjoy it immediately as a side dish or a modest meal with steamed rice.

NOTE

Kang kong has sharply pointed leaves and thin hollow stems. The lower leaves on the stem are the woodiest; I trim those and the smaller stems away from the main trunk before cooking. You can find the vegetable at Asian grocery stores or farmers' markets. It's a fairly delicate green, so cook it the same day you buy it.

LISTEN
The Dead Weather, *Horehound*—this bluesy rock from Jack White, et al., can hang with the intensity of sambal belacan.

DRINK
Sazerac—lean, focused drinking. There's a reason this cocktail shows up elsewhere in this book. Chill a short rocks glass. Pour 2 ounces **rye** and ½ ounce **simple syrup** into a shaker with **ice**. Stir well, add 5 dashes **Peychaud's bitters** and 2 dashes of **angostura bitters**, and stir some more until the shaker has frosted. Rinse the rocks glass with ½ ounce **absinthe**, then strain and pour your drink. Rub the rim of the glass with a piece of **lemon peel**, then drop it in.

NASI ULAM

This is a highly seasoned rice salad, common to the rural, predominantly Muslim areas of Malaysia, where it's often the main dish along with some raw or blanched veggies and *sambal*. I love the complexity: three different types of processed seafood provide the base salinity, turmeric brightens the color, and herbs and lemongrass lend high notes. It's an elegant use of rice that isn't typical in the West. Of all the recipes in this book, this one has the most full-on Asian shopping list, so if you're following it to the letter, a Chinatown trip is required. Or you can use the ingredients as a guide—just one of the seafood ingredients along with some fish sauce would be enough to make it taste authentic.

SERVES 4 TO 6 AS A SIDE

¼ pound salt mackerel
3 tablespoons neutral oil, such as grapeseed or canola
¼ cup dried shrimp
¼ cup Kerisik (page 319)
2 tablespoons chopped fresh turmeric
1¼ tablespoons belacan, toasted (page 333)
5 cups steamed jasmine rice
1 tablespoon freshly ground black pepper
1½ teaspoons sugar

Sea salt
4 shallots, thinly sliced
1¼ tablespoons thinly sliced lemongrass
1¼ tablespoons thinly sliced galangal flower, if you can find it
18 fresh Vietnamese mint (rau ram) leaves
12 fresh Thai basil leaves
12 fresh mint leaves
8 fresh kaffir lime leaves, stems and center veins discarded and leaves thinly sliced

1. Rinse the salt fish very well with cold water. Peel off the skin and remove the bones, keeping only the flesh. Add the flesh to a bowl, cover with cold water, and refrigerate overnight, changing the water once.

2. Drain the fish, pat it dry, then thinly slice it. Heat the oil in a small pan over medium-high heat. Fry the fish, flipping it once, until golden, about 4 minutes. Transfer to a paper-towel-lined plate to drain thoroughly, then break it into small pieces.

3. Soak the dried shrimp in warm water for 10 minutes, then drain and let dry on a towel for 10 minutes.

4. Working with one ingredient at a time, use a mortar and pestle to pound (see page 12) the kerisik, dried shrimp, turmeric, and belacan, transferring each to a mixing bowl once it's thoroughly pounded before adding the next. Toss them all lightly to combine.

5. Gently stir the rice into the pounded ingredients, add the salt mackerel, then season with the pepper, sugar, and 1½ teaspoons salt. Add the remaining ingredients and toss lightly to blend the flavors until the rice salad is beautiful to behold. Serve right away.

LISTEN
Mirage, "Lady Operator." Whenever I listen to it, I feel like I've just landed on a faraway, happy planet.

DRINK
Cold, sour buttermilk. The acidity with the warm rice and funky fish bits is so good.

ARUGULA AND BOILED PEANUT SALAD WITH CHILI VINEGAR

I grew up eating roasted peanuts, so the texture of the boiled version common at roadside stands in the South was all new to me. Boiling turns the crunch into beanlike creaminess—after all, peanuts are legumes. This bright, simple salad is a great complement to any roasted protein, but I especially like it alongside sausage-gravy-poached chicken!

SERVES 4 TO 6

2 pounds raw unshelled peanuts (you'll have some extra for snacking)

⅓ cup kosher salt

2 generous handfuls of arugula

2 cups thinly shaved radicchio

¾ cup chili vinegar (page 106)

Fleur de sel

1. Rinse the peanuts and then put them in a large pot with 8 cups water and the salt. Bring the water to a boil and let them boil away for about 3 hours, adding more hot water as necessary to keep the peanuts covered. Crack one of the peanut shells open and have a taste. It should be salty, soft, and creamy, like a perfectly cooked bean. I've heard that some people boil their peanuts for even longer. I don't know why; maybe they don't have teeth? Anyhow, 3 hours is plenty of time. Shell enough of the peanuts to give you about 2 cups. Save the rest for snacking.

2. Toss all the salad components together, season with fleur de sel to taste, and eat with your hands.

LISTEN
Ten Years After, *Ssssh*—the whole album rocks . . . and the version of "Good Morning Little Schoolgirl" is on the money.

DRINK
Rotenberger from Domaine Marcel Deiss—a wine from Alsace that's light and sweet, and I mean that in the best possible sense of those adjectives.

SNACKS

When one should snack: late at night, for sure. Definitely in the afternoon. Around dinner, too. Oh, and late morning! Fuck it, early morning, too. In other words, all the time. I find that some of my favorite meals are actually just snacks anyway, which, either on purpose or not, end up killing hunger with small bursts of delicious flavor. All the recipes in this chapter are a starch and a veg, or another snack, away from a full-on feast.

FRIED MORTADELLA SANDWICH

If you've never heard of a fried bologna sandwich, bear in mind that there are people who've never heard of eating the mellow, spongy cold cut any other way. Mortadella, a most exquisite bologna from Bologna, Italy, is pale pink, like its American cousin, but the similarities end there. Mortadella is infinitely more delicious—delicately spiced, studded with lard, and dotted, too, with pistachios or olives. This sandwich merges this fine Italian product with one of the American South's greatest culinary quirks. Patè di capperi is a salty Sicilian condiment that stands in for mustard and mayo and should be made the day before you plan to fry the mighty meat.

MAKES 4 SANDWICHES

FOR THE PÂTÉ DI CAPPERI
1 cup salted capers, well rinsed, or vinegar-packed capers, drained
¾ cup white wine vinegar
⅓ cup olive oil (the best you can afford)
Pinch of hot red pepper flakes

FOR THE SANDWICHES
2 fresh eggs, lightly beaten
1 cup all-purpose flour
2 cups panko bread crumbs
2 cups neutral oil, such as grapeseed or canola
Four ⅓-inch-thick slices mortadella, about 6 inches in diameter
Sea salt and freshly ground black pepper
4 brioche hamburger buns or good ciabatta or baguette
1 cup fresh whole-milk ricotta

MAKE THE PÂTÉ DI CAPPERI
Put the capers into a small bowl and add the vinegar, olive oil, and hot pepper flakes. Refrigerate overnight. Pulse the mixture in a food processor or blender to form a rough paste. You can store it, covered, in the refrigerator for up to 2 weeks. Bring it to room temperature before you use it.

MAKE THE SANDWICHES
1. Line up 3 shallow bowls next to the stove, one with the beaten eggs, one with the flour, and one with the panko.
2. Heat the oil in a large straight-sided sauté pan over medium-high heat until 375°F and oil ripples appear across its surface but before it begins to smoke. Meanwhile, cut each slice of mortadella into quarters to make four approximate triangles.
3. Dredge the mortadella slices in the flour, then the beaten egg, then the panko.

LISTEN
Black Devil *Disco Club* EP—you'll need to dance before, during, and after eating this sandwich or your ass will look like the ricotta.

DRINK
An old fashioned, from Dottore Dave Wondrich and his definitive book, *Imbibe!* In the bottom of a whiskey glass, dissolve ½ teaspoon **sugar** in ½ teaspoon **water**. Add 2 dashes of **angostura bitters**, a **cube of ice**, a **lemon twist**, and 2 ounces of **whiskey**.

Working in batches, fry the mortadella, flipping it once, until each side is golden brown, 6 to 8 minutes total. Transfer it to a paper-towel-lined tray to drain. Season the fried mortadella with salt and pepper.

4. Spread each side of the buns with 1 tablespoon pâté di caperi (2 tablespoons per sandwich). Place the mortadella on top of one bun half and then add a liberal scoop of the ricotta. Top with the other half of the bun and serve immediately.

SARDINE OMELET, p. 273

KIELBASA BRUSCHETTA

Sikorski Meat Market is one of the last great Polish butchers in Greenpoint, Brooklyn. It has a massive, two-door, roll-in smoker made of cast iron, which they use to smoke all of their own sausage, belly, and pork loin. It's the kind of thing you just don't see anymore. I used to roll by early in the morning, fresh faced and with an empty bag ready to fill with smoked meats. The guys who ran the place were generally in the back, singing, shooting vodka, and grinding meat after a long night of drinking. By the time I arrived, they were usually in a state of giddy delirium that made it nearly impossible to get focused service but always resulted in generous "tastings" during my wait.

The kielbasa bruschetta I made from their peerless sausage was on the menu at the Chickenbone Café, well loved by the both the old guard and the new non-Polish denizens who began taking over Williamsburg in the early nineties. On the night of the famous 2003 blackout, we set up a grill outside the restaurant, and I cooked whatever we had in house out on the sidewalk. Hot, tired, and hungry people trekked over the Williamsburg Bridge and were greeted by Billy Campion, who had a band called Vic Thrill (maybe he still does?), in a silvery, glittered turban. He powered his musical gear with the engine of his ancient Suburban and put on a show next to my grill. He played one continuous jam strung together with looped recordings of him tempting the crowd to eat the "kielbasa bruschetta . . . it's really . . . quite remarkable." You said it, Billy.

SERVES 4 AS A SNACK

Two ½-inch-thick slices fresh country bread, halved

2 teaspoons olive oil (the best you can afford)

½ pound smoked kielbasa, cut into ¼-inch dice

1 sour pickle, cut into ¼-inch dice

2 tablespoons Pulaski stone-ground mustard

2 tablespoons finely chopped fresh dill

Coarse sea salt and freshly ground black pepper

1. Preheat the oven to 375°F. Put the bread directly on the oven rack and toast until the surface is golden and crispy and the interior is still plenty squishy, about 10 minutes. Set the bread aside.

2. Heat the oil in a sauté pan over medium heat. Add the kielbasa and cook, stirring occasionally, until it's just warmed through (it's already cooked). Meanwhile, dump the pickle, mustard, and dill into a medium bowl and stir to combine. Mix in the kielbasa gently with a wooden spoon until you feel good about it.

3. Spoon the kielbasa mixture onto the toasts and season with the salt and pepper. Eat.

LISTEN
Greg and Duane Allman, "Morning Dew"—the brothers recorded this in the late sixties. It's got some love.

DRINK
A bottle of Polish vodka with a Zywiec beer back.

SARDINE OMELET

This is a snack for kings! Or if I were king, it would be my royal snack. Because as you know by now, this king's favorite fish is the sardine, and he adores the omelet's topping of crunchy pork. The playful presentation—fish heads poking out of an eggy blanket—always makes the king smile.

MAKES 1 OMELET

2 whole fresh head-on sardines, scaled and cleaned
Sea salt and freshly ground black pepper
2 tablespoons olive oil (the best you can afford)
2 fresh eggs
1½ teaspoons freshly ground green peppercorns

1 garlic clove, minced
½ medium shallot, minced
1 teaspoon minced fresh cilantro root
One 2-inch-square piece guanciale, cut into matchsticks
1 teaspoon trout roe
Small handful of fresh cilantro leaves

1. Season the sardines liberally on both sides with salt and black pepper. Heat 1 tablespoon of the oil in an 8-inch nonstick or black steel sauté pan over medium-high heat until it's hot but not smoking. Sear the sardines on both sides until golden, about 3 minutes per side. Transfer them to a plate and set aside.

2. In a small bowl, whisk the eggs with ¼ teaspoon salt, the green peppercorns, garlic, shallot, and cilantro root.

3. Heat the remaining tablespoon of oil over medium heat in the same pan in which you cooked the sardines. Throw in the guanciale and cook, stirring occasionally, until it's lightly browned and some of the fat has rendered, 2 to 3 minutes.

4. Pour in the egg and stir briefly. Cook, undisturbed, for about 20 seconds, then stir again, letting the liquid egg flow under that which has set. Sprinkle the roe over the egg. When the edges of the egg begin to pull away from the pan and the egg is set but still jiggly, slide the still round omelet onto a serving plate. Put the sardines on the egg, each with its head extending past the edge of the omelet. Fold the omelet over the fish to wrap them in their blanket. Garnish with the cilantro leaves.

LISTEN
Daniel Wang, "Pistol Oderso"—electro-disco that reminds me of a forty-eight-hour bender I had in Bangkok a while back.

DRINK
Sinner's Buck, a Fatty concoction made with Mekhong, keeping the Thai spirit alive. Shake 1 ounce **Mekhong Thai spiced rum**, ½ ounce **Chartreuse**, and the juice of 1 **Meyer lemon** briefly with **ice** (about 3 shakes and that's it) and strain into a highball glass. Top off with 2 ounces **Boylan ginger ale**. Stir gently and add fresh ice. Stab **candied ginger** with a black toothpick; garnish glass.

JÁMON IBÉRICO AND SHISHITO PEPPERS

As chili season approaches toward the end of August and early September, I start craving this snack of the gods. When I'm feeling spendy, I'll buy a leg of the dear pata negra, the air-dried hams of the acorn-grazing black beast of the Extremadura, in preparation for the arrival of the vegetal, mildly spicy, thin-skinned shishito pepper. (If you can't find them, its almost interchangeable Spanish cousin, the padrón, works too.) When they do arrive, it's straight into the hot pan they go, until they blister, dramatically puff up, then deflate. Then the ham is taken from its dark, cool hiding place and the snacking begins. Eat the peppers and ham by hand; there's no other way.

SERVES 2

¼ cup olive oil (the best you can afford)
6 ounces shishito peppers
Fleur de sel

3 ounces Jamón Ibérico, thinly sliced into small irregular pieces, preferably by hand

1. Heat a cast-iron pan over medium-high heat until it's nice and hot, then pour in the oil and heat it. Add the peppers and let them spit and blister, periodically shaking the pan, until they puff up and then, as if taking one last breath, deflate, about 4 minutes.

2. Season the peppers with the fleur de sel, then spill them into a pretty, rustic bowl. With the casual elegance of a cultured gentleman (or gentlewoman) farmer, toss the thin-sliced ham on top, drive a wooden spoon into the center of the peppers, and stir just enough to get a little chili oil to coat the fatty ham slices. Eat with your hands.

LISTEN
Pere Ubu, *Dub Housing*—like jámon Ibérico, this album is pure inspiration.

DRINK
A cold bottle of Txakoli, preferably poured in a long, thin stream from on high.

OTAK-OTAK

Otak is the Malaysian word for brain. *Otak chai* means "hot or melted brain," a comical diagnosis for absentmindedness that shifts blame from person to equatorial location. Say "otak" twice and you're referring to this banana-leaf-wrapped combination of sliced fish and fish paste. I guess it bears some resemblance to brain. In lieu of fresh mackerel, I use salted mackerel to make the fish paste and appease my desire for the extra-funky, then I roll the paste into balls and deep-fry them (no banana leaf necessary), which gives you a crunchy exterior that encourages sustained drinking.

MAKES ABOUT 40 FISH BALLS

FOR THE SAMBAL

2 fresh Thai bird chilies, minced
1 garlic clove, minced
1 shallot, minced

Juice of ½ lime
1 tablespoon cincalok

FOR THE FISH BALLS

1 lemongrass stalk, woody outer layers and bottom 1½ inches removed, tender inner stalk thinly sliced
4 fresh Thai bird chilies, thinly sliced
2 inches fresh turmeric, peeled
1 tablespoon ground coriander
¼ teaspoon freshly ground white pepper
4 shallots, thinly sliced
4 fresh kaffir lime leaves, stems and center veins discarded
1 pound cod fillets, cut into 1-inch chunks

¼ pound salt mackerel, boned and skinned, or 4 oil-packed anchovies
2 fresh eggs
⅔ cup well-stirred coconut milk, preferably Aroy-D brand
2 tablespoons rice flour
About 6 cups neutral oil, such as grapeseed or canola
2 cups panko bread crumbs, finely ground in a food processor

MAKE THE SAMBAL

Stir together all the sambal ingredients. Set the mixture aside or refrigerate if you're making it more than 5 hours in advance.

MAKE THE FISH BALLS

1. Use a mortar and pestle to pound (see page 12) the lemongrass, chilies, turmeric, ground coriander, pepper, shallots, and lime leaves to a smooth paste, pounding each ingredient thoroughly before adding the next. Transfer the chili paste to a medium bowl.

2. Pulse the cod and salt mackerel in a food processor to chop and combine. Add

LISTEN
Frank Zappa, "Directly from My Heart to You"—electric fiddle blues from an unmitigated, audacious genius.

DRINK
Nothing less than the full bouquet and luscious mouthfeel of a Corton-Charlemagne.

the eggs and pulse briefly. Add the chili paste and pulse briefly. Add the coconut milk, and, yep, pulse briefly. Gradually add the rice flour, a tablespoon at a time, pulsing to incorporate each addition, just until you can form a ball with the mixture (you might not use all the rice flour).

3. Fill a wide straight-sided sauté pan with 3 inches of oil and heat it over medium-high heat until the oil reaches 375°F (measured on a deep-frying thermometer).

4. Use wet hands to roll the cod mixture into 2-inch balls. Roll the balls in the ground panko to coat them evenly, then transfer them to the hot oil in batches. Fry the balls, occasionally prodding them so they rotate in the oil, until they're golden brown all over, 3 to 4 minutes. Use a slotted spoon to transfer them to a paper-towel-lined tray to drain. Serve in a bowl with the sambal alongside to dip in.

THREE LITTLE FISHES

ROUGET SANDWICHES

Bright red with yellow highlights, rouget (also known as red mullet) is a strikingly sexy, boldly flavored little fishy. It deserves your full attention in the pan, because it can dry out on you like "clk!" (That was me, snapping.) The rouget and my rouillesque potato emulsion are high-class for sure, but the hot dog bun is delectably low-brow, so the sandwich is like a princess wearing a Snuggie.

MAKES 4 SANDWICHES

FOR THE ROUILLE

3 medium Yukon Gold potatoes, peeled

7 garlic cloves, 4 crushed and peeled and 3 minced

Sea salt

1 tablespoon saffron threads, plus a pinch more

1 egg yolk

2 tablespoons pastis

½ cup olive oil (the best you can afford)

1 lemon

TO FINISH THE SANDWICH

4 Pepperidge Farm hot dog rolls, toasted

8 skin-on rouget fillets

About 2 tablespoons olive oil (the best you can afford)

Coarse sea salt and freshly ground black pepper

1 fennel bulb, outer layer discarded

MAKE THE ROUILLE

1. Add the potatoes and crushed garlic to a large pot of salted water and bring it to a boil. Cook at a lazy boil for 45 minutes, then add 1 tablespoon of the saffron to the cooking water and cook until the potatoes offer no resistance to the poke of a paring knife, about 5 minutes more. Drain the potatoes in a colander, reserving the cooking liquid.

2. Discard the garlic cloves and pass the potatoes through a ricer into the bowl of a stand mixer fitted with a whisk attachment (or into a food processor). Add the minced garlic, egg yolk, the remaining pinch of saffron, and the pastis and mix on low speed to blend.

3. When the mixture is well combined, raise the speed to medium and drizzle in the oil, whisking until smooth and creamy. Stir in a squeeze of lemon juice.

MAKE THE SANDWICH

1. Heat a cast-iron or stainless-steel pan over medium-high heat.

2. Lightly toast the hot dog buns and then spread them liberally with the rouille.

LISTEN
Herb Alpert & the Tijuana Brass, *South of the Border*—a good-time, horn-blowin' fiesta!

DRINK
Pallagrello Bianco, preferably Terre del Principe from Caserta in Campania, Italy. It's a wine made for seafood with strong Mediterranean flavors.

3. Rub the rouget with some of the olive oil and season with salt and pepper. Pour 1 tablespoon of oil into your hot pan. Cook the fish skin side down until almost all of the flesh has gone from iridescent to opaque, about 2 minutes. Flip the fish over onto a plate so they can cool for a minute or two, skin side up.

4. Slice the fennel paper-thin on a mandoline.

5. Put 2 rouget fillets on each hot dog bun. Top each with the sliced fennel, coarse salt, and freshly ground black pepper.

SARDINE SANDWICHES

Like Pasta con Sarde (page 90), this sandwich celebrates the flawless combination of sardines, pine nuts, and raisins but with a different starch. I do this not for lack of other ideas, but because this trinity is a powerful force in the universe. I must obey.

MAKES 4 SANDWICHES

2 tablespoons pine nuts
2 tablespoons raisins
½ cup olive oil (the best you can afford)
1 medium white onion, thinly sliced
2 garlic cloves, crushed and peeled
1 fennel stem, thinly sliced, fronds chopped and reserved for garnish

3 tablespoons tomato puree (page 28 or store-bought)
8 fresh sardine fillets
Kosher salt and freshly ground black pepper
4 Pepperidge Farm hot dog buns
½ cup roughly chopped fresh flat-leaf parsley
Zest of ½ lemon

1. Preheat the oven to 350°F. Spread the pine nuts on a baking sheet and lightly toast them in the oven, shaking the pan once until they're lightly colored and aromatic, about 3 minutes. Spill them onto a plate to cool.

2. Meanwhile, soak the raisins in warm water until they plump up. (I like to season the water with ½ teaspoon sugar and a splash of booze like anisette or cognac. Totally optional, though.)

3. Heat 3 tablespoons of the olive oil in a large sauté pan over medium heat. Add the onion, garlic, and fennel stem and cook until they're soft and translucent, about 6 minutes. Add the tomato puree and bring it to a simmer. Cook until it has thickened slightly, about 6 minutes. Strain the sauce through a sieve, discarding the solids, and set it aside. (This sauce will keep covered and refrigerated for up to 2 days. Warm it before you use it.)

4. Drain the raisins, pat them dry with paper towels, then mix them with the toasted pine nuts.

5. Heat a cast-iron or stainless-steel pan over medium-high heat. Rub the sardine fillets on both sides with 2 tablespoons of olive oil. Add the remaining 3 tablespoons of oil to the pan, tilting it to cover the surface. Season the fillets on both sides with salt and pepper, then add them skin down to the hot pan. Cook until the flesh turns opaque, about 3 minutes, and then flip them over; count to 10 and transfer them to a plate to cool.

6. Toast the hot dog buns in a toaster or on a griddle and spread the tomato-fennel sauce inside each one. Put 2 sardine fillets in each bun and garnish with the toasted-pine-nut-raisin mixture, a sprinkling of chopped parsley, fennel fronds, and some lemon zest.

LISTEN
Jimi Hendrix, "Second Time Around"—early, raw Hendrix. Hits a groove and sticks. It's actually a sort of version two of "Get That Feeling."

DRINK
The same Pallagrello Bianco you drank with your rouget sandwich.

ANCHOVY SANDWICHES

Anchovy, that which gives flavors unto others and asks for nothing in return. Anchovies are either spurned or adored, so with this recipe you're either in or out. Obviously I'm in, especially with high-fat butter, fresh, crisp radishes, and pricey-but-worth-it Sicilian anchovies.

SERVES 4

16 oil-packed Sicilian anchovy fillets
8 tablespoons (1 stick) high-fat
   French butter, softened
4 small ciabatta rolls
4 breakfast radishes, very thinly
   sliced

Coarse sea salt
¼ cup roughly chopped fresh flat-
   leaf parsley

1. On a cutting board, chop the anchovy fillets, almost mashing them to a paste with a knife. Mash together the anchovies and butter.
2. Spread both sides of each roll with the anchovy butter. Add a thin layer of radishes and a sprinkling of the salt and parsley. You'll be a superstar if you have plates of these little sammies for guests to nosh on. Nosh on, I say; nosh on.

LISTEN
Le Tigre, "Deceptacon" (the DFA remix)—jumpy, irreverent fun to get your party hoppin'.

DRINK
More Pallagrello Bianco.

OYSTER BANH MI

I served a vaguely traditional pork sausage banh mi back in the days of the Chickenbone Café. This is not that. It has mortadella standing in for the mysterious cold cuts you often see beneath the pickled carrots and daikon and cilantro in authentic banh mi. And it's piled, po' boy-like, with fried oysters. Working within the permissive banh mi format, just about anything is possible. To the version available at the Upper West Side Fatty Crab, we added braised pig's feet. (I turn my head for one minute and that rascal Corwin has shmeared one side of the bread with a pork skin and sardine nam prik!) Now you know why the sandwich creeps on to my menu just about everywhere I go. Maybe I'm paranoid, but I think it's after me.

SERVES 4

FOR THE PICKLES
3 tablespoons fish sauce
1 cup rice vinegar
5 tablespoons honey
1 tablespoon ground dry-roasted
    chili, such as cayenne

One 6-inch daikon radish, julienned
1 large carrot, julienned

FOR THE OYSTERS
4 cups neutral oil, such as
    grapeseed or canola
2 cups all-purpose flour
1 cup cornstarch

3 tablespoons kosher salt
3 dozen oysters, shucked
Sea salt

FOR THE SANDWICHES
Four 6-inch pieces light, crusty
    baguette, split
½ cup Sambal Aïoli (page 309)

8 thin slices mortadella
1 cup fresh cilantro leaves

MAKE THE PICKLES

1. In a small saucepan over medium-low heat, heat the fish sauce, vinegar, honey, and ground chili, stirring occasionally, until the honey is dissolved. Adjust the seasoning, if necessary, so the liquid is sweet, salty, and sour. Let the mixture cool to room temperature.
2. Put the daikon and carrot in separate containers and divide the liquid equally between them. Cover and refrigerate for at least 1 hour and up to a day. Mix them together when you're ready to use them.

FRY THE OYSTERS

1. Heat the oil in a medium saucepan to 375°F (measured on a deep-frying thermometer).

LISTEN
!!! (Pronounced chick-chick-chick), *Louden Up Now*—proving that post-punk never died; it just got so much fucking better!

DRINK
Step up to the cool, crisp taste of a giant Asahi. Take a sip!

2. Sift together the flour, cornstarch, and kosher salt. Gently dredge the oysters in the flour mixture. Dust off the excess flour and fry the oysters, in batches, until they're golden brown, about 2 minutes per batch. Transfer the oysters as they're fried to a paper-towel-lined plate to drain and season with sea salt. Sample an oyster or 2 (you need 8 per sandwich, but you have 36; see, I got you extra. Who loves you?).

MAKE THE SANDWICHES

Lightly toast the bread. Liberally smear the inner sides with the sambal aïoli. Add 2 slices of mortadella to each roll, followed by 8 fried oysters, ¼ cup drained pickles, and a generous sprinkling (about ¼ cup) of cilantro leaves. Eat with a knife and fork. Kidding.

PICKLES AND PRESERVES

I think I've tried to pickle every ingredient I've ever met. Because in my endless quest to introduce palate-resuscitating, richness-assaulting acidity to my food, pickles are my action hero. Unlike lime juice and vinegar, for example, they bring more to the party than just liquid. And once you've made them, you have three toys to play with—the tasty pickling liquid, the pickled ingredient's texture, and the pickled ingredient's fundamental flavor. It allows you to make an entire awesome, complex-tasting dish, if you want to, from just two main ingredients: a protein and a vegetable (in both its pickled form and not). Your acid-infused ingredients can even be the main event if you find the proper partner to offer textural and flavor contrast.

That's why pickles are everywhere in this book, embedded in larger recipes and here in this chapter without any compulsory application. All of them are great to keep on hand, to spark your imagination, to be played with. And as always, these are just ideas. From this launching pad, pickle whatever is fresh, whatever you have, and whatever is here now but won't be when the season changes. It's the reason I give you an awesome Standard Pickling Solution.

Perhaps it's too obvious to note that I am my own greatest pickling project. With the amount I drank last night, I'm probably about halfway there. More precisely, I'm on brine, waiting to be slow smoked at my wake.

No individual tunes recommendations in this chapter. Just start a long Led Zeppelin playlist or Seventies Dead show and get down to business.

A NOTE ON STERILIZATION AND PROCESSING

None of the recipes in this chapter require jarring and processing as long as you are going to eat them in a timely manner—let's say within one month. They'll be delicious, but keep in mind that some of these pickles won't have peaked by then. Processing your jars will ensure that they keep for a long-ass time until you're ready to serve them (you don't even need to take these extra steps for kimchi because it's already fermented and will keep in the fridge for up to two months).

How to sterilize your jars (Note: These instructions are for 8-ounce jars):

Bring a large canning pot with a rack for the bottom of the pot to a boil.

Hand wash your jars, seal caps, and screw bands in very hot soapy water and rinse them well in hot water. Just before you are ready to fill the jars with your prepared ingredients, boil the jars in the boiling water for 5 minutes, fully submerged, and boil the seal caps for 2 minutes. You do not need to boil the screw bands. Remove the items from the water and transfer to a rack with a towel underneath to drain. While the jars are still hot, dry with a lint free towel and immediately fill the jars with the warm prepared pickles and liquid, leaving a 1/2 inch of space from the top of the jar. Tap the jars lightly to release any air bubbles and ensure the liquid has worked its way to the bottom of the jar. Cover the jar with the seal cap followed by the screw band. Screw the band to seal the jar firmly, but don't go all Hulk crazy; they should be "fingertip tight" only (as tight as your fingers can get without exerting any extra force). If you twist it on too tight, you will create a false seal. Put the filled, sealed jars back into the boiling water. The water should cover the jars by at least 2 inches; if it's not covering to that level, top it off with more boiling water.

Boil the jars for 10 minutes in the water. Remove the jars and let them cool on the cooling rack, top side up, at room temperature until they reach room temperature. This will take hours and you should hear lots of *pops* as the caps seal. When the jars have reached room temperature, test the seal by turning each jar upside down and giving one firm shake downward. If the cap stays depressed, it's sealed; if it pops up, it's not.

If a jar doesn't seal properly, you can repeat the entire process above, but I really don't encourage it because you will further break down the ingredient structure you are preserving, or just do what I do and close the jar, pop it in the fridge, and eat it within one month.

Store the sealed jars in a cool dark place; there is no need to refrigerate them until they are opened.

PINEAPPLE PICKLE

The meaty flesh of pineapple and the crispness of cucumber become a mighty pickle, sweet and tangy and a little hot, that's just made for a giant hunk of pork shoulder, preferably smoked. Processing is not recommended for this pickle.

MAKES 3 CUPS

½ pineapple, peeled
1 English cucumber, halved, then sliced ⅛ inch thick
2 long red chilies, such as Anaheim or Hungarian Wax, thinly sliced crosswise

2 shallots, very thinly sliced (preferably using a mandoline)
1 teaspoon sugar
1 teaspoon sea salt
¼ cup rice vinegar

1. Cut the pineapple lengthwise, cut away and discard the core, and cut the fruit lengthwise into thirds. Cut each third crosswise into ¼-inch-thick pieces.
2. Toss the pineapple, cucumber, chilies, and shallots together in a bowl.
3. In a small bowl, whisk the sugar, salt, and vinegar together until the sugar has dissolved. Pour the mixture over the pineapple mix and toss to combine. Let the mixture sit in a cool place for at least 1 hour before serving.

YOUR OPTIONS

1. Eat it immediately.
2. Put it in an airtight container and consume it within a week.

KIMCHI

I make the glorious fermented pickle called *kimchi* from time to time in the restaurants and at home, typically in the early fall, when I'm acutely aware of the coming winter. So I buy up tons of stuff at the farmers' market and start playing around. In this version, for instance, black kale (aka *lacinato* or *Tuscan kale*) stands in for the staple cabbage. I like my kimchi like I like pretty much everything else: spicy and funky. If this makes you afraid, opt out of the cincalok and reduce the amount of chilies. No need to process this sucker. It'll keep in the fridge for several months.

MAKES 8 CUPS

4 cups kosher salt

1 pound whole tender inner leaves black kale, plus 6 to 8 large outer leaves

3 garlic cloves, peeled

2 tablespoons cincalok, drained and juice reserved

6 dried red chilies, such as cayenne, dry-toasted and then ground

1½ inches fresh ginger, peeled and thinly sliced

¼ cup fish sauce

5 fresh long red chilies, such as Anaheim or Hungarian Wax, stemmed, seeded, and julienned

1 bunch of scallions (about 5), cut crosswise into thirds and julienned

10 breakfast radishes, quartered lengthwise, tossed with salt, and drained in a colander for 1 hour

1 medium daikon radish, grated

1 medium white onion, grated

1. In a large bowl combine 2 gallons water with the salt and stir to dissolve. Add the kale to the water and let it soak overnight, but no more than 12 hours, making sure it's completely submerged the whole time. Drain the kale and rinse it thoroughly under cold running water. Drain the kale in a colander for 30 minutes, then separate the large outer leaves from the rest and dust those with some salt.

2. Add the garlic, cincalok, ground toasted chili, ginger, and fish sauce to a blender and blend until you have a fine paste, using a bit of water to smooth it out. Transfer the mixture to a bowl, and mix in the fresh chilies, scallions, breakfast radishes, daikon, and onion. Rub the kale (except for the large outer leaves) with the ingredients, coating each side well.

3. Using a container with a tight lid large enough to fit all the ingredients without much room at the top, stuff the saucy kale leaves into the container first and push them down so there are no air pockets remaining at the bottom of the container. Top them with the salted outer leaves, pressing the mixture down a bit. Cover the container and store in a cool, dark place—anywhere from 40° to 50°F is perfect—for at least 3 weeks. (I store mine in a little wine refrigerator in the basement in my place in upstate New York that's probably about 57°F, but as I've said, I like things funky.) Once you open it, keep it in an airtight container in the fridge for up to 3 months. This is really good shit.

SALTY OIL-CURED CHILIES

I am addicted to chilies. I definitely get grumpy when several meals pass without some present. After a week I might even get the shakes, but I've never found out, because I always have a stash of these cured chilies on hand. A few years back I had a surfeit of chilies and tried packing them in salt, as Chinese cooks do. They were supertasty but incredibly salty, more of a seasoning agent than a condiment. But then Jori came up with this method, which produces preserved chilies with gentler salinity and an aromatic, flavorful oil. They were an immediate hit with everyone who tasted them.

As you get used to having them around, you'll make the surprising discovery that they're fantastic with almost everything, adding heat, brightness, and color to eggs and salads and sandwiches and tasty roasted things. Any kind or combination of chilies will do. My chili hit parade: Thai, cayenne, long red, Holland, cherry, serrano, jalapeño. Buy, pick, or steal them—whatever you have to do to get your fix.

MAKES 2 CUPS, DEPENDING ON THE CHILIES

1 pound assorted chilies, stemmed
½ cup kosher salt

1 to 1½ cups oil, such as flavorful olive oil or grapeseed

1. Slice all the chilies crosswise into uniform rounds about ⅛ inch thick.
2. Put them in a bowl and toss them with the salt. Don't pussyfoot around—really season the chilies well. Transfer the salted chilies to a colander or a fine-mesh sieve set over a bowl and let them drain for about an hour or so. The salt will have dissolved at this point, and you should have quite a bit of chili water gathered in the bowl (see Note for ways to use it). Rinse the chilies well under cold running water. Transfer the rinsed slices to a paper-towel-lined tray, pat dry, then transfer them to a heatproof bowl (or sterilized jars if you're rolling like that).
3. Heat the oil in a saucepan over medium-high heat (as a guideline, you want the oil to be about 325°F, so use a deep-frying thermometer if you have one), and carefully pour it over the chilies. You will hear a happy sizzle. Let the chilies come to room temperature.

YOUR OPTIONS

1. Wait a day, then eat! They'll keep in the refrigerator for about a month as long as they're covered with oil. If the oil level gets low, just top it off with more straight from the bottle.
2. Process according to the method on page 290.
3. Keep them in sterilized jars, unprocessed, in the fridge and consume within a couple of months.
4. Split the finished product into three batches and complete options 1, 2, and 3.

NOTE

Don't just toss that chili water! Use it in brine for meats. Last summer I made a puree of it, basil, parsley, scallion, and garlic to brush on a baby lamb we roasted on a spit. Fucking awesome!

PICKLED THAI CHILIES

Salty Oil-Cured Chilies (preceding recipe) provide salinity and slick chili goodness. This pickle, however, is all about tartness, a little crispness, and the mouth-scalding, party-starting heat of Thai chilies.

MAKES 5 CUPS

1½ pounds fresh Thai bird chilies, slit (but not split) lengthwise almost to the stem
5 garlic cloves, crushed and peeled
2 inches fresh ginger, peeled and crushed

1½ cups apple cider vinegar
3 tablespoons kosher salt, or pickling salt for a slightly less cloudy product
1 tablespoon sugar

1. Drop the chilies into sterilized pickling jars (page 290) along with the crushed garlic and the ginger.
2. In a saucepan, bring the vinegar, salt, sugar, and 2 cups water to a boil over high heat. Remove it from the heat once the salt and sugar have dissolved. (If you're feeling creative, add a sachet to the saucepan—perhaps coriander seeds, black peppercorns, and bay leaf—and leave it in there to steep for 30 minutes once the pot comes off the heat. Bring the solution back to a boil before proceeding.)
3. Carefully pour the boiling solution over the chilies, letting the liquid work its way down through the chilies to the bottom. Fill the jars to about ¼ inch from the top. Cover the jars with the prepared caps and lids and seal them fingertip tight. Wait at least an hour before you eat them.

YOUR OPTIONS
1. Eat immediately.
2. Process according to the method on page 290.
3. Keep the pickles in the jars, unprocessed, in the fridge and consume within a couple of months.
4. Split the finished product into three batches and complete all of the above.

STANDARD PICKLE SOLUTION

This super solution can be poured over most hardy garden vegetables to make great pickles. The key is to pour the hot solution over the raw product. This makes the result snappy rather than mushy and overcooked. Following is a list of a few of the fruits and veggies from my garden that I've soaked in this enchanted liquid, along with how to prep them.

Carrots: Cut carrots on a bias into ¼-inch-thick, 1-inch-long pieces. Leave baby carrots whole (no peeling necessary), just trimmed of the stem and washed well. Add some carrot greens to the jar, because they taste great pickled and look pretty next to the orange.

Celery: Wash the stalks very well and peel the outer layer to get rid of those stringy fibers. Cut the stalks, crosswise on a bias, into ½-inch-thick pieces. Add the leaves, even the bitter inner yellow ones, which give the solution a wonderful aroma and taste great.

Cucumber: Cut in half lengthwise, then cut crosswise about ¼ inch thick.

Fennel: For small bulbs, peel the outer layer and pickle them whole. For larger bulbs, peel the outer layer and cut the remaining bulb in half lengthwise. Trim off the base and cut each half lengthwise into about six pieces. Add the fronds, too, because they're tasty and damn pretty.

Garlic: Peel and separate the cloves. For spring garlic, cut the green tops to mimic the size of the cloves and mix them in too.

Green Beans: Trim the tip, sit them upright in the jar, and pickle them whole.

Green (Unripe) Tomatoes: Use ¼- to ½-inch slices or cut them up however you want.

Onions: Peel the onion and cut it into ¼-inch-thick rings. Or go ahead and cut any shape (half-moons, chunks) you like.

Peppers: Such as jalapeños, long red and greens, serranos, Hollands, anything hearty or even all of the above. Cut them however you want, though I do like my rings ⅛ inch thick.

Radishes: Leave them whole if they're bite-sized; halve them lengthwise if they're larger.

Rhubarb: Peel and cut in the same way you would celery. *Just please don't use the leaves. They're toxic, and you could get pretty sick.*

Scallions: Peel the outer layer, trim the root end, and cut into 1-inch-long pieces.

Tomatoes: I generally pickle only whole cherry and grape tomatoes. If you cut into tomatoes and pickle them, they get mushy.

YIELD WILL DEPEND ON THE VEGETABLE USED

1½ cups distilled white vinegar

3 tablespoons pickling salt or kosher salt

1 tablespoons sugar

1 tablespoon black peppercorns

2 teaspoons coriander seeds

2 teaspoons fennel seeds

1 teaspoon yellow mustard seeds

1 small fresh thyme sprig

About 1½ pounds vegetables (see opposite page for some options), washed really well

Bring all the ingredients except the vegetables, and 2 cups water to a boil in a pot. Remove it from the heat and let it sit in the pot for about 30 minutes while the aromatics infuse the solution. Strain the liquid into a saucepan, discarding the solids, and bring it back to a boil. Pour it over the vegetables in sterilized jars. Cover the jars with the prepared caps and lids and seal them fingertip tight. They're pickle-tastic after 1 day.

YOUR OPTIONS

1. Eat immediately.
2. Process according to the method on page 290.
3. Keep them in the jars, unprocessed, in the fridge and consume within a couple of months.
4. Split the finished product into three batches and complete options 1, 2, and 3.

PICKLED RAMPS

When these slender wild leeks arrive in the markets, you can be sure spring is here. Not only are they a harbinger of the coming market bounty; they're also damn tasty and complement all things savory. Because of their short season, everyone I know pickles them like there's no tomorrow—or, more accurately, like there's a whole lot of tomorrows. That way you get to enjoy them through summer into fall's bounty and then winter's bleakness . . . until they arrive again.

MAKES ABOUT 4 CUPS

2 pounds ramps, cleaned well, greens cut off and reserved for another tasty purpose
½ cup kosher salt
1½ cups apple cider vinegar

3 tablespoons fish sauce
1 tablespoon pickling salt
3 tablespoons local honey
3 tablespoons pink peppercorns
3 garlic cloves, crushed and peeled

1. Put the ramp bulbs in a bowl and cover them with 1 cup cold water and the kosher salt. Stir gently and well to dissolve the salt. Let them soak for 30 minutes or so.
2. While the ramps soak, bring the remaining ingredients to a boil in a saucepan. Remove it from the heat and let it sit for about 30 minutes while the aromatics infuse the solution.
3. Drain and rinse the ramps under cold running water, then pat them dry and add them to the sterilized and prepared jars.
4. Strain the liquid into a saucepan, discarding the solids, and bring it back to a boil. Pour the boiling liquid over the ramps. Cover the jars with the prepared caps and lids and seal fingertip tight. After 1 day, they're pickle-tastic.

YOUR OPTIONS
1. Eat immediately.
2. Process according to the method on page 290.
3. Put in an airtight container in the fridge and consume within a couple of months.
4. Split the finished product into three batches and complete options 1, 2, and 3.

CLEANING RAMPS

Fill a large bowl with water. Using a paring knife, trim the roots from the ramps. Swish the trimmed ramps in the cold water and drain in a colander. Refill the bowl with fresh clean water. Working out of the colander, peel the outer layer from each ramp (1 or 2 layers down, depending on how dirty they are). After peeling, drop the ramps into the fresh water. Move them around in the water and drain in a colander again.

CELERY MOSTARDA

While technically not a pickle, this sweet-savory, mustardy condiment can be processed in jars in the same manner. I've enjoyed mostarda with many a bollito misto over the years, but unsurprisingly I like it with a bit more spicy zing than the traditional version. I slip some fish sauce in there too. I love celery's texture, but you can replace it with carrots and raisins, rhubarb, pear, quince, apple, even citrus.

MAKES 2 TO 3 CUPS

5 dried red chilies, such as cayenne
½ cup local honey
2 tablespoons fish sauce
3 star anise
2 cloves

4 celery stalks, peeled and cut on
   the bias into ½-inch pieces
1 tablespoon sea salt
2 tablespoons unsalted butter
3 tablespoons mustard oil

1. In a dry pan over medium heat, toast the dried chilies until they take on a dark color, pressing them down with a wooden spoon to increase contact with the pan, about 3 to 4 minutes. Be careful not to inhale over the toasting chilies.
2. Combine the honey, fish sauce, star anise, cloves, toasted chilies, and ½ cup water in a bowl.
3. In a small bowl, toss the celery with the salt.
4. Melt the butter in a large sauté pan over medium heat. Add the celery and cook for a minute, then pour in the honey mixture and stir well. Bring the mixture to a simmer, reduce the heat to low, cover the pan, and cook at a very low simmer until the celery is tender but still has a slight bite, 7 to 10 minutes.
5. Transfer the celery with a slotted spoon to sterilized and prepared jars. Increase the heat and cook the liquid in the pan, uncovered, until it's as thick as maple syrup. Whisk in the mustard oil, then pour the mixture over the celery and seal the jars.

YOUR OPTIONS

1. Eat immediately.
2. Place in an airtight container in the refrigerator and consume (at room temperature) within 3 weeks.

GINGER AND PAPAYA PICKLE

This quick pickle makes an awesome partner for Steamed Loup De Mer (page 32), but it'll brighten up simpler fish dishes too. Roast chicken wouldn't throw it out of bed either. You should not process this pickle.

MAKES 2 CUPS

4 inches fresh ginger, peeled
½ green papaya, peeled and seeded
1 cup rice vinegar

3 tablespoons palm or brown sugar
Juice of 1 lime

MAKE THE PICKLE

1. Carefully slice the ginger and the green papaya lengthwise on a mandoline into paper-thin ribbons. Set each aside in a separate bowl.

2. Put the rice vinegar, 1½ tablespoons of the palm sugar, and 1 cup water in a saucepan and add the sliced ginger. Bring the liquid to a simmer over medium heat and cook, stirring occasionally, until the palm sugar has dissolved and the ginger is tender but still slightly toothsome. (The ginger should have absorbed the sweet and sour flavors.) Transfer the ginger and liquid to a bowl to cool.

3. In a medium bowl, combine the remaining 1½ tablespoons palm sugar and the lime juice, stirring to dissolve the sugar. Add the papaya to the sweetened lime juice, stir, and let it sit until the papaya softens slightly and absorbs some flavor, about 20 minutes. When the ginger has cooled and the papaya is ready, combine them and their juices and stir. Drain the liquid when you're ready to use it. Store up to 1 week.

PRESERVED LEMONS

Preserved lemon, like fresh chili and sea salt, is a highly valued "finisher" in my kitchen. It adds the aroma of citrus, an awesome bitter flavor, and a bit of salt and funky depth that seems to eke out a bit more from most dishes. Usually preserved lemons are cured simply with salt. I ask for more from my preserved lemons and add a bunch of coriander seed and bay leaves. They're easy to make, but they do require some space and time to mature. Don't consider using them until they've cured for about a month. When you're ready to use one, rinse it well under cold running water. Now you have a powerful weapon in the battle for braises or roasts, which are awesome with preserved lemons, either whole or cut into chunks. Or julienne the zest and use it as a finisher. But, I do not recommend processing these lemons.

MAKES 20 LEMONS

6 cups kosher salt
⅔ cup freshly ground black pepper
1 cup coriander seeds, dry-toasted
    and cracked

6 dried bay leaves, crumbled
20 lemons, rinsed and dried

1. Mix the salt and spices.
2. Trim ½ inch off the stem end of each lemon. Then cut the lemon in half lengthwise, stopping about ¼ inch before the end. Turn the lemon and make a similar lengthwise cut, stopping ¼ inch before the end. Each lemon should still be in one piece but with four lemon prongs.
3. Rub the salt mix all over each lemon, inside and out.
4. Put the lemons in a plastic or glass container with a lid. Cover them with any leftover salt mix. Cover the container and refrigerate for 2 weeks. Then shuffle the lemons around, cover again, and refrigerate for another 2 weeks. Congratulations: you have added a new item to your pantry. Rinse the lemons under cold water before you use them.

PRESERVED LEMON PULP SAUCE

Most of my recipes call only for the zest of the preserved lemon. But this doesn't mean you shouldn't take advantage of the pulp. Soak the preserved lemon in cold water for 1 hour, drain it, and discard the seeds. Then blend it with ¼ cup Japanese brown rice vinegar, 1 or 2 fresh Thai bird chilies, and 1 clove garlic for every ¼ cup of pulp. Once it's smooth, strain it through a sieve and you have a condiment for meat, fish, or whatever else you think would benefit from a salty, spicy hit!

BLACK PEPPER RHUBARB PICKLE

Delicious with vanilla ice cream or a simple steamed fish, or even a hearty braised meat. However, do not process these.

MAKES 1½ CUPS

3 rhubarb stalks, peeled and cut into 1-inch-long matchsticks (peels reserved)

1 cup sugar

2 tablespoons freshly ground black pepper, ideally Indonesian long pepper

1. Combine the reserved rhubarb peels with the sugar and 1 cup water in a small saucepan. Bring to a simmer, stirring, until the sugar is dissolved, then strain into a medium saucepan, discarding the solids.

2. Warm the syrup over medium heat until it's just hot to the touch, add the rhubarb and the black pepper, and take the pan off the heat. Let it sit for at least an hour or up to many. Keep it in the liquid, covered, up to a few weeks in the refrigerator, until you're ready to use it.

CONDIMENTS

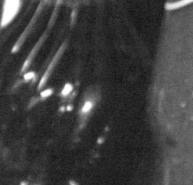

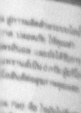

SAMBAL BELACAN

Sambal is ubiquitous in Malaysian cuisine, served in bowls at the table at every meal to be spooned on everything but ice cream. The composition and flavor varies from region to region, and from cook to cook, though every version packs some fieriness from chilies. This fish-funky version is named for the ingredient that gives it its pungent backbone: belacan ("BLA-chan"), or dried shrimp paste. To make the sambal, you've got to toast the belacan. If you have an exhaust fan or oven hood, be sure it's on high. The aroma is . . . the bouquet has a . . . fuck it, this stuff stinks!

MAKES ½ CUP

2 teaspoons belacan, toasted
   (see page 333)
8 long red chilies, such as Anaheim
   or Hungarian Wax, stemmed
5 fresh red Thai bird chilies,
   stemmed

1 garlic clove, crushed and peeled
Juice of 1 to 3 limes
Sea salt

Use a mortar and pestle to pound (see page 12) the toasted belacan, chilies, and garlic to a coarse paste, pounding each ingredient thoroughly before adding the next. Add lime juice to taste and season with salt to brighten the flavors. Store the sambal, covered, in the refrigerator, for damn near ever. Bring it to room temperature and freshen it with more lime juice before you use it.

AÏOLI AND SAMBAL AÏOLI

First we have the aïoli. And then we add a bit of the fishy Sambal Belacan (preceding recipe) for a whole new taste sensation. Spread the love anywhere you'd normally use mayo!

MAKES 2 TO 2½ CUPS

1 large egg yolk
2 small garlic cloves, minced
2 cups grapeseed oil
1 teaspoon brown rice vinegar
1 teaspoon fresh lime juice

Sea salt
1 tablespoon Sambal Belacan (preceding recipe) for Sambal Aïoli

Put the egg yolk and garlic in the bowl of a food processor and pulse, using a rubber spatula to scrape any yolk that gets stuck to the sides of the processor back toward the blades, until smooth. Then puree, slowly adding the oil while the machine is running until the aïoli has emulsified. Add the vinegar and lime juice and process to combine. Season with salt to taste. Cover and refrigerate until you're ready to use it or stir in the sambal belacan.

SAMBAL IKAN BILIS

When we were opening the first Fatty Crab, I tasted all the wine I was considering buying for the restaurant alongside spoonfuls of this sambal. I figured the wine had to complement the flavors of the food, and this is a great example of the Fatty palate. More mellow than Sambal Belacan (page 306), this sambal shows off the deep, muted salinity of ikan bilis (tiny dried anchovies). I eat a nice big spoonful of it on rice at least twice a week as a snack. It's a great condiment to have sitting in your fridge.

MAKES ABOUT 2 CUPS

3 dried red chilies, such as cayenne
2 garlic cloves, thinly sliced
3 medium shallots, minced
¼ cup candlenuts or macadamia nuts
¼ pound belacan, toasted (see page 333)
2 cups ikan bilis

2 tablespoons neutral oil, such as grapeseed or canola
1 large white onion, thinly sliced
¼ cup unsweetened tamarind paste
¼ pound palm sugar (2⅔ rounds gala jawa), crushed, or ⅓ cup brown sugar
2 tablespoons tomato paste

1. Remove the seeds from the chilies by cracking them in a mortar and pestle (or with gloved hands), transferring them to a colander, and shaking the colander over the sink until all the seeds fall through the holes.
2. Use a mortar and pestle to pound (see page 12) the dried chilies, garlic, shallots, candlenuts, belacan, and ikan bilis to a very smooth paste, pounding each ingredient thoroughly before adding the next.
3. Heat the oil in a sauté pan over medium heat. Add the onion and cook, stirring occasionally, until soft, about 3 minutes, then add the chili paste and cook, stirring, until the mixture is fragrant, about 2 more minutes. Add the tamarind paste, palm sugar, and tomato paste and bring the mixture to a simmer. Cook, stirring, until the sugar is completely dissolved and the mixture has thickened slightly, 2 to 3 more minutes. Remove from the heat and let it come to room temperature. Transfer to a blender or food processor and puree until smooth. Store, covered, in the refrigerator, for damn near ever.

CHILI SAUCE #1

I found a basic recipe for this phenomenal sweet, spicy chili sauce in a 1970s Thai cookbook I bought in Chiang Mai. After a few tweaks I knew I'd come upon a condiment that I would never tire of. I suggest you make it a permanent part of your pantry. Make a shitload, because it keeps more or less forever. Check the next recipe for its sibling sauce.

MAKES ABOUT 5 CUPS

1¼ tablespoons sea salt
¾ cup fresh cilantro roots, rinsed, scraped, and rinsed again
15 fresh long red chilies, such as Anaheim or Hungarian Wax, stemmed

About 18 garlic cloves, peeled
1¾ cups palm or brown sugar
1¼ cups fish sauce
1¼ cups fresh lime juice
⅔ cup brown rice vinegar

Use a mortar and pestle to pound (see page 12) the salt with the cilantro roots, chilies, and garlic to a smooth paste, pounding each ingredient thoroughly before adding the next. Add the palm sugar, fish sauce, lime juice, and rice vinegar and pound to achieve a smooth sauce. If you like it a bit sweeter, feel free to incorporate some more palm sugar.

CHILI SAUCE #2

1 cup fresh cilantro leaves
½ recipe Chili Sauce #1 (preceding recipe)
2½ fresh kaffir lime leaves, stems and center veins discarded and leaves finely julienned

Fresh lime juice to taste
Palm or brown sugar to taste
Sea salt

Use a mortar and pestle to pound the cilantro leaves to break them down a little. Add the chili sauce, pounding to blend the ingredients together. Stir in the kaffir lime leaves and season with lime juice, palm sugar, and salt to taste.

CHILI SAUCE #1, p. 309

PINEAPPLE PICKLE, p. 291

PINEAPPLE RED CURRY, p. 314

PINEAPPLE RED CURRY

We recently made a mountain of this, enough to serve with a 225-pound pig that we smoked in my backyard. I'd opt out of a three-way just to have that meal! Either warm from the pot or at room temperature, pineapple and red curry adds both sweetness and heat and rocks as a condiment for grilled meat or fish.

MAKES ABOUT 4 CUPS

1 star anise
1 tablespoon coriander seeds
4 small green cardamom pods
1½ inches fresh ginger, peeled
5 fresh long red chilies, such as
   Anaheim or Hungarian Wax,
   stemmed
3 fresh Thai bird chilies, stemmed
3 shallots, sliced
5 tablespoons unsalted butter

1 pineapple, peeled, cored, and cut
   into ½-inch chunks
1 tablespoon palm or brown sugar
One 14-ounce can coconut milk,
   preferably Aroy-D brand, shaken
2 lemongrass stalks, outer layer
   removed and stalk crushed with
   a blunt object
1 teaspoon sea salt

1. Toast the star anise, coriander seeds, and cardamom pods in a dry pan over medium heat, swirling and shaking them until they crackle lightly, just begin to color, and release their aromas, about 3 minutes. Grind them to a fine powder in a spice grinder.

2. Use a mortar and pestle to pound (see page 12) the ginger, then add both types of chilies and pound until the skins are pulverized. Add the shallots and pound to a paste. Sprinkle in the ground toasted spices and pound thoroughly to combine well.

3. In a large saucepan, melt 2 tablespoons of the butter over medium heat. Add the chili paste to the pan and cook, stirring occasionally, until fragrant, 3 to 4 minutes, then transfer the paste to a mixing bowl. Increase the heat to medium-high and melt the remaining butter in the saucepan. Add the pineapple chunks and sauté them until they're browned, about 5 minutes. Return the chili paste to the pan and stir to combine.

4. Mash the palm sugar with a few tablespoons of the coconut milk to soften it. Add the rest of the coconut milk, the softened palm sugar, the lemongrass, and the salt to the pan. Reduce the heat and cook at a low simmer, about 20 minutes. Eat it warm or at room temperature. Or cover the cooled curry and store it in the fridge for about 1 week.

FISH SAUCE AND PALM SUGAR SYRUP

Another pantry staple in the Pelaccio household, this versatile salty-sweet syrup can be used on its own, turned into a dressing with the addition of lime juice, or spiked with sliced chilies and set out on the table, as it is at Fatty 'Cue. If you want to take it to another level, put it uncovered in a low barbecue for a couple of hours until it picks up some smoke.

MAKES ABOUT 2 CUPS

2 cups palm or brown sugar

1½ cups fish sauce

Brown rice vinegar (optional)

Thai chili (optional)

Put the palm sugar in a pot and use the fish sauce to moisten it, breaking it up slightly with a spoon. Heat the mixture over low heat, stirring, until the sugar is completely dissolved. Let it cool in the pot and then pour into pint or quart containers. This will keep for an eternity either in the fridge or at room temperature.

If you want, add a couple tablespoons of brown rice vinegar to the mix to give it a touch of acidity and it becomes the Asian version of a Southern U.S. style BBQ dippin' sauce. Add some sliced fresh Thai chili for heat if you so desire.

A SIMPLE GREEN CURRY

There are already a number of recipes for curries in the book. But this one is comparatively simple, the ingredients not terribly obscure. I even suggest using a blender rather than the mortar and pestle. This way, if the other curry recipes are too involved for you, you won't miss out on the experience of making your own curry. The flavor is peerless.

Even with this accessible ingredient list, you may not be able to find one or two of the things you need. That's OK. That's how cooking should be: dependent in some part on your location. So play around a bit. If you can't find cilantro with roots, use the stems instead. If you can't find lemongrass, use basil stems. If you can't find Thai bird chilies, use jalapeños. If those chilies aren't hot enough, add more. The result is excellent spooned over fish, meat, even roasted vegetables, or used as the cooking liquid for those very things.

MAKES ABOUT 4 CUPS

1 tablespoon white peppercorns
1½ tablespoons coriander seeds
1 tablespoon fennel seeds
3 shallots, chopped
5 garlic cloves, crushed and peeled
2 inches fresh ginger, peeled and
    chopped
4 fresh Thai bird chilies, stemmed
3 long green chilies, such as
    Anaheim or Hungarian Wax, or
    even 5 to 6 jalapeños, stemmed
10 fresh cilantro roots, rinsed,
    scraped, and rinsed again, or 40
    fresh cilantro stems, minced

Sea salt
2 tablespoons neutral oil, such as
    grapeseed or canola
2 lemongrass stalks, outer layer
    removed and stalk crushed with
    a blunt object
Two 14-ounce cans coconut milk,
    preferably Aroy-D brand, shaken
Juice of 1 lime, or more to taste
1½ tablespoons fish sauce, or more
    to taste
¼ cup fresh basil leaves

1. In a dry sauté pan, combine the white peppercorns, coriander seeds, and fennel seeds and toast over medium heat, swirling the pan occasionally, until the spices smell amazing, about 3 minutes. Grind them to a powder in a spice grinder and set the mixture aside.

2. In a blender, puree the shallots, garlic, ginger, chilies, and cilantro roots with a pinch of salt and just enough water to get it going and form a smooth paste.

3. Heat the oil in a heavy medium pot over medium heat. Add the puree and cook, stirring a bit, until it's very aromatic, about 3 minutes. Then add the ground spices and lemongrass and continue cooking for 1 minute more. Add the coconut milk and bring it to a gentle simmer and add lime juice and fish sauce. Cook for 30 minutes, then add a little more lime juice and fish sauce until it tastes really good. Tear the basil leaves and sprinkle them in.

SWEET CILANTRO SAUCE

This sauce is so, so good with greasy, fatty, roasty beef and pork. It's *the* sauce for Fatty Brisket (page 238). It wouldn't suck with chicken or fish either.

MAKES 1¾ CUPS

½ cup palm or brown sugar
½ cup brown rice vinegar
2 cups packed fresh cilantro leaves
8 fresh Thai bird chilies, chopped

½ cup fresh lime juice
Sea salt and freshly ground black pepper

Soften the palm sugar with a little of the vinegar, then puree the cilantro, chilies, and lime juice in a food processor or blender. Season with salt and pepper to taste. You can also adjust the acidity, heat, and sweetness—find your sweet spot!

CHILI OIL

Here's a dead-simple condiment to drizzle over whatever could use the aromatic punch and heat of chilies. Any type of oil will do—canola, grapeseed, extra virgin olive—though I prefer using peanut oil in Asian recipes.

MAKES ABOUT 4 CUPS

4 cups oil (your choice)
12 dried red chilies, such as cayenne

Dump the oil and chilies into a blender and blend well. Pour the blended mixture into a saucepan, put it over low heat, and cook for 20 minutes. Let it cool, then pour it into a glass or plastic container and cover. Wait a day before you use it. You can strain out the solids or leave them in and strain for each use. It will hold in a shaded spot for a month, no worries.

KERISIK

You'll find kerisik in Malaysian salads and sprinkled on top of rendangs, but there's no end to the applications for the grated fresh coconut, slowly toasted until it's golden brown. Think outside the Asian box, and you'll start putting it on ice cream and roast chicken, in your coffee and tea, or on the rim of your cocktail glass.

MAKES ABOUT 1 CUP

> 1 cup shredded fresh coconut, from about 1 mature coconut (you might need another to reach 1 cup), or store-bought unsweetened shredded coconut

1. If you're shredding your own coconut, use an old cleaver, machete, hammer, or other instrument of destruction to crack open the fruit. Then use a paring knife to cut and pry the white flesh away from the hard shell. Remove the thin brown skin left on the meat with a vegetable peeler or paring knife. Use the large holes of a box grater to grate the fresh coconut flesh.
2. Sprinkle the grated coconut in no more than a ½-inch-deep layer (work in batches if necessary) in a large pan over medium heat. Toss the coconut every 30 seconds. Once the coconut starts to color lightly, start tossing more often. When most flakes have turned a golden brown color, give the pan a few shakes over the heat, then a couple more tosses and a few shakes again, like some superstitious ritual that keeps the coconut-burning gods at bay while stealing a few more precious moments of cooking time. Pull the pan from the heat and toss it nervously just to prevent those burning gods from following you out of the fire. Spread the toasted coconut on a platter or cookie sheet to cool.

STOCKS

MASTER STOCK

If I can have only one stock, let it be Master, said Confucius. Or maybe that was just the weird lady who hangs out in Confucius Plaza in Chinatown. Either way, he or she was right! This stock, essentially chicken stock fortified with duck necks, pig's feet, and other glories, is at once versatile and deeply flavored, with the flexibility to participate in lighter sauce making when veal stock can't, but with the heavy-lifting abilities of beef- and lamb-based broths.

MAKES ABOUT 12 CUPS

3 pounds duck necks
½ cup rendered leaf lard (see page 196) or neutral oil, such as grapeseed or canola
1 recipe Chicken Stock (page 324)
2 tablespoons olive oil (the best you can afford)
1 small carrot, halved crosswise
1 celery stalk, cut crosswise into thirds
1 white onion, quartered
1 head of garlic, split crosswise
¼ cup Shaoxing wine or dry sherry
2 pig's feet, split in half lengthwise
1 ham hock or ½ pound prosciutto rinds
1 hand fresh ginger, cut into 4 pieces
5 scallions
1 tablespoon black peppercorns
1 tablespoon coriander seeds
1 fresh thyme sprig

1. Preheat the oven to 450°F. Slide a dry roasting pan into the oven to get it hot.
2. Toss the duck necks with the lard or neutral oil. When the roasting pan is hot, add the duck necks and return the pan to the hot oven. Cook, turning the bones every 5 minutes or so, until there's a wonderful caramelized color on all sides, about 15 minutes.
3. Meanwhile, heat the chicken stock in a large saucepan over medium-low heat until it's warm.
4. Heat the olive oil in a large stockpot over medium-high heat. Add the carrot, celery, onion, and garlic and cook, stirring occasionally, until they're almost tender and roasty brown on all sides, about 10 minutes. Add the Shaoxing wine and let it bubble, scraping up any brown bits with a wooden spoon. Add the duck necks to the pot along with the pig's feet and ham hock or prosciutto rinds. Do not stir—the less you mess with your ingredients now, the clearer the stock will be when it's ready. Add enough of the warm chicken stock to reach the necks, feet, and hock.
5. Bring the stock to a boil, then immediately reduce the heat so the liquid simmers. Cook, skimming any gunk that forms on the surface, for a couple of minutes, then add the ginger, scallions, peppercorns, coriander seeds, and thyme.
6. Simmer the stock for about 5 hours, skimming the top often. When the stock

is ready, it should be roasty brown and bold in flavor with a wonderfully rich mouthfeel.

7. Strain the stock twice, first through a wide-mesh sieve or colander, discarding the solids, then again through a fine-mesh sieve. Let the stock cool completely and skim the fat from the surface.

8. Refrigerate the stock for 5 days or store it in the freezer for up to 3 months in an airtight freezer container or bag (or divided among several).

CHICKEN STOCK

Back away from the canned and boxed stuff—slowly, slowly, that's right. Now, get a big pot, get a chicken, and get to work. This recipe makes 8 cups of stock, so if you need more—maybe you're making Master Stock (page 322) or Double Chicken Stock (page 325)—you can just double, triple, or quadruple the recipe.

MAKES 8 CUPS

1 whole chicken (3 to 4 pounds), hacked into 3-inch pieces, or the same weight in chicken parts (neck, backs, wings)

1 celery stalk, cut crosswise into thirds

1 white onion, quartered

1 head of garlic, halved crosswise

1 tablespoon black peppercorns

1 tablespoon coriander seeds

1 fresh thyme sprig

1. Rinse the chicken pieces very well, especially the backbone pieces, to get rid of any junk, in a colander under cold running water. Add the chicken to a large stockpot along with the rest of the ingredients and fill it with just enough water to submerge the bones and innards.
2. Bring the water to a boil over high heat, then immediately reduce the temperature so it simmers. Cook the stock for 2 hours, skimming the surface often to remove any gunk that develops.
3. Strain the stock first through a wide-mesh sieve or colander, discarding the solids, then again through a fine-mesh sieve. Let the stock cool completely and skim the fat from the surface, reserving it—for it is schmaltz, a very valuable culinary currency.
4. Refrigerate the stock for 5 days or store it in the freezer for up to 3 months in an airtight freezer container or bag (or divided among several).

DOUBLE CHICKEN STOCK

It's stock made with stock—dark, delicious, and double the chicken flavor!

1 whole chicken (3 to 4 pounds), hacked into 3-inch pieces, or the same weight in chicken parts (neck, backs, wings)

3 tablespoons olive oil (the best you can afford) or rendered schmaltz
1 recipe Chicken Stock (preceding recipe)

1. Preheat the oven to 450°F. Slide a dry roasting pan into the oven to get it hot.
2. Rinse the chicken pieces very well, especially the backbone pieces, to get rid of the junk, in a colander under cold running water. Dry the chicken pieces well, then toss them with the oil or schmaltz.
3. When the pan is hot, add the chicken and return the pan to the hot oven. Cook, turning the pieces every 5 minutes or so, until there's a wonderful dark caramelized color on all sides, about 15 minutes.
4. Heat the chicken stock in a saucepan over medium heat until it's warm. Transfer the roasted chicken to a large stockpot and add the warmed chicken stock.
5. Bring the stock to a boil over high heat, then immediately reduce the temperature so it simmers. Cook the stock for 2 hours, skimming the surface often to remove any gunk that develops.
6. Strain the stock first through a wide-mesh sieve or colander, discarding the solids, then again through a fine-mesh sieve. Let the stock cool completely and skim the fat from the surface. If you value happiness, for God's sake save it—it's schmaltz!
7. Refrigerate the stock for 5 days or store it in the freezer for up to 3 months in an airtight freezer container or bag (or divided among several).

SIMPLE FISH STOCK

All the flavors of those lovely fish heads and bones are distilled into this light, flavorful stock.

MAKES 8 CUPS

1 teaspoon white peppercorns
1 tablespoon coriander seeds
1 star anise
Peel of 1 lemon
3 to 5 pounds bones and heads of
    white-fleshed fish, such as cod
    or haddock

1 large onion, cut into eighths
1 small fennel bulb, quartered
2 heads of garlic, halved crosswise
1 cup dry white wine

1. Make a sachet by wrapping the white peppercorns, coriander seeds, star anise, and lemon peel in a square of cheesecloth; tie it closed with kitchen twine.
2. Chop the fish bones into approximately 2-inch pieces. Split the fish heads in half lengthwise and remove the gills, brains, and other gunk. Rinse the bones and heads very well under cold water.
3. Put the bones and heads in a very large stockpot along with the onion, fennel, garlic, and sachet.
4. Add the wine, then add enough water to just submerge the fish bones.
5. Bring the water to a boil, then immediately reduce the heat so it simmers gently. Simmer for about 1 hour, skimming the surface often.
6. Strain the stock through a fine-mesh sieve, discarding the solids. Let it cool completely to room temperature and then skim the surface of the stock.
7. Refrigerate the stock for 5 days or store it in the freezer for up to 3 months in an airtight freezer container or bag (or divided among several).

LOBSTER STOCK

I've seen people who are otherwise in their right mind spend a ton on lobster and then casually toss out the shells. Never do this. Make stock with those shells and let the lobster flavor live on.

MAKES ABOUT 8 CUPS

¼ cup neutral oil, such as grapeseed or canola
1 large white onion, cut into eighths
2 heads of garlic, halved crosswise
3 shallots, halved
Shells and heads of 6 lobsters, hacked into 2-inch pieces

½ cup Shaoxing wine or dry sherry
½ cup Armagnac
8 mixed stems fresh parsley, Vietnamese mint (rau ram), Thai basil, and/or cilantro

1. Heat 2 tablespoons of the oil in a Dutch oven or stockpot over medium-high heat. Add the onion, garlic, and shallots and cook, stirring occasionally, until they're golden brown, about 5 minutes. Use a slotted spoon to transfer the vegetables to a large plate.
2. Increase the heat under the pot to high, add a touch more oil, and when it's hot, throw in a single layer of lobster shells. Cook the shells until their color brightens to a magnificent orange and the pieces touching the pan start to roast and darken, about 10 minutes. Then crush the shells with a wooden spoon and cook for another minute. Transfer the cooked shells to the plate with the roasted vegetables and repeat the process until all the shells are cooked.
3. Reduce the heat to medium and pour in the Shaoxing wine and the Armagnac, letting them bubble and scraping up all the brown bits on the bottom of the pot with a wooden spoon. Cook off the alcohol, about 4 minutes.
4. Return the roasted shells and vegetables to the pot along with the herb stems. Add just enough water to reach the top of the shells but not enough to cover them completely.
5. Bring the liquid to a boil and immediately reduce the heat so it simmers gently. Let it simmer for about 2 hours, skimming the surface often.
6. Strain the stock through a fine-mesh sieve, discarding the solids. Let it cool completely at room temperature and skim the surface fat.
7. Refrigerate the stock for 5 days or store it in the freezer for up to 3 months in an airtight freezer container or bag (or divided among several).

CRAB STOCK

A beautiful, Asian-inflected stock is the only rational response to a glut of blue crabs.

MAKES 6 CUPS

1 tablespoon black peppercorns
1 tablespoon coriander seeds
3 pounds blue crabs, cut in half and bottom plates removed
1 head of garlic, halved crosswise
5 shallots, halved
4 fresh Vietnamese mint (rau ram) stems

3 fresh Thai basil stems
5 fresh cilantro roots, rinsed, scraped, and rinsed again, or 20 fresh cilantro stems
1 lemongrass stalk, outer layer removed and stalk crushed with a blunt object

1. Make a sachet by wrapping the peppercorns and coriander seeds in a square of cheesecloth and tying it closed with kitchen twine.
2. Rinse the crab pieces well under cold running water.
3. In a large stockpot, combine the crab pieces with the sachet, garlic, shallots, herb stems, cilantro roots, and lemongrass. Add just enough water to reach the top of the shells but not enough to cover them.
4. Bring the water to a boil, then immediately reduce the heat so it simmers gently. Simmer for about 1 hour, skimming the surface often.
5. Turn off the heat, and remove the herb stems, lemongrass, and sachet from the stock and discard. Use an immersion blender or food processor to lightly pulse the stock and the shells, breaking up the shells a bit until they're the size of cornflakes. Strain the stock through a fine-mesh sieve lined with cheesecloth, discarding the solids. Let it cool completely to room temperature and then skim the surface of the stock.
6. Refrigerate the stock for 5 days or store it in the freezer for up to 3 months in an airtight freezer container or bag (or divided among several).

DESSERTS

EAT FR

ESH FRUIT!

GLOSSARY

ASSAM GELUGOR

This Malaysian fruit, which is yellow-orange and looks like a mini pumpkin, is often mistakenly identified as tamarind skin. It is rarely, if ever, eaten fresh. Instead it's thickly sliced, dried in the sun, and used to provide a uniquely awesome sourness to balance sweet and salty flavors. Look for it at Asian grocery stores. If you must, you can substitute tamarind, which is a bit sweeter, or the fleshy pits of unripe mangoes.

BAO

These pillowy, spongy, steamed Chinese buns made from rice flour provide a soft, featherweight bed for meat or vegetables. You'll typically find bao, filled with sweet, fatty pork, as part of dim sum menus. Look for them at Chinese bakeries.

BELACAN (pronounced BLAH-chan)

Sold in small bricks and used to flavor sambals, this dried and fermented shrimp paste is always toasted before using. Like all fermented products, the flavor and aroma of belacan is impossible to ignore. I love to watch the reactions of the people on the basketball courts across from the downtown Fatty Crab as the fumes of toasting belacan waft gently across Hudson Street.

   Toasting Belacan: It's important to note that toasting belacan creates a powerful, stinktastic odor. At Fatty Crab, we regularly piss off neighbors four doors down when we get to toastin' belacan. If you have an exhaust fan or hood, for god's sake, turn it on!

   Put the belacan in a dry pan (you can also do it in a baking sheet under the broiler) and put the pan over medium heat. Once the belacan begins to smoke, in 4 to 5 minutes, use a spoon to crush it and disperse the crumbs across the pan. Open doors and windows, turn on fans, do whatever you can do to get the air flowing and the stink of toasting belacan out of your kitchen. Continue cooking until it's a darker color and has become dry and crumbles easily, about 3 minutes. Don't let it burn. Pull the pan from the heat, dump it into a bowl or mortar, and let it cool until it's easy to handle.

BUDU SAUCE

Also called *nam budo*, this extremely pungent Southeast Asian condiment that looks like cloudy dishwater, smells like fish rotting on a shipwreck, and when used correctly, tastes like heaven, is produced by packing freshwater fish into earthenware pots with rice husk dust and letting it ferment. Then it's cooked and strained. Look for it in bottles at Asian grocery stores.

GALANGAL

GALANGAL FLOWER

GINGER

IKAN BILIS

THAI EGGPLANTS

CANDLENUTS

LEMONGRASS

TURMERIC

THAI RED CHILIES

DRIED SHRIMP

LONG RED CHILIES

PORK FLOSS

TAMARIND PASTE

ASSAM SKIN

BLACK PEPPER

TOASTED COCONUT

DRIED CHILI

ROCK SUGAR

SICHUAN PEPPERCORNS

PALM SUGAR

GULA JAWA

PRESERVED BLACK BEANS

CANDLENUTS

Native to Indonesia and used often in Malaysia, these nuts were originally used to make—yep—candles. Today the oily nut is ground to a paste and used to enrich curries, sauces, and sambals, giving them distinctive texture. You can substitute an equal number of macadamia nuts (a distant relative), but keep in mind that candlenuts aren't as sweet.

CILANTRO ROOTS

The whitish roots of the cilantro plant add an earthy version of cilantro flavor without the green color. Look for coriander with the roots attached at farmers' markets and Asian or Indian markets that sell vegetables. Or grow your own, which is highly rewarding. If you can't find them, substitute four cilantro stems for every root.

CINCALOK (pronounced CHIN-cha-loke)

Used throughout Malaysia, cincalok is made from fermented krill (a tiny shrimplike creature that you'll see suspended in liquid in the bottle) and has a downright pungent flavor and a concentrated deep-sea complexity.

COCONUT MILK

When you steep the grated meat from a mature coconut in hot water and strain it, you get coconut cream, a lovely, fatty substance used to fry curry pastes. Add more hot water and strain again and you'll have coconut milk for thinning curries, making soups, and about a thousand other tasty things.

Alas, typically in our climate, we have to get them both from a can. The Aroy-D brand from Thailand is the best I've found and what we use at Fatty Crab. Chaokoh is a quality brand too. Whatever you do, don't use the Coco Lopez brand, which is sweetened cream and not what you're after.

CURRY LEAVES

Not related to the spice mix "curry powder," these dark green leaves from a Southeast Asian plant have a complex aroma—a little like curry powder—when they're crushed or heated. They're commonly found in bunches in Asian and Indian markets.

FERMENTED TOFU

Sold in small jars at Asian markets, the pale yellow cubes of mold-fermented tofu have a creamy consistency and a pronounced funky flavor. They smell like a cross between ripe Camembert cheese and anchovies.

GALANGAL

Pleasantly spicy, lemony, and aromatic, galangal is a rhizome that, like ginger, you peel and thinly slice, then pound or mince before using. It has an intense, almost floral flavor that holds its own with the boldly flavored spices with which it's usually paired. Many Southeast Asian grocery stores sell galangal frozen, but you can certainly find it fresh as well. It looks a lot like ginger, but with pale skin and often a pinkish hue. Other common names are *blue ginger*, *Siamese ginger*, and *Thai ginger*.

GALANGAL FLOWER

The flower from the galangal plant has vibrant pink petals, sometimes specked with purple. But galangal flowers aren't just pretty—they're tasty too, with a lovely astringent flavor similar to the galangal rhizome, but without the heat. Look for it at Asian markets, from those with a Southeast Asian focus to those with a Japanese one.

GINGER AND YOUNG GINGER

Just about everyone knows about ginger root (technically, it's a rhizome), but not everyone is familiar with young ginger, which I call for often in this book. It is what it sounds like: nubile, juvenile ginger has pale, almost pink flesh and has yet to become fibrous. It has a stronger ginger flavor but less tongue-stinging heat.

GULA JAWA

See Palm Sugar.

IKAN BILIS

These little dried anchovies sold in big bags are one of my favorite seasonings. Rinse them, fry in oil until crispy, and use to garnish soups and salads or as part of a spice mix. I also love them as a snack—ikan bilis tossed with peanuts and chili powder might be the Chex Party Mix of the future.

KAFFIR LIME LEAF

These glossy leaves of the trees that produce bumpy-skinned kaffir limes are incredibly fragrant when julienned for salads or added whole to curries and soups. Don't even mess with the dried or frozen leaves. You can find them fresh at any good Thai grocery store or online.

KANG KONG

Not to be confused with the giant monkey that terrorized Manhattan, this delicious green (also called *Chinese water spinach*) has long, slender dark green leaves and tender, hollow stems. It cooks up quickly like American or New Zealand spinach and has the heartiness to stand up to bold flavors.

KECAP MANIS (pronounced KEE-chop MAHN-eese)

Yes, this is where the word *ketchup* comes from, and this syrupy bottled sauce made of soy sauce, palm sugar, garlic, and star anise might be even more delicious. Brands such as ABC or Hamal can easily be found at Asian grocery stores, but you'll spot it at many supermarkets too.

KERISIK

You can buy prepackaged kerisik, grated fresh coconut toasted slowly in an oilless pan until it's a golden-brown color. But this essential topping for rendangs and addition to Malaysian salads is best when made yourself (see page 319).

LEAF LARD

See page 196.

LEMONGRASS

Thanks to the pan-Asian craze of the nineties, everyone is familiar with this woody and highly aromatic stalk. Lemongrass has a muted lemon flavor but a strong lemon aroma. The stalks should be firm and creamy beige to pale green (not brown). There are several ways to prep lemongrass. For some recipes, you'll chop off and discard the bottom 1½ inches, then peel and discard the woody outer layers. You're left with the tender inner stalk, which you thinly slice and use to make dressings and sambals. In others, you'll peel only the outermost layer, then bruise the stalk (whack it with a meat tenderizer or the back of a knife) and steep it in broths.

LONG CHILIES

When I call for "long chilies," I mean any variety of chili that's longer than, say, a jalapeño or serrano and has a little heat and some great flavor. Anaheim and Hungarian wax peppers are two particularly good examples. I usually call for a particular color—either red and ripe or green and unripe—but if you can't find red, use green!

LONG PEPPER

Like tiny pinecones or cattails tops, these fruits of the long pepper plant are dried and used throughout Southeast Asia. The flavor shares some attributes (especially the warm tingle) with black peppercorns, but is even more complex with a hint of anise. Good spice stores sell it. It's also a piece of pie to find online.

MSG

One of science's finest contributions to food, MSG is like umami distilled. It's a seasoning agent to add to your cupboard next to the salt and sugar, contributing a mouth-filling depth of flavor to sauces and stocks. Sadly, it has yet to shake its stigma as a substance to be avoided at all costs. Look for it at Asian grocery stores (it comes in bags of white crystals) or supermarkets, and employ it judiciously. Like many things, it's best in moderation.

MUSTARD OIL

A staple oil in Indian cooking, you'll spot it at Indian grocery stores. There will often be an encouraging note on the bottle that reads, "Not for human consumption." Keep calm. You'd need to eat a terrifying amount for you to have a problem. Trust me, I haven't died yet.

NARDELLO PEPPERS

Named for Jimmy Nardello, a true American hero who brought this pepper's seeds from Italy to the United States, Nardellos are sweet and mild with a bit of citrus tang. If you have to substitute, use an equal ratio of red bell and long red peppers.

PALM SUGAR

Palm sugars are made all over Asia, each region offering its own idiosyncratic flavor and local name: *gula melaka* in Malaysia, *nam tan peep* in Thailand, and *gula jawa* in Indonesia. Each has its own subtleties, and sweetness is just the starting point. They're made from the sap of various types of sugar palm trees, which is boiled down to a dark syrup and poured into bamboo cylinders, where it dries into a cakey dark disc of sugar (some are smoked). In this book, I call for palm sugar (the light tan stuff that's really easy to find) and gula jawa (the dark brown unrefined palm sugar that takes a little more effort). Sold in small clear bags, the disks of palm sugar can be cut into pieces and crumbled or softened with a little water. Could you use brown sugar in place of palm? Sure, but you will be sacrificing the depth and mystery that palm sugar adds to savory dishes.

Gula Jawa Syrup: Combine 2 cups gula jawa sugar and 1 cup water in a small pot and gently heat the mixture until the sugar is completely dissolved and you have a dark brown syrup. You may want to break up the sugar with a spoon to speed the process along. Let it cool and put it in a container with a tight lid. Make some today so you'll always have it on hand. It keeps for up to a year in the fridge.

PICKLED MUSTARD GREENS

Most Asian markets stock these tasty, khaki-colored pickles, either set out in bins or on shelves in clear plastic packages floating in yellowish brine. Drain, rinse lightly, and pat dry before using.

PRESERVED BLACK BEANS

Chinese black beans, fermented black beans, salted black beans—they're all the same product: small black soybeans that have been preserved in salt and have a very strong flavor. They require rinsing and soaking for at least an hour in cold water before being used in a dish.

SALT MACKEREL

Look for steaks of salt mackerel sold in Cryovac packages at Asian markets. Buy cross-cut steaks—that way you'll be sure to get plenty of meat.

SAVAGNIN WINE

Savagnin is a grape from the Jura region of France. My favorite comes from the Arbois appellation and is made by Jacques Puffeney, the so-called "Pope of the Arbois." It has a slightly nutty, bitter flavor with a touch of petrol and a lingering complexity. It tastes a bit like sherry, actually, which makes a fine substitute for cooking if not for drinking.

SHAOXING WINE

The Chinese both drink and cook with this fermented rice wine, though what you often find at Asian markets here in the States is salted, so taste it first before adding to a dish. You can also successfully sub a good dry sherry.

SICHUAN PEPPERCORNS

The dried berries of a shrub, Sichuan peppercorns are not technically peppercorns. They're used in Sichuan cooking to deliver a wonderfully weird numbing, tingly sort of spiciness called *ma la*. You'll find them in bags at many Chinese grocery stores and some good spice shops.

SIL GOCHU

These dried red chili threads are sold in tangles in plastic bags at Korean grocery stores and make a fantastic garnish. They're flavorful, not fiery. You could, if you must, substitute biber or Aleppo chili flakes.

TAMARIND PASTE

Made from the sun-dried and processed interior of the pods from the tamarind tree, this paste is dark, sweet, and a little sour. Look for it in plastic jars that are sometimes labeled as paste or as "tamarind concentrate."

THAI BASIL

This variety of basil has purplish stems and a strong flavor reminiscent of licorice. Nowadays it's sold at some locations of Whole Foods as well as at Asian markets—how times have changed! If you must, you can use regular basil instead, but come on . . .

THAI BIRD CHILIES

Sometimes called "bird's eye" chilies, these bastards are about 4 inches long and extremely hot—anywhere between 50,000 to 100,000 Scoville units (jalapeños clock in at only around 5,000). If you can't find them, fresh cayenne chilies make good stand-ins.

TURMERIC ROOT

This rhizome (commonly called a root) is most familiar in its ground form, but the whole fresh root offers so much more than the tasteless yellow powder. Fresh turmeric has an enthralling, almost carroty flavor. You can occasionally find it fresh, but I often use the stuff I find in Cryovaced bags in the freezer sections at Southeast Asian or Indian grocery stores.

VIETNAMESE MINT (RAU RAM)

Despite its look and smell, Vietnamese mint is not related to the mint family; technically it's a variety of cilantro. Known in Malaysia as *daun kesom* or *daun laksa* (laksa leaf), it's essential for an authentic laksa. Slightly tart, peppery, and very tannic, the herb has no substitute, though if you can't track it down, you could use a combination of mint and basil, just to replicate the freshness it provides.

SOURCES

Much of the time, the way I cook is to combine the tricks of my travels with the local offerings of my two neighborhoods: New York City's Chinatown and a bucolic stretch of the Hudson Valley. Chinatown offers inexpensive fish, imported strange fruits, and ingredients that I developed a taste for while working in Malaysia. In the Hudson Valley I build relationships with local farmers—the one who raises the pigs, the one who kills the chickens, the one who grows herbs. And, of course, that's where I grow herbs and veggies myself. I'm always juggling my conflicting desire for the far-flung ingredients that have had such a huge influence on my cooking and my increasing desire to eat only what is raised locally and sustainably. I like to think that these desires are less a source of conflict than a way to embrace the gifts that long-haul shipping can offer when integrated into daily local living. Whatever it may be, to cook many of the recipes in this book you will need to venture into an Asian market and purchase a few imported products.

Walking into an Asian market is, in many ways, a mini trip abroad. As in Asia, an American can feel a version of the culture shock that one enjoys while traveling: How can I find an ingredient when I can't read the packages? This can be the moment when one realizes that actually looking at the ingredients is more revealing than looking at the signs underneath them. It's analogous to turning off your goddamn GPS, pulling your nose out of the simulated landscape, and looking for real landmarks while you're driving. Visually identifying your food automatically puts you more in touch with it and is the surest way to know you have arrived. Of course, you can always just ask somebody who works at the market! Don't let fear of seeming ignorant stop you from learning something new (and making something delicious). These ingredients sometimes require a little detective work, and in the bowels of Chinatown, common verbal communication can present a challenge, provided your fluency in Mandarin and Cantonese is none.

If you're not lucky enough to live near a gaggle of Asian grocery stores, fret not, the Internet is here! Here are a few sources to get you started:

- Temple of Thai, www.templeofthai.com: For fresh ingredients, like herbs, chilies, and lemongrass, and bottled sauces, like budo sauce, fish sauce, and just about everything else called for in this book
- Grocery Thai, www.grocerythai.com: Another source for Asian ingredients of all sorts, particularly fresh ingredients like kaffir lime leaf, galangal, green papaya, turmeric, and chilies
- Holland's Best, www.hollandsbest.com: This Dutch store has plenty of Indonesian ingredients (the cultures have a long history), which means you can buy a variety of hard-to-find Asian ingredients like palm and gula jawa sugar and duan salam

- Online Food Grocery, www.onlinefoodgrocery.com: Yet another site to pore over on your search. Here you'll find belacan, different types of soy and fish sauces, Aroy-D brand coconut milk, noodles, Asian flours, and more
- Le Sanctuaire, www.le-sanctuaire.com: A great source for spices, this Santa Monica storefront's online operation stocks Indonesian long pepper as well as more common spices of especially high quality
- Gustiamo, www.gustiamo.com
- Zingerman's, www.zingermans.com
- Formaggio Kitchen, www.formaggiokitchen.com

This book calls for Italian and French ingredients, too, that you might not find at your local deli. These are just a few companies that will ship fine olive oils, salt-packed anchovies, and top-notch cheese to your door:

- La Boîte, laboiteny.com
- Malaysian Food.net Market, malaysianfood.net/products.htm
- Heritage Foods, HeritageFoodsUSA.com

INDEX

Note: Page reference in *italics* refer to photographs.